Democratizing the European Union

MANCHESTER
UNIVERSITY PRESS

PERSPECTIVES ON DEMOCRATIZATION

The series presents critical texts on democratization processes and democratic theory. Written in an accessible style, the books are theoretically informed and empirically rich, and examine issues critical to the establishment, extension and deepening of democracy in different political systems and contexts. Important examples of successful democratization processes, as well as reasons why experiments in democratic government fail, are some of the issues analysed in the series. The books in the series make an important contribution to the ongoing debates about democracy, good governance and democratization.

Series editors: SHIRIN M. RAI and WYN GRANT

already published

Funding democratization
PETER BURNELL AND ALAN WARE (editors)

Globalizing democracy
KATHERINE FIERLBECK

Democracy in Latin America
GERALDINE LIEVESLEY

Democratization in the South
ROBIN LUCKHAM AND GORDON WHITE (editors)

Democratizing the European Union

Issues for the twenty-first century

CATHERINE HOSKYNS
and MICHAEL NEWMAN   editors

MANCHESTER UNIVERSITY PRESS
Manchester and New York

distributed exclusively in the USA by St. Martin's Press

Published by Manchester University Press
Oxford Road, Manchester M13 9NR, UK
and Room 400, 175 Fifth Avenue, New York, NY 10010, USA
http://www.man.ac.uk/mup

Distributed exclusively in the USA by
St. Martin's Press, Inc., 175 Fifth Avenue, New York,
NY 10010, USA

Distributed exclusively in Canada by
UBC Press, University of British Columbia, 6344 Memorial Road,
Vancouver, BC, Canada V6T 1Z2

British Library Cataloguing-in-Publication Data

A catalogue record for this book is available from the British Library

Library of Congress Cataloging-in-Publication Data applied for

ISBN 0 7190 5665 9 *hardback*
0 7190 5666 7 *paperback*

First published 2000

06 05 04 03 02 01 00   10 9 8 7 6 5 4 3 2 1

Typeset in Trump Medieval
by Servis Filmsetting Ltd, Manchester
Printed in Great Britain
by Bell & Bain Ltd, Glasgow

Contents

Contributors

Sue Cohen is Co-ordinator of the Single Parent Action Network (SPAN), a grass-roots multi-racial network of single parents working locally, nationally and in Europe, set up in 1990 under the EC's Third Poverty Action Programme. She also works with the European Anti Poverty Network (EAPN) and has done research at Bristol University on women's perspectives on social solidarity in the EU.

Stefano Fella is researching a PhD thesis at the University of North London on the Labour Party's European policy, with special reference to the Intergovernmental Conference of 1996/97. He has previously worked in the House of Commons and the European Parliament, and at South Bank University. He is the author of *The 1996–97 Intergovermental Conference and the Treaty of Amsterdam – a Thwarted Reform* (South Bank European Paper 1/99).

Sverker Gustavsson is Jean Monnet Professor of European Political Integration at Uppsala University in Sweden. His recent publications include 'Double Asymmetry as Normative Challenge' in A. Føllesdal and P. Koslowski (eds), *Democracy and the European Union* (Springer, 1997), and 'Defending the Democratic Deficit' in A. Weale and M. Nentwich (eds), *Political Theory and the European Union* (Routledge, 1998). He is the editor (together with Leif Lewin) of *The Future of the Nation State* (Routledge, 1996).

Catherine Hoskyns is Jean Monnet Professor of European Studies at Coventry University. She teaches on European Union politics and gender studies and is the author of *Integrating Gender: Women, Law and Politics in the European Union* (Verso, 1996). She is currently studying the application of deliberative democracy to the EU.

Mary Kaldor is Programme Director of the Centre for Global Governance at the London School of Economics and Co-chair of the Helsinki Citizens' Assembly. She is the author of *New and Old Wars: Organised Violence in a Global Era* (Polity, 1999) and is the editor (with

B. Einhorn and Z. Kavan) of *Citizenship and Democratic Control in Europe* (Edward Elgar, 1996).

Richard Kuper lectured in European politics at the University of Hertfordshire until he took early retirement in 1997. A former publisher with Pluto Press, he is now working with an organic farming, research and education eentre in France while continuing to research and write about policy formation, the democratic process and the EU. His publications include *Democracy and the European Union* (European Dossier Series, University of North London Press, 1996) and *The Politics of the European Court of Justice* (European Dossier Series, Kogan Page, 1998).

John Lambert is a freelance journalist who has worked in Brussels since the 1970s. He was Secretary General of the Technical Co-ordination Group in the first directly elected European Parliament and thereafter of the Rainbow Group and the Green-Left Group. He is a co-founder of the Agenor network, which works for understanding and contact among the left in Europe. He is the author of *Solidarity and Survival: a Vision for Europe* (Avebury, 1994).

Valerio Lintner is Reader in European Economics at London Guildhall University and visiting lecturer at the Universities of Perugia and Montpellier. He has written a number of articles on the economics of European integration and on the European economy and is the author (with David Edye) of *Contemporary Europe: Economics, Politics and Society* (Prentice-Hall, 1996).

Michael Newman is Jean Monnet Professor in European Integration Studies and Director of the London European Research Centre at the University of North London. He is the author of *Democracy, Sovereignty and the European Union* (Hurst, 1996), and of *Socialism and European Unity: the Dilemma of the Left in Britain and France* (Hurst, 1983). He is currently working on a biography of Ralph Miliband.

Acknowledgements

This book originated in a conference entitled 'Democratizing the European Union: Beyond Institutional Change?' which was held in London in May 1997. It was organized jointly by the London European Research Centre of the University of North London and Centre for International and European Studies of Coventry University with additional support from the University Association of Contemporary European Studies and the Jean Monnet Project. We are grateful to the sponsors of the conference for making the event possible and to the participants for making it a success. We also want to thank all the authors of this volume for collaborating with us, and Sol Picciotto and Ines Newman for their helpful comments and suggestions. We are grateful to the series editors, Shirin Rai and Wyn Grant, and Manchester University Press for editorial advice and support.

Catherine Hoskyns
Michael Newman

Abbreviations

CAP	Common Agricultural Policy
CEEC	Central and East European countries
CFSP	Common Foreign and Security Policy
COSAC	Conference of European Affairs Committees (of national parliaments)
EAPN	European Anti Poverty Network
EC	European Community
ECB	European Central Bank
ECHR	European Court of Human Rights
ECOFIN	Committee of Finance Ministers
ECSC	European Coal and Steel Community
ECU	European currency unity
EEC	European Economic Community
EMI	European Monetary Institute
EMS	European Monetary System
EMU	Economic and Monetary Union
EPP	European People's Party
ERM	exchange rate mechanism
ESCB	European System of Central Banks
ETUC	European Trade Union Confederation
EU	European Union
GDP	gross domestic product
GLC	Greater London Council
GRAEL	Green Alternative European Link
IGC	intergovernmental conference
IRC	independent regulatory commission
JHA	justice and home affairs
MEP	Member of the European Parliament
NATO	North Atlantic Treaty Organization
NGO	non-governmental organization
PDS	Democratic Party of the Left (Italy)
PES	Party of European Socialists
PR	proportional representation
QMV	qualified majority voting

SDP	Social Democratic Party
SEA	Single European Act
SEM	Single European Market
SPAN	Single Parent Action Network
SPD	Social Democratic Party (Germany)
UK	United Kingdom
UNICE	Union of Industry Associations and Employers' Federations
US	United States (America)

1
Introduction

MICHAEL NEWMAN

In the final year of the twentieth century two very different epi-
sodes in European Union (EU) affairs highlighted issues of
democracy. The first, in January, was the establishment of
Economic and Monetary Union (EMU) among eleven of the
member states. This simultaneously raised questions about
democracy both within the states and at EU level. If governments no longer possess traditional levers of macro-economic
policy, this implies an important new stage in the erosion of
domestic autonomy. At the same time the independence of the
European Central Bank will limit the possibilities of intervention by the governments or the European Parliament at the EU
level. Thus EMU could weaken democratic control of economic
policy within the member states without establishing any new
form of European political intervention. The second, unplanned,
event came two months later when the European Parliament
forced the resignation of the whole Commission over allegations
of fraud and corruption. Previously termed the Parliament's
'nuclear weapon' – on the grounds that it was too powerful ever
to be used – the threat to dismiss the whole Commission put
democratic accountability of the institutions at the forefront of
the politics of European integration. However, neither EMU nor
the crisis of the Commission reveals the full extent of the difficulties involved in democratizing the EU, for the problems are
deeply embedded in its historical development.

The historical context

The structure and policy-making system of the EU bear the
imprint of the early post-war years when political and economic

elites constructed European integration on the basis of a 'permissive consensus'. Convinced of the imperative need to establish peace, particularly by overcoming the historic conflict between between France and Germany, and to create economic interdependence as a basis for growth, the 'Six' built institutions which reflected these priorities. Certainly, the European Coal and Steel Community and the European Economic Community (EEC) also included parliamentary assemblies but, as each country nominated its members to these bodies, the system paid little more than lip service to democratic principles. While the electorates of the member states appeared to support the construction of a 'new Europe', and believed that they were deriving benefits from it, the Community's policy-making system was generally accepted. However, the accession of states, such as Britain, which were less *communautaire* than the original members, and recurrent economic recessions after the end of the long boom in the early 1970s, progressively undermined the tacit public support which had provided the basis of the integration process.

The first reaction by the Community to this growth of indifference and hostility was to seek greater legitimacy, rather than to enhance democracy. This resulted in some tangible benefits, particularly when Jacques Delors sought a more active social policy, partly as a means of enhancing popular support for the Community. However, some of the responses to the problem were of a more symbolic nature, such as the provision of passports of the same size and colour in all countries, the use of the blue and yellow flag as the Community logo, and the adoption of Beethoven's ninth symphony as its anthem. Emulating the process by which national identities were cemented, the hope was that such appeals to emotion would create a similar bond between ordinary people and the 'European project'. A further development of this kind, with far greater potential importance, was the establishment of EU citizenship, realized for the first time in the Treaty of European Union (TEU, the Maastricht Treaty) which took effect in 1993. Since a condition of acquiring this status was citizenship in a member state, and the majority of the rights of EU citizens had already been acquired in earlier phases of the integration process, the innovation was again largely symbolic. Moreover, while citizenship (at least of certain kinds) may be related to democracy, it is not inherently democratic. The new articles introduced in the Maastricht

Treaty should therefore be viewed as part of the continuing attempt to enhance the legitimacy of the EU. Given the continuing growth of 'Euro-scepticism' and nationalist populism in many of the member states during the 1990s, these efforts have clearly been unsuccessful.

Calls for the democratization of the Community increased throughout the 1980s. Both the demands of directly elected MEPs for greater power and the evident impact of European policies on the domestic domain led to demands for a fundamental transformation of the decision-making system. These, coupled with the need for greater legitimacy and efficiency, resulted in a series of gradual changes. The Single European Act, which was implemented in 1987, went some way to meet the claim of the European Parliament that an enhancement of its legislative role would reduce the 'democratic deficit'. A new co-operation procedure was introduced and extended with the establishment of 'co-decision' in the Maastricht Treaty. The enunciation of the ambiguous doctrine of 'subsidiarity' in this treaty, with its emphasis on taking decisions as closely as possible to the citizen, also had potential democratic relevance. Moreover, the Amsterdam Treaty, signed in 1997, has taken some more significant steps. First, it has reduced and simplified the previously complex and numerous procedures of decision-making in which the European Parliament is involved, and has broadened the scope of the simplified co-decision procedure. Second, the Parliament was given the right of approval of the Commission president, while the Commission president's own role was also strengthened. This combined process represented a significant step in defining clearer lines of accountability, which the Parliament used with such dramatic effect in March 1999. Third, there was also a stronger commitment to transparency in decision-making (which had been foreshadowed at Maastricht and at the Edinburgh summit in 1992). It was thus agreed that the minutes of Council meetings when acting in a legislative capacity, together with the votes and an explanation of them, would be made public, and that there would be a right of access to all Council, Commission and Parliament documents related to EU decision-making. The Amsterdam Treaty introduced new articles in areas concerning human rights. It provided new sanctions (ultimately including suspension of membership) against member states violating the principles of democracy and human rights, and the Court of Justice was also granted jurisdiction to ensure that the Community institutions respected fundamental rights as guaranteed by the European Court of Human Rights. Finally, provision for legislation against racism (and other forms of discrimination) was included in the treaty.

All these were significant changes, although it is also easy to detect weaknesses in each of them. For example, past practice does not suggest that the theoretical commitment to transparency will be implemented satisfactorily in practice; it will be extremely difficult to secure a Council decision in favour of sanctions for human rights abuses, given the requirement of unanimity; and the implementation of effective anti-discrimination legislation will depend on governments demonstrating a political will which is not currently in evidence. However, there is a further fundamental problem with the steps towards democratization taken by the Community thus far. *Piecemeal changes have occurred without any thoroughgoing discussion of the nature of the democracy that is being sought.* Yet the difficulties involved in democratizing the EU are not only the practical ones of securing the necessary changes, but are also theoretical. For it is not at all obvious how a democratised Union is even to be conceptualized.

We hope that this book makes an important contribution to the debate over such problems. Its approach differs from most of the existing literature, which tends to concentrate on the EU institutions, or on interest group activity, or on rather abstract and esoteric theory. Our purpose has been to cross these boundaries by bringing together theorists and campaigners, and those who take a 'national' perspective with those who consider the issues transnationally. It also argues that democratization must be understood in relation to values as well as procedures, and that this requires acceptance of complexity. The following sections elucidate the issues addressed within the volume.

Definitions of democracy

The initial problem is that there is, of course, no agreement about the definition of 'democracy' itself. Yet different concepts will imply quite different policy prescriptions about the way in which the EU might be democratized. It is therefore necessary to begin by clarifying the assumptions of the editors on these issues, which provided the starting point for the book. We accept the basic features of the liberal democratic model – such as the freedoms of opinion, expression and organization, universal suffrage, a choice of political representatives and the separation of powers – as important elements in any viable conception of democracy. However, democracy is not simply a set of procedures, but also incorporates substantive values, and our position in relation to three key debates about values and relative priorities must be elucidated, for these underlie the themes of the book.

The first concerns the relationship between liberty and equality. Most would accept that both concepts are constituent elements of democracy, but also that there are tensions between them. Our position on liberty accepts the traditional catalogue of liberal civil and political freedoms but rejects neo-liberal definitions of liberty on the grounds that these effectively defend the privileges of those who already possess power and privilege. In our view, one of the main functions of public authorities is to use political power to redistribute resources in favour of the disadvantaged. Otherwise they are negating equality, which is both a condition and a goal of democracy. However, if equality is elevated to become the *sole* principle, it can lead to the elimination of fundamental liberties. It follows that democracy implies some form of balance between the goals of liberty and equality, and that in present circumstances democratization requires a move towards greater equality.

Second, we regard the empowerment of ordinary people as a crucial aim Unlike some theorists who see the debate between the advocates of 'democratic elitism' and 'participatory democracy' as procedural, we therefore believe that greater participation is a substantive value as an aspect of empowerment. This does not mean that 'direct democracy' is possible in large and complex societies. We regard representation as indispensable, and political parties as necessary agencies for articulating and implementing policies and providing leadership. However, these must not be viewed as substitutes for active participation at all levels. Protest is also a legitimate political activity, and organizations and channels of mass involvement should be nurtured both because of their effects upon the participants and their impact in bringing about change.

Third, the book is based on the view that democratization demands a move towards greater 'inclusiveness'. It therefore rejects notions of democracy that stress the interests of the 'insider' against those of the 'outsider', the dominant nation against the minority nation, and traditional roles and values against those that challenge stereotypes. We assume instead that democracy must be as inclusive as possible in relation to ethnicity, religion, gender and sexuality. In this respect the recent work on 'deliberative democracy', elaborating an ideal in which all those affected by decisions should be able to participate equally and openly in the deliberative process by which policy outcomes are determined is helpful (Bohman and Rehg 1997).

Application to the EU

Yet even among those who share these values there is a further fundamental conceptual difficulty in the subject matter of the book: is the democratization of the EU an appropriate aim? Many argue against the idea on the grounds that democracy is working, or that it could and should work, within the confines of the 'nation state'. In Britain this view is now mainly associated with the last Conservative government and 'Eurosceptics' of the right. However, there are left-wing variants of the position and, as Sverker Gustavsson explains, one of these is common among Social Democrats in Sweden (Chapter 3). Their argument is that democratizing the EU would strengthen its supranational power, thereby giving it more scope to encroach on the domestic polity. This in turn would weaken democracy within the 'nation state', since it would diminish the control of the elected government over policy-making. It therefore follows that it is better to restrict supranational democracy by maintaining the EU as a union of independent states.

Since the notion that the *demos* should rule within the polity lies at the core of the concept of democracy, the defenders of independent states appear to have a strong argument in their favour. Their case is often reinforced by the claim that the *demos* is constituted by the nation, which has the right to self-government without external interference. Furthermore this doctrine may also be underpinned with the argument that particular values, such as social and economic equality and empowerment, are pursued by 'nation states'. For it may then be concluded that certain forms of supranationalism make it increasingly difficult for such goals to be achieved. As Valerio

Lintner argues, this may certainly be the case in relation to the Maastricht project for EMU (Chapter 5). However, there are also major weaknesses in the state-centred doctrine.

Challenges to the state?

In the first place, it can certainly be challenged on normative grounds. States which claim to represent a particular *demos* may in fact be controlled, to a great extent, by economic and political elites rather than by the people as a whole. Similarly, there is room for considerable scepticism about the claim that states are always 'nation states'. Certainly in the UK a particular nation has dominated the state, while minority nations have largely been excluded from power. In such circumstances, rather than maintaining democracy, the state-centred doctrine may simply mean the continued dominance of the current elites. In contrast, a democratic alternative might be to establish effective political power at a regional level, with smaller and minority nations controlling their own affairs. Finally, it may be argued that more cosmopolitan forms of democracy are desirable on principle. Thus many of those who favour democratizing the EU regard this as an important goal in its own right on the grounds that exclusivism and intolerance are immanent dangers within the 'nation state', which could be overcome in a transnational form of democracy.

There are also good reasons for maintaining that the state-centred doctrine is no longer tenable in practice. The EU has already encroached on the domestic sphere. Community law takes precedence over state legislation, there is Community competence over an ever-increasing range of policy areas, and there is a high level of economic interdependence and interpenetration. It is therefore hardly plausible to draw a rigid distinction between inter-state relations and the domestic polity, and it is evident that much policy-making evades democratic participation or control at *any* level. If democratization is a fundamental goal, it cannot therefore be pursued solely in relation to the member states and must also involve the EU as a whole.

Some commentators appear to believe that the answer lies in transferring a federal model of liberal democracy to the EU itself. This might involve the conversion of the Commission into a democratically elected executive, with the Council of Ministers and the European Parliament acting as a bicameral legislature, respectively representing the member states and the people. However, it must surely be acknowledged that the EU is not at present a state, even of a federal kind. The governments maintain decisive power in key areas of policy and some of the states are major actors in the international system in their own right. And if the EU were ever to evolve into a supranational democratic state there would be further theoretical and normative problems to consider: would the comparative rigidity of a federal system be compatible with the fluidity of the current world? If not, any constitutional settlement might be anachronistic as soon as it came into operation. Could Community structures, procedures and assumptions be tailored to the plurality of peoples, languages, political consciousness and traditions within its domain? If not, the federation would contradict the goal of inclusiveness, which suggests that diversity should be tolerated and fostered. Such questions may need to be answered in the future but, in the present circumstances, it seems more helpful to accept that the EU is a complex entity, with power distributed unevenly between levels and across policy areas, and to ask how stronger elements of democracy may be introduced into it.

Approaches to democratization

Yet even if state-centrism and federalism are both rejected as representations of the present situation, at least three different possible perspectives on democratizing the EU remain. The first (Approach 1) might suggest that political and social movements should operate in regions, countries and in EU institutions to advance democracy, and that it it is necessary to work on different levels for different policy areas. This approach does not begin with a blueprint for the EU institutions but assumes that they will be shaped by the interactions between the movements and by continuing conflicts over the distribution of power. Those who adopt this as their starting point may happily accept the possibility that the EU will remain an inchoate and untidy entity.

The second perspective (Approach 2) might hold that certain necessary changes follow from both basic liberal principles and the substantive values outlined above. Liberalism would require the EU to reform its own procedures – for example, by introducing greater transparency and freedom of information. The goals of inclusiveness and a move in the direction of equality would imply a broader conception of the rights to be guaranteed by the Court of Justice: for example, the implementation of effective anti-discrimination laws, and the definition of a minimum level of social provision. This approach would therefore view the EU as a guarantor of rights, the conception of which may be enlarged over time.

The third perspective (Approach 3) would go beyond this, holding that there is a potential *demos* in the EU but that it needs to be given consciousness and the means to make its 'voice' effective in existing and new institutions. This transformation would enable the Community to undertake policies which are necessary but currently inconceivable. For example, if EMU leads to greater inequality between regions and countries, the goals of equality and social justice would require redistributive measures at EU level to counterbalance these negative effects. However, a condition of large-scale social transfers would (it is argued) be the establishment of a common democratic consciousness by the population of the Community. For only that would provide the sense of belonging to a 'community of destiny' that allegedly exists within nation states. This would not require the conversion of the EU into a quasi-state, but such an approach implies that it can and should become a democratic polity – at least to an extent.

The contributors to this book have not explicitly taken a position on these approaches and would not necessarily agree as to which is the most profitable route towards democratization. Some chapters link all three approaches. For example, Richard Kuper implies that active citizens campaigning for changes at local level might bring about constitutional demands which ultimately establish a conception of a democratic polity in which further developments become possible (Chapter 8). Other contributors remain more cautious, adopting a stance of 'piecemeal reform' or concentrating on more specific issues and remaining within the framework suggested by the first or second approach. All offer some fruitful suggestions.

Creating the 'substance of politics'

In 1966 Altiero Spinelli, the Italian resistance fighter and strong proponent of a European federation, wrote of the early stages of European integration:

> There were lacking the traditions, the institutions, and a common political language, that is to say the very instruments which are necessary to transform sentiments into the substance of politics. (Spinelli 1966)

The implication was that one key element of democratization would be the establishment of the 'substance of politics' at European level. More than three decades later, there has been comparatively little progress in this respect. Indeed, even in the limited areas in which a democratic space has been created, it is evident that there are serious weaknesses. Thus John Lambert argues that the European Parliament has been managed to a considerable extent by a consensus between Christian and Social Democrats, which has excluded a whole range of alternative views (Chapter 5). Similarly, while the EU has established and facilitated the activities of transnational networks of NGOs, Sue Cohen shows that the Commission has ensured that awkward issues have been kept off the agenda and has maintained its own control over the process (Chapter 2). It is therefore clear that it is now necessary to push transnational politics beyond the limits set by those who view it as nothing more than elite exchange and professional lobbying. But how might ordinary people become involved so as to bring about this transformation?

Richard Kuper stresses the importance of the republican tradition, with its emphasis on active citizens as the source of law (Chapter 8). Because of the size, diversity and complexity of the EU, and the fact that it has developed thus far without popular legitimation, he argues that the idea of a single constitutional enactment is impracticable. But he suggests that an on-going *constitutionalizing* process might be possible if people came to see the connections between the EU and their own concerns. And Mary Kaldor argues that such links might be forged across Europe as a whole so that the peoples of East Central Europe take control of their own future rather than being 'managed' by the existing Community. However, she also argues that the European citizenry will become fully engaged only through the elaboration of their own 'projects' to set against those of the political and economic elites (Chapter 7).

Kuper also argues that a real breakthrough depends upon a double conceptual disengagement: of citizenship from nationality and ethnicity, and of democracy from territory. On the other hand, successful transnational democracy is dependent upon vibrant democratic politics in all its component parts. Those who seek to change the EU therefore also need programmes of domestic reform and, in this context, Stefano Fella's explanation of the Labour Party's general approach to the issue of democratization is of particular importance (Chapter 4). Moreover, simultaneous action is often necessary at the different levels. For example, visible ethnic minorities face exploitation and discrimination both within states and in the EU as a whole. It is clear that effective policies must be implemented both at state and EU level if democracy is to have any meaning for the current victims of European racism.

If, as seems probable, the EU remains an amalgam of supranational, state and sub-state power, democratization must involve not only multi-level governance but also acceptance of the fact that different degrees and types of democracy will operate at the different levels. Furthermore, this does not simply involve territorially based institutions, for there also needs to be a democratic response to the transnational impact of the EU by the creation of vibrant issue-based organizations that bring together peoples from the Community as a whole. Whether this degree of complexity means that the EU will remain untidy and inchoate (approach 1), whether it can become a guarantor of rights (approach 2), or whether it can ultimately become a democratic polity (approach 3) remain open questions.

Catherine Hoskyns returns to these approaches in Chapter 9, when summarizing the main themes of the book and making some specific proposals for reform. Naturally, we do not claim to have 'the solution' to all these intractable problems, but we do believe that it is necessary to move beyond the models of democracy derived from the theory and practice of states if we are to democratize the EU in the twenty-first century.

References

Bohman, James, and William Rehg, eds (1997), *Deliberative Democracy. Essays on Reason and Politics*, Cambridge MA, MIT Press.

Spinelli, Altiero (1966), *The Eurocrats. Conflict and Crisis in the European Community*, Baltimore MD, Johns Hopkins University Press.

2

Social solidarity in the Delors period: barriers to participation

SUE COHEN

The political era from 1985 to 1994, when Jacques Delors was President of the European Commission, is commonly called the Delors period. This was a period in the history of the European Union (EU) which saw not only the introduction of the Single European Market but also the proliferation of programmes and consultative committees designed to strengthen social cohesion. Representatives of non-governmental organizations (NGOs) from all parts of the EU were drawn into these initiatives, to inform the social agenda and provide models of action to combat poverty and social exclusion.

As the Delors period gained political momentum the concept of a social Europe was increasingly translated by the European Commission into notions of social solidarity, social cohesion, partnership and participation. I was one of many NGO representatives involved in various working parties designed to put these notions into practice, and would use the terminology in the documents I wrote for my own organization.

Although it felt an enormous privilege to be part of such networks and programmes, and although I was attracted to and intrigued by the notion of social solidarity and the potential for grass-roots participation in EU initiatives, I soon felt uneasy. It seemed to me that those of us involved in the social action had committed ourselves to an ideology that was hardly debated – in theory, action or in process. It is true that extensive research, evaluation and monitoring of these different programmes took place, with numerous papers written on the themes of partnership, participation and multi-dimensionality, and on many different aspects of social policy. DG V in the European Commission dedicated its energies to wide-ranging consultations with different social representatives from all parts of the

EU (Poverty 3 1992; EAPN 1994). However, the evaluation that took place was generally undertaken as part of the Commission's own agenda, as part of its political relationship to the Council of Ministers and the European Parliament, whilst the nature of the underlying ideology which prompted these measures, or the rationale for them, was barely addressed.

My desire to explore the political ideology of the period developed out of my involvement with grass-roots women in EU-funded programmes and networks designed to achieve social cohesion. Why did we experience so many problems and in some areas so much resistance to enacting social solidarity in practice (Cohen 1998)?

This chapter explores the limitations of consensus politics within the politics of the EU and the problems experienced by grass-roots organizations when questioning dominant beliefs and practices. In an attempt to explore these contradictions, it examines the similarities between the political discourse of the Delors era and the theories of the French social theorist Emile Durkheim, particularly with regard to social corporatism, social solidarity and the separation of the private from the political.

Drawing on interviews which I carried out with grass-roots women active in European networks, I discuss the problems in addressing feminist/socialist concerns within a political culture which bows to dominant institutions, agencies and decision-making bodies. I suggest that if the Union is to become more participatory and democratic, then political knowledge and action will need to be informed by grass-roots activists as well as corporatized agencies, by work in the home as well as paid employment, by the private as well as the public.

The EU movement for social solidarity

Social solidarity as a notion is imprinted with political and emotional contradictions: support/fight, comfort/struggle, community/self-interest, interdependence/antagonism, stability/disruption. Liberal, social democratic and socialist theorists have developed very different interpretations of the concept, but the contradictions described do not fall neatly between these different political philosophies. Rather they interweave in complex ways, creating enormous confusion for those involved in different political groupings which yearn for the general harmony that social solidarity appears to promise, then wonder at the dissent that is embodied in the process.

Yet at the beginning of the twenty-first century the notion of social solidarity continues to hold special promise in an era of international economic competition, apparent chaos and fragmentation, lost socialist visions and increasing division between rich and poor – both nationally and globally. Whilst those experiencing particular oppression continue to join together in different social movements, principles of social responsibility, social solidarity and communitarianism are being reworked by liberal and social democratic politicians in many different contexts (Young 1990).

The movement towards European economic union from the mid-1980s onwards is one of these contexts. The potential for social solidarity within such a broad union is exceedingly problematic, and any attempt at implementation a complex affair. Yet the need to 'govern' this ever-growing, diverse union appears to have pushed social solidarity higher up the EU agenda during the Delors period.

There are a number of reasons for this. EU policy-making is by its very nature multi-faceted. One major consideration during this period was that economic convergence within the EU would need to rely to some extent on a common social infrastructure. Ross states that 'social' programmes were as much a response to the needs of capital in the development of the Single European Market as they were to pressure for a more balanced Union (1995: 7–8).

The overriding influence of the economic lobby in the creation of the Single European Market also meant that the poorer countries in the Southern block needed guarantees that they would not suffer in the process. At the same time, the left and centre left parties in the more powerful countries worked to counterbalance the economic lobby with the introduction of social initiatives and programmes.

In developing its social agenda the Commission became increasingly influenced by corporatist models in Germany and the Netherlands, by the French model of worker participation in decision-making and by the concept of the corporate state. In liberal and social democracies the state helped to resolve 'the inevitable conflicts between competing interests in diverse pluralist societies composed of many different groups, classes, regions and so on' (Wise and Gibb 1993: 40). This process echoed a culture of decision-making in the Council of Ministers based on negotiated consensus rather than open conflict.

Powerful leaders also play their part in the development of a political ethos in the EU, particularly those who come from countries which have the highest number of votes in the Council of Ministers – France, Germany, Italy and the UK. Jacques Delors was a committed Europhile. He brought to the Commission his own history, which included a leading role in Mitterrand's government, as well as the position of social affairs adviser to the Gaullist Prime Minister Jacques Chaban-Delmas in the aftermath of student protests in Paris in 1968. In France he had worked to develop a platform which combined economic competition with a more just social order. This included the structuring of a 'social dialogue' between representative bodies of employers and employees. Delors believed that the free market could not:

> guarantee equity, a moralized social order, or full economic success. These things depended upon 'dialogue' among different groups – employers and labor in particular – to reach clearer understandings of mutual needs about what had to be done and what could be shared. (Ross 1995: 18)

As President of the European Commission Delors took a special interest in drawing the non-governmental organizations into this dialogue. I was one of many gripped by the vision of a social Europe. This vision had no place in UK political settings at the time. We lived in a society in which the leader of the country had proclaimed that there was no such thing as society. Individualism and competition were lauded, high unemployment levels were systematically built into structural economic policies and, despite the ever-increasing gap between rich and poor, social movements appeared unable to develop a successful counter-strategy.

In this political climate, the concept of social solidarity at an international level felt like a new way forward. What was not possible at a national level might become possible if collective pressure was put on governments in a European arena, doubling back on the nation state with a European social agenda developed through the EU social action programmes of the Delors period.

In 1984 the EC summit meeting at Fontainebleau had agreed a social action plan, heralding a new era in the political development of the EU with the announcement that:

> the Community will not be able to strengthen its economic cohesion in the face of international competition if it does not strengthen its social cohesion at the same time. Social policy must therefore be developed at community level on the same basis as economic and industrial policy. (Venturini 1989, quoted in Wise and Gibb 1993: 147)

This new action programme, agreed by the European Parliament in 1985, included provisions which promoted social dialogue and increased protection in the working environment. Following on from these initiatives, the Delors package presented in 1987 proposed the co-ordination of the three structural funds, and the doubling of revenue for these combined social/economic objectives.

'Social solidarity' soon became a widely adopted umbrella term, but many other concepts proliferated during this period: 'social cohesion' as opposed to 'social exclusion', 'partnership', 'participation', 'integration'. They became part of a discourse embodied in policy documents, funding initiatives and platform speeches. See for example the EU Inter-institutional Declaration 'Towards a Europe of Greater Solidarity respecting Human Dignity and rejecting Exclusion' (European Union 1993).

The two initiatives that I would like to focus on to illustrate these principles in practice are the European Poverty Programme, which was strengthened during the Delors period, and the European Anti Poverty Network, which was set up to have an impact on the social agenda.

The European Poverty Programme

The First and Second European Poverty Programmes, 1975–80 and 1984–88, had a relatively low profile. I was involved in the Second Programme as the co-ordinator of a small inner-city project and experienced the dizzying acceleration of activity when as co-ordinator of the UK Single Parent Action Network (SPAN) I became involved in the Third European Poverty Programme in 1989, at a time when Delors was at the peak of his influence. I also experienced the demise of the programme as his influence began to wane towards the end of 1994.

The Third Poverty Programme was larger, more ambitious,

had more researchers attached to it, and was more centrally controlled by DG V than any of the earlier programmes. Moreover, whereas the Second Poverty Programme brought organizations working with people in poverty together into separate working groups which centred on a particular disadvantage, e.g. the long-term unemployed, homeless people, rural poverty, single parents – the Third Programme crossed these boundaries by drawing organizations together to work on what were effectively the principles of social solidarity.

The three major themes of the Third European Poverty Programme were *partnership, participation* and *multi-dimensionality*. Initially many of us were amused by the constant reiteration of these 'buzz words' and then, as the programme developed, increasingly intrigued as to why it should have been organized in that way. It was only as the Delors period began to come to an end and the Poverty Programme itself became threatened that it became clearer to me that *partnership, participation* and *multi-dimensionality* were in fact the hard-fought underlying principles of a social democratic Europe.

The European Anti Poverty Network

The European Anti Poverty Network (EAPN) was set up during the same era. This exciting new organization put poverty on the political agenda of the EU, acquiring ever-increasing status as a negotiating body on issues of social policy. However, as with the Poverty Programme itself, it was at the time unclear to those involved why poverty had suddenly risen so rapidly up the EU agenda.

It is difficult to describe the unsettling combination of bewilderment, privilege and suspicion felt by those grass-roots activists who in 1990 were invited to a meeting in Brussels funded by the European Commission to set up the EAPN as a network of NGOs across the EU. Or why Delors himself should have been so keen to negotiate with this network on issues of social policy. Or why networks focusing on particular issue groups such as the European Network of One Parent Families should have had their funding cut around the same time and be told that it should be channelled instead into umbrella organizations such as the EAPN. Many of us were left with questions, reservations and frustrations because so little of the broader political context was explained.

Consensus politics

Questioning the consensus

A great deal is said about the accessibility of the European Commission as a political institution. But for grass-roots groups involved in emancipatory action there can also be huge barriers when working with emerging EU systems of social democracy, barriers which are in themselves hard to define. The rhetoric promises so much – participation, solidarity, inclusion – whilst the reality can feel quite the opposite. This is the difference between 'espoused theory' and 'theory in use' (Argyris and Schon 1978).

Anyone who has attended formal presentations by the European Commission will be familiar with the stultifying atmosphere of some of the meetings. It becomes difficult to challenge the accepted wisdom in these settings, especially if the Commission is your project's funding body. Very little debate takes place, although particular individuals may make stabs at it. Most of the time, however, participants are required to suspend their disbelief as 'consensus' politics takes over from reality.

In the sphere of anti-poverty measures, presentations by the Commission are often underpinned by assumptions such as 'We can cure poverty without needing to redistribute wealth,' 'One day we will attain a society within capitalist systems where no one suffers social exclusion.' It is a scenario akin to the emperor's new clothes. Every now and then some brave individual will not be able to contain her or himself and will stand up and state the obvious, some apparent insight which a good percentage of people were thinking but didn't have the nerve to say. For example, 'If a small number of people get the majority of the wealth, then inevitably a large number of people are going to get a lot less.' There will be a sigh of collective relief, then often a dead silence when no one speaks up in support. Afterwards, however, the person will be congratulated, as though they had delivered some startling new analysis. If the insight is considered to be too controversial by the Commission, then the speaker may very well find that his or her contribution has been edited out of the records.

My decision to research the underlying ideology of what was going on in these settings was grounded in the problems I and other grass-roots representatives experienced in raising issues that were not part of the prevailing agenda. I had so many questions:

- Why did the direct involvement in these processes of grass-roots women, black people and those in poverty become such a contentious issue?
- Why was it a never-ending fight to put anti-racist initiatives on the agenda in the late 1980s and early 1990s?
- Why were the efforts to set up all-women working parties given such a hard time?
- Why did the thematic group on participation deteriorate so badly in the Third Poverty Programme?
- Why did many of those from grass-roots groups feel excited about the work they were involved in and at the same time experience such terrible feelings of isolation, anger, grief?

And yet we still wanted to carry on. What could we learn about the context we were working in, and from each other, that would help us to understand more about the dilemmas we were trying to deal with?

I use 'we' here but the 'we' were never a static group. Concern about the different issues varied according to race, gender and class, according to the complex interrelationship of these social constructions, the context we were working in and according to the individual concerned. Nevertheless, I also felt that there was a commonality of experience amongst the grass-roots women I worked alongside, which I wanted to explore.

Uncovering the theory

The work I undertook to help me understand these dilemmas initially led me down two very different paths and into two very different areas of knowledge – to the extent that at times I wondered whether I had undertaken two entirely different and incompatible pieces of work. They were what some feminists might refer to as male and female paradigms. The first concentrated on the public world of European politics, in particular suprastate corporatism, and examined the underlying ideologies that have in the past left women very much unaccounted for. The second involved interviewing women who represented grass-roots organizations in Europe, and through this uncovering the 'private' world of women – domestic work, the physical and emotional investment in bringing up children, the exploitation of the body, the experiential and the emotional. I experienced enormous problems in 'marrying' the two.

Cynthia Enloe, a feminist writer on politics, states that 'the international is personal and the personal international'. With my personal engagement in the politics of the EU I became fascinated by how personal experience of this kind linked into broad, international political processes. If the personal is political, how could I explain the dilemmas we faced, the emotions we felt? What were the politics at play?

To be involved in the movement for social solidarity in the EU *felt* as though we were playing a part in enacting a grand theory, whatever the reality of the theory in practice. However, this instinct was confounded by my inability to find any analysis in EU documentation of what social solidarity actually meant. It seemed that those using the terminology deliberately dissociated themselves from any identifiable political ideology.

It was only after some time that I was signposted to the work of the social theorist Emile Durkheim. He had examined the concept of social solidarity in great depth in the late nineteenth century and was a major influence on the construction of modern concepts of liberal and social democracy. There was much in his work that resonated with the movement towards social solidarity under Delors, particularly on the relationship between organic solidarity and social corporatism. I could not stop reading him. Yet the more I read the more depressed I became. I realized later that I had become locked into a classical 'male' political discourse, handed down from Aristotle and only lately being challenged by feminist writers, where the body and emotion, the domestic and the home, the personal and the private, had been deliberately and systematically abstracted from the political theory.

I was only able to break out of this intellectual straitjacket when I acted on an instinct and applied a feminist perspective to Durkheim's life and work. I became fascinated by the role of his wife, who was either absent or appeared as a mere footnote in most of the studies of his life and works. My mind cleared, my intellectual energy returned and I had the physical sensation of being able to breathe again.

The Delors/Durkheim connection

Using Durkheim as a reference point for the Delors period is not to suggest that his ideas have been imprinted on the EU, only that they are part of a legacy of thinking, still current in both liberal and social democratic ideology and practice, which informs us about some of the modern-day undercurrents in the movement towards social solidarity in Europe. As Eagleton says, 'Ideology is a text woven of a whole tissue of different conceptual strands; it is traced through by divergent histories' (1991: 1).

Durkheim's thinking is only one of many strands which make up the text of social solidarity, but it is, I believe, a significant strand. Most of Durkheim's areas of interest resonate in their different ways with the contemporary discourse on social solidarity in the EU. For the purposes of this chapter I shall concentrate on his discussion of corporatism, organic solidarity and the division between body and mind, the personal and the political.

Corporatism

The history of the notion of social solidarity in the EU is very recent, and as yet there is little political analysis of the term. Many of the sources one might use are from recent policy papers and funding programme documents. However, some political writers highlight how the development of concepts such as participation, partnership and social integration are part of the discourse involved in both federalist and suprastate politics. Slater writes:

> Almost by definition the building of a political community means the creation of a sense of community or solidarity among the people of a given region. It is this sense of solidarity which gives legitimacy to the Community's institutions. A viable political community needs the allegiance of its mass public as well as that of elites. (1994: 155)

This seems to be an underlying rationale for the Delors concept of solidarity, exemplified in his keynote speech 'A Necessary Union' at Bruges in 1989 (Nelsen and Stubb 1994: 52) and expanded in many public addresses and policy papers since that date. The discourse which framed these speeches and papers suggested that if the European market was to thrive, then federal and suprastate institutions and networks would need to be developed so that international capital did not become divorced from the realities of people's daily existence. Suprastate corporate strategies helped to ensure that common policies reflected mainstream 'consensus' within an international capitalist system.

Delors himself did not come from the socialist left in France, but from a politics rooted in the social democrat/Christian democrat European tradition. Ross states that Delors's ideals owed a great deal to the Catholic anti-individualism of Mounier, the early twentieth-century French philosopher. Mounier believed that:

> Society grew from delicate interdependence in which different social groups owed one another active solidarity. . . . The state had a role, but in facilitating rather than substituting for the active agency of groups and moralized individuals working together. (Ross 1995: 17)

This philosophy is reflected in the Commission's thinking on the development of social partnerships to further European union during the Delors period, with representative bodies selected by government to negotiate on behalf of different sectors of society. The discourse suggests that the free market cannot on its own guarantee morality, social order or social cohesion. At the same time the Commission was being accused of being over-bureaucratic and distanced from the realities of the people. It was also faced with a proliferation of interest groups lobbying for their own particular agenda. By drawing these interest groups together into cohesive bodies and encouraging them to talk to each other the European institutions, it was felt, could help to circumvent the problems of pluralism. Dialogue with and between corporatist institutions became a way of furthering cohesion between these pluralist interests in a competitive, capitalist society.

Schmitter traces this thinking, so characteristic of Delors, back to Durkheim,

> with his concept of professional corporations as the main institutional basis of 'organic solidarity' in modern societies characterised by a highly developed division of labour . . . which have prepared an ideological basis, often via social democracy for the growing importance of associations and organizational concertation. (Schmitter 1979: 10)

Durkheim believed that the state played a central role in regulating both sides of industry. The state needs to be strong and independent but also

> in close communication with the ideas of the mass of the population. . . . The more that deliberation and reflection and a critical spirit play a considerable part in the course of public affairs, the more democratic the nation. (Giddens 1972: 60)

However, the state alone could not guarantee this democracy, for it was distant from the complex groupings in society: it did not have its finger on the pulse. Nor was participative democracy involving the majority of the population feasible, given the divergent views of the mass of individuals which make up society. Attempting to represent each and every one would lead to confusion, uncertainty and chaos.

Durkheim's thinking is very much reflected in the discourse of the European Commission. Social Affairs Commissioner Paidrig Flynn, in his introduction to the Green Paper *European Social Policy. Options for the Union*, states:

> The rich diversity of the cultures and social systems within the European Union is a competitive advantage in a fast changing world. . . . But diversity may deteriorate into disorder if the common goals which embody the distinctive values of European society and are set out in the Treaty on European Union, are not defended by the efforts of the member states and by people themselves. (CEC 1993: 7)

Durkheim believed that his own economic era was in crisis. With the growth of capitalism, consumers and producers became more separate, with dangerous consequences.

> The fusion of different segments draws the markets together into a single market which embraces almost all society. . . . The result is that each industry produces for consumers spread over the whole surface of the country or even of the entire world. . . . The search for increased profit in this environment knows no boundaries. . . . Accordingly production becomes unchecked and unregulated. . . . From this comes the crises which periodically dislocate economic life. (Giddens 1986: 75)

Durkheim warned that 'under such conditions moral equilibrium is unstable: it requires but a slight blow to disrupt it' (Giddens 1991: 175).

In order to overcome this moral turpitude, Durkheim thought that the economic apparatus, and the various agencies involved in its functioning, should be regulated in a way that those affected believed to be just, with the rights and duties of those involved determined according to their particular economic role.

Again, this correlates with the thinking of Delors. Like Durkheim, Delors placed his faith in the mediative capacity of corporative institutions. By working with the state, these institutions would help to construct a balance of power based on common, co-operative values, rather than on the values of individual greed and self-interest. There is growing evidence to suggest that it was the influence of this kind of argument that led to the Commission's decision to set up and help fund the EAPN, and other similar NGOs (Hinds 1990; Harvey and Kiernan 1991).

Durkheim himself had been vague as to how the corporation or 'occupational association' would be constituted but was more specific about its political role. He believed that a moral equilibrium would not happen naturally under capitalism but would be achieved only if the state was in consultation with representative bodies which were close enough to the people they represented to know their main interests and how these were likely to change.

The corporation also had to be in touch with the realities of economic life under capitalism. In the late nineteenth century Durkheim was far-sighted enough to predict international corporatist developments in the EU: 'Since the market, formally localised in the town, has become national and international, the corporation must expand to the same degree' (Giddens 1986: 77). Although he predicted that these corporations would include employers and employees, what he could not predict was that they might also include networks and initiatives representing the poor and unemployed, such as the EAPN.

Organic solidarity in theory

Not only does Durkheim write extensively on the harmonious potential of 'corporations' to negotiate with the state on behalf of different sectors, he links this with the much broader concept of 'organic solidarity', which he considers to be the naturally cohesive quality of a democratic capitalist society. Durkheim's work 'The Division of Labour' (Giddens 1991) draws together many of the undercurrents in his thinking on solidarity. Through the division of labour capitalist society evolves organic solidarity. This develops because those involved in separate and yet interdependent activities are less likely to be in competition than to value and uphold the harmony that may be derived from mutual interdependence. Individuals would not survive in a society based on self-interest; instead the individual 'depends on society because he depends on the parts which comprise it' (Lukes 1973: 153).

The division of labour, Durkheim argued, had an economic rationale, but also furthered a morality of co-operation in capitalist societies. It was inherently a source of solidarity once it was morally regulated. Durkheim believed that the existence of class conflict indicated that the realization of organic solidarity was incomplete. This led to *anomie*, alienation from a sense of morality, and the use of coercive power by one class upon another. Corporations helped to mediate between groups of people and the state in sorting out these tensions.

This political discourse remains as significant within the EU as it did in Durkheim's time. Lehmbruch writes:

> Liberal corporatism rests on the theoretical premise that there exists strong interdependence between the interests of conflicting social groups in a capitalist economy. This 'interdependence of interests' image of society is clearly opposed to a 'conflict of interests' image which (as in the Marxist concept of class conflict) stresses the ultimate incompatibility of antagonistic demands. (Lehmbruch 1979: 55)

For Durkheim, class conflict indicates that change is needed. But class conflict does not in itself enhance the possibility of progressive change, rather it inhibits it. In this lies a key difference between the ideologies of liberal and social democracy and those of a Marxist persuasion. For Marx, class struggle was the key to progressive change. The structural relationship between classes was one of inherent antagonism rather than potential harmony.

Marx argued that, if the division of labour is inherently a source of solidarity, why the determined need for moral regulation (Draper 1977: 306)? Is it that the tensions and conflicts which result from the division of labour are ameliorated in ways that control and contain rather than liberate and enfranchise? Whereas Marxists argue that the division of labour creates fundamental inequalities due to the unequal acquisition of wealth, and that these carry with them a constant internal dynamic of resistance, activism and praxis, Durkheim argued that the division of labour is inherently co-operative and potentially harmonious.

Organic solidarity in practice

A Durkheimian ideology certainly appears to underpin the Commission's determination to bring the economic and social partners to the negotiating table. However, *cross-sectoral* partnerships were not very successful under Delors. The three-way dialogue promoting social solidarity between employers, employees and the Commission never really got off the ground. Clearly, there are ideological differences between the European

Trade Union Confederation (ETUC) and the Union of Industrial and Employers' Confederations of Europe (UNICE). Although the Commission referred to them as social partners and in the early 1990s began to include NGOs in the consultation process, particularly with the development of the Social Policy Forum, it is debatable whether any long-lasting partnerships have yet been formed between the three different sectors represented by employers, trade unions and NGOs.

At the Val Duchesse talks in 1984 between UNICE and the ETUC the employers refused to be bound by any legislation that might be suggested. During the rest of the 1980s they showed themselves unwilling to commit themselves to the *grand rendezvous* envisaged by Delors (1986).

Broad alliances were much more common *within* the social sectors, in some instances encouraged and funded by the Commission itself, with these alliances then drawn into consultation with the Commission on different aspects of current policy. They include, for example, the EAPN, as already discussed, and more recently the Platform, a broad-based pressure group consisting of transnational NGOs working in the European arena.

Although the broad alliances developed by NGOs and the trade union movement would claim to be independent and to be developing their own agendas from their diverse constituent bodies, some have recently begun to adopt the discourse on social solidarity in their policy statements (ETUC 1995). Do the social partners who commit themselves to this principle have an understanding of the ideological issues at play? I would suggest that there has been little theoretical debate independent of the Commission, and that those involved in the action are often left struggling to implement a concept that in practice has many contradictions.

Even within the social sector of NGOs there has often been a radical division of interests between the large, corporatist organizations and smaller, more radical groups (Cohen 1998). It would seem that theories of social solidarity within the EU dramatically oversimplify the unity of interests as well as the power differentials between those involved in building 'organic solidarity'. The power of the rhetoric appears to have overtaken the political analysis. Not only are class interests at issue here, but also the interests of those experiencing a combination of oppressions, in particular women and black people.

Durkheim believed that 'moral rules are shaped by society under the pressure of collective needs' (Giddens 1971: 69). He tended to argue that what was 'normal' in society had a positive moral value. That which is normal is deduced from that which is prevalent (*ibid.*: 93). One could counter this by arguing that that which is normal is generally that which is dominant, whether moral or not.

What may be considered by many as 'normal' in modern-day capitalist society is a hegemony that tends to exclude women's interests, if not their presence, and certainly excludes black people and those with the least economic power. Networks drawing together plural groups within this socio/economic environment have a tendency to reflect, if not mirror, hegemony within their constituent membership. If such is the case, then little has changed since Durkheim's time, as I hope the following snapshot of his life will reveal.

The private as political

Durkheim's theories on solidarity excluded women, black people and those in poverty. They also excluded the body and emotion and rejected the idea of the personal as political. All these, as I shall later argue, are in danger of remaining excluded from the dominant ideology and practice of the EU. Durkheim stated that 'no theory or analysis which begins from the 'individual' . . . can successfully grasp the specific properties of social phenomena' (Giddens 1971: 87). It is the synthesis of individuals coexisting that needs to be studied, not the individual as such. His own life belies this theory.

Durkheim was born in 1858 in Epinal in Lorraine. His was a traditional orthodox Jewish family which cultivated in him a sense of duty and respect for the law, disdain for wealth achieved without hard work and social responsibility to others, and belief in the moral influence of family life, education and community. In short, Durkheim had some commitment to organic solidarity from the outset.

Being a Jew may have given Durkheim a perspective on life common to a number of Jewish thinkers of this period, that of the outsider looking on (Bauman 1989). He acknowledged that the Jewish community developed tighter social bonds to sustain its members against antisemitism. This 'incitement to hatred' he felt could be made a criminal offence (Lukes 1973: 299).

Durkheim's views on antisemitism are far-sighted and

yet out of step with his analysis of other common senti-
ments/discriminations in society, which he tended to view as
'normal'. Though singling out antisemitism as symptomatic of
society's ills, other forms of discrimination – classism, patriar-
chy and racism against black people, for example – he appeared
to regard as part of the natural order. Could it be that he was able
to connect his own oppression with the concept of social solidarity only because it was real for him? Is a strong identity with
a political cause ontologically based?

Durkheim developed his ideas within the closeted academic
environment of university life. Perhaps this drew him to analysis of the *status quo* rather than to analysis informed by interaction with different social groupings, as was the case with
Gramsci, who developed a very different concept of social solidarity. Gramsci examined how radical movements might
counter the hegemony of social democracy by working to
develop a counter-hegemony informed by those most oppressed
by dominant political and economic structures (1978).

Durkheim studied long hours, was of a serious and staid dis-
position, but was to find great happiness once he married.
Louise Durkheim took complete responsibility for the care,
education and emotional well-being of their two children
(Lukes 1973). For Durkheim too, she was a constant support,
helping him in the editing of his work, and maintaining an
engaging and lively outlook. Durkheim's nephew, Marcel
Mauss, admired her spirit immensely, especially given the
social restrictions she had to endure. 'My uncle made her lead a
life that was more than austere, but she led it with gaiety' (*ibid.:*
99).

Smith writes of how the Aristotelian categories of mind and
body are kept separate for such a male philosopher by:

> a woman who keeps house for him, bears his children, washes his
> clothes, looks after him when he is sick and generally provides for
> the logistics of his bodily existence. . . . At almost every point
> women mediate for men the relation between the conceptual mode
> of action and the actual forms in which it is and must be realised
> and the actual conditions upon which it depends. (Smith 1987:
> 89–90)

The more men are separated from the domestic and emotional
realities of life the less likely they are to include them in an
analysis of material reality.

Mauss writes that his aunt removed Durkheim from 'every

material care and all frivolity' (Lukes 1973: 99). Louise Durkheim's intellectual, practical and emotional responsibilities, that work which has been the work of women through the ages, are barely represented in Durkheim's writings, other than in the institution of marriage and the family, which he saw as 'unexcelled as a territory for feminine activity' (ibid.: 209).

Durkheim acknowledged that women might very well gain little from marriage, but that for men it was a central institution within the notion of social solidarity, for it controlled their lustful and individualistic desires and gave them security and a link with wider society.

At that moment in history the wife's subordination to the man was the 'necessary condition of family unity' (ibid.: 209). Durkheim wrote that women might in the future gain equal legal status within marriage but that it was not appropriate given the social construction of society in his time. Louise Durkheim would not figure in his theories of the division of labour, for she was not paid for domestic work. Women's unpaid labour appeared to Durkheim to be conceived as one of the 'spontaneous manifestations of natural inequalities in society' (Giddens 1991: 182).

It seems that Durkheim did not regard these 'natural inequalities' as necessarily static:

> If the institutions of classes or castes sometimes gives rise to frictions instead of producing solidarity, this is because the distribution of social functions on which it rests does not correspond, or rather no longer corresponds, to the distribution of natural talents. (Ibid.: 180)

This is a consequence not of the division of labour, as such, but of economic and social changes which alter relationships within the division of labour.

Durkheim's thinking here is central to his theories of social solidarity. Rather than society creating oppressive inequalities, these are seen as part of a natural order. The dominant social divisions tend to be regarded as normal and therefore morally acceptable in that era. In a contemporary European setting, a Durkheiman argument might run, women have now advanced to take more of a place in society through economic and social change.

Louise Durkheim, like many other women of her period, had not advanced sufficiently to be playing a role in the division of labour. For Durkheim, she was present in the private but not in the political sphere. However, whilst women in contemporary society may now have a greater public presence, they continue to carry the major responsibilities of work in the private and are increasingly divided by the dominant inequalities inherent in race and class.

The EU experience

Public and private realms

This separation of the private from the political remains a constant in the development of EU solidarity programmes. Levitas (1998) argues that the Commission is in the process of developing a 'new Durkheimian hegemony' reflected in the discourse on social cohesion, solidarity and integration.

The very fact that the legal instruments of the EU focus primarily on the world of work within a capitalist economic system means that women's work in the private 'world' is more likely to be excluded from the agenda. Likewise, the social and economic interests of those fighting emancipatory causes will have difficulty being placed on the agenda of a political system which refuses to consider the radical redistribution of wealth.

That which is dominant is that which is normal. Those emancipatory struggles which are hidden from view tend not to be addressed until they become mainstream concerns. An example is the fight to combat racism and xenophobia by various grass-roots organizations and networks, which was systematically taken off the agenda by representatives of the European Commission, until it was taken up as a concerted strategy by members of the European Parliament (Hoskyns 1996).

Gramscian theory on the development of a counter-hegemony rooted in collective social movements, as well as feminist/socialist theory on the personal as political, helps to counterbalance the liberal and social democratic ideologies which appear to underpin the movement towards social solidarity in the EU. These more radical critiques helped me to unravel the contradictions, frustrations and problematics which are embedded in EU social solidarity programmes.

I was already conscious as a participant in seminars of how much is edited out of written material at an EU level, particu-

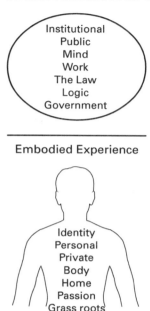

Figure 2.1 Political exclusion

larly from minutes and written reports. I believed that this discarded information would be key to my research. A great deal of relevant material is in people's heads, especially those of marginalized groups, who are not normally given a voice. I decided to concentrate on interviewing women active in grass-roots organizations in European settings and work with them to explore that hidden material as a basis for uncovering what might be happening within the social solidarity programmes under Delors.

What emerged from these interviews was the remarkable dissociation in EU arenas of the private from the public, grass-roots politics from EU politics, embodied experience from formal debate, the personal from the political (Cohen 1998). The classical tradition of separating the public world of politics from private concerns, work from the home, the intellect from passion and experience, government and the law from grass-roots action, continues to prevail within EU social solidarity programmes. Thus the very programmes which have as their object to counter social exclusion can continue to perpetuate the process (Figure 2.1).

Women's exclusion has been doubly reinforced by an epistemological tradition which insists that all rational thought in the
political arena should be disembodied, that it would otherwise
be tainted by body and emotion. Cavarero comments that 'male
into neutral or universal is a very ancient matter: yet the ration-
alising abstractive capacity of modern theory brings it to its
maximum fulfilment' (1992: 36).

In contrast to this rationalist, disembodied tradition in political thinking, most feminist epistemologies regard knowledge
as subjective and believe that through a process of consciousness-raising we can work to understand more about ourselves
and the world around us. Stanley argues that the Durkheimian
insistence on sociology's scientific objectivity stems from 'a set
of intellectual practices for separating people from knowledge of
their own subjectivity' (1990: 11).

Feminist/socialist thinking drew me towards engaging with
women more likely to have experience of discrimination,
towards considering commonalities and difference, and examining ways in which structural systems of domination may or
may not interlink.

> Many people have noted that being 'other' brings with it the posses-
> sion of knowledge concerning 'rulers' and their ways, but also the
> different and subversive knowledge that accrues to the 'ruled', as a
> consequence of seeing the 'underside' of oppression. (*Ibid.*: 30)

Patterns within complexity

Some feminist postmodernists argue that we can never know
another person's reality and that we are such diverse and indi-
vidually complex beings that to place us in categories of race,
class, gender, etc., stereotypes rather than informs (Weedon
1987). Although this is to some extent the case, one does not
have to look far to see that there are great material differences
between groups of people: that some are much more likely to
benefit whilst others are more likely to suffer.

So, for example, unskilled workers, black people, single-
parent mothers are more likely to be in poverty in the EU than
white ruling-class men. This indicates that not only does the
material world favour some more than others, but that we will
all also be socially conditioned by the experience of this
material reality and assumptions about it. So that, although
thoughts and feelings can never be experienced in the same way,
there can still exist a commonality of experience within various

groupings in society (Collins 1990). Thus, as my interviews with grass-roots women developed, and despite the enormous complexity of the political, social and economic fabric of the EU, some consistent patterns began to emerge. These patterns demonstrate ways in which European networks and programmes are required to work in political settings deeply embedded in the politics of liberal and social democracies.

The main conclusions from the interviews are as follows:

- In using society's systems to set up a network, the European network can begin to reflect those systems. The grass roots feel dominated by the large professional organizations, the South by the North, women by men, black people by white people and those in poverty are not even there.
- Networking generally tends to adopt an organizational culture based on apparent consensus, which means that the dominant interests usually end up controlling the agenda. Because those interests are less likely fundamentally to challenge the *status quo*, the network itself can take a non-confrontational political stance. Rather than being worked through, dissent and division are more usually buried or repressed. There appears to be consensus but in fact there is hidden repression.
- Negotiated consensus develops a culture of social corporatism where, for example, charitable organizations representing the most disadvantaged in society remain within boundaries which do not challenge the root causes of disadvantage. As the root causes become more hidden, so they become more difficult to confront. If one does confront them one is being disruptive. All manner of people can feel unsafe if that happens. Better the security of repression and order.
- The rhetoric promises equality and participation. There may be a large number of women – sometimes they are in the majority. But there remains a huge gap between 'espoused theory' and 'theory in use', as already discussed. Women very often operate within the confines of 'male' traditional ways of organizing and do not draw on the experience of organization in the women's movement, by addressing issues of class and race. Instead, embedded ways of working control presence, emotion, voice and identity. In doing so they control and marginalize the participation of women, black people and those from grass-roots organizations.

Conclusion

The tensions, divisions and inequalities outlined above are comparable to the problems faced by most grass-roots movements within the European nation states. It may be, however, that the European Commission's rhetoric promises rather more than that of national politicians. In an attempt to engage the citizens of Europe in this 'European experiment', sentiments of participation, social solidarity and egalitarianism abound. In particular, the Commission has placed much emphasis on the need to give those in poverty a voice. Some of us involved in grass-roots movements naively believed this rhetoric and got upset when actions did not match the words.

Yet groups in poverty are rarely given powers of decision-making in liberal and social democracies. What is notable is that some *do* get that opportunity in EU programmes and networks. The final conclusions of the women I interviewed on social solidarity indicated that, although the EU is governed by a hidden ethos that is predominantly male, white and economically competitive, there is a political dynamic taking place that is rather more than social corporatism. Even if the social initiatives proliferated to help sustain political and economic cohesion within a capitalist system, there is nevertheless a small amount of slippage which can provide emancipatory movements with space for manoeuvre.

To understand why this may be the case, I return to the political and economic context of the movement towards a social Europe. Although a primary concern was the need for social cohesion within the context of economic union, it included the need to engage with the concerns of those countries and political interests that had less to gain from the Union. Left and left-of-centre parties, which include within their constituency emancipatory movements, along with countries less equipped to engage in transnational economic competition, demanded some space and presence within the Union. This has meant that the conflicting politics of corporatism and socialism, as well as the divisions between North and South, are to some extent played out in social networks.

In the post-Delors period these networks continue to press for a social agenda. Their work is supported by some sections in DG V in the European Commission and by such bodies as the bi-annual Social Policy Forum held in Brussels, and the 'Comité des Sages', which has consulted voluntary sector representatives in different countries on their role in Europe. Yet, in the general run of things, these consultations still carry relatively little weight in a Europe dominated by the Council of Ministers. The 1996 Treaty of Amsterdam made some concessions to a social agenda, but none that would have a major impact on the engagement of social movements across the EU.

EU social initiatives funded by the European Commission may state that they wish to encourage the empowerment of those facing poverty and social exclusion, yet the political institutions restrict, if not deny, that potential. The politics of the EU, as well as of individual nations, continue to exert control in ways which reflect existing systems of dominance within and between race, class and gender. This means, for example, that larger corporatized NGOs are more likely to acquire funding at the expense of grass-roots, emancipatory organizations.

If the EU is to become more participatory, institutions will need to break with the political tradition that confines political knowledge exclusively to the public domain. Conversely, those involved in social movements need to break out of the narrow political confines current in the late twentieth century, which place individual experience above all else, avoiding the connection with broader economic, political and social developments. Political knowledge comes from the relationship between the private and the public.

It could be argued that some of the more emancipatory and democratic EU initiatives are those that combine the political understandings of the private and the public, as illustrated in Figure 2.2. However, given that these initiatives are more likely to integrate an analysis of ways in which the discriminations inherent in race, class and gender consign disadvantaged groups of people to the very margins of society, they are sure to have a long uphill struggle in effecting any significant change in the way power and resources are distributed within the EU.

There exists a tension between the 'top-down' approach of dominant political institutions which draw 'civil society' in to reinforce the *status quo* and the 'bottom-up' approach of many social movements led by the disadvantaged in society which act as potential agents of change (Cox 1999: 7). With the development of alliances involving participatory ways of working around race, class, gender and disability, some social movements may be in the process of developing an alternative social

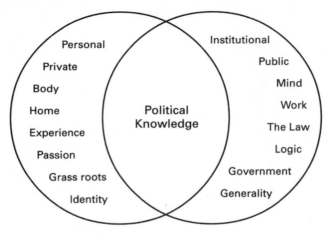

Figure 2.2 Political knowledge

solidarity which challenges rather than colludes with the political and economic hegemony.

The grass-roots women I interviewed were uncertain whether solidarity could ever be built within the EU social networks, given the power differentials in civil society which those networks tend to mirror. They nevertheless felt engaged in a political process which was living, dynamic, in process. This process often took place in alternative sites to the political hegemony, settings which were disparate, seemingly fragmented, hidden from view. However, when women involved in social action moved into a political arena, there were times when their combined understandings formed a body of experience that seized the moment, claimed the space, changed the political direction.

Women's solidarity in a grass-roots context may appear amorphous, but that is not necessarily a contradiction. Margo described the process vividly.

> Social solidarity is by its nature very fluid. You can't pin it down and that makes it hard to organize. The way I see social solidarity, it seems like it's almost spontaneous but it's not. It's a combination of a lot of ideas, networks, informal and formal organizations that are not really visible. It seems to take off spontaneously and then vanishes in the same way. It only emerges when there is a reason for it, and it's like the tip of the iceberg, and the rest of it is hidden for most of the time. And then it vanishes – but an iceberg did wreck the *Titanic*, didn't it?

References

Argyris, C., and D. Schon (1978), *Organizational Learning. A Theory in Action Perspective*, Reading MA, Addison-Wesley.

Bauman, Z. (1989), *Intimations of Postmodernity*, London, Routledge.

Cavarero, A. (1992), 'Equality and sexual difference. Amnesia in political thought' in G. Bock and S. James (eds), *Beyond Equality and Difference*, London, Routledge.

Commission of the European Communities (1993), *European Social Policy. Options for the Union*, Brussels, CEC.

Cohen, S. (1998), 'Body, space and presence. Women's social exclusion in the politics of the EU', *European Journal of Women's Studies* 5 (3–4), 367–80.

Collins, P. (1990), *Black Feminist Thought. Knowledge, Consciousness and the Politics of Empowerment*, London, Routledge.

Cox, R. W. (1999), 'Civil society at the turn of the millennium. Prospects of an alternative world order', *Review of International Studies* 25, 3–28.

Delors, J. (1986), *The Single Act and Europe. A Moment of Truth*, Luxembourg, Office of Official Publications of the EC.

Draper, H. (1977), *Karl Marx's Theory of Revolution I, State and Bureaucracy*, London, Monthly Review Press.

Eagleton, T. (1991), *Ideology. An Introduction*, London, Verso.

European Anti Poverty Network (1994), *NGO Forum on European Social Policy, Brussels, 8–9 April 1994*, Brussels, EAPN.

Enloe, C. (1989), *Making Feminist Sense of International Politics. Bananas, Beaches and Bases*, London, Pandora.

European Trade Union Confederation (1995), *For a Strong, Democratic and Open European Union built on Solidarity*, Brussels, ETUC.

European Union (1993), *Declaration 'Towards a Europe of Greater Solidarity respecting Human Dignity and rejecting Exclusion'*, Brussels, the Council, the Parliament, the Commission, the Economic and Social Committee and the Committee of the Regions.

Giddens, A. (1971), *Capitalism and Modern Social Theory. An Analysis of the Writings of Marx, Durkheim and Max Weber*, Cambridge, Cambridge University Press.

Giddens, A., ed. (1972), *Emile Durkheim. Selected Writings*, Cambridge, Cambridge University Press.

Giddens, A., ed. (1986), *Durkheim on Politics and the State*, Oxford, Polity Press.

Giddens, A., ed. (1991), *Emile Durkheim. Selected Writings*, Cambridge, Cambridge University Press.

Gramsci, A. (1978), *Selections from the Prison Notebooks*, ed. Hoare and Nowell Smith, London, Lawrence & Wishart.

Harvey, B., and J. Kiernan (1991), *Poverty: a Challenge to us all. The Foundation of the European Anti Poverty Network, from Working Group to Launch*, Belfast, Northern Ireland Council of Voluntary Associations.

Hinds, B. (1990), in *European Anti Poverty Network. South West Region Conference Report*, Bristol, Single Parent Action Network.

Hoskyns, C. (1996), *Integrating Gender. Women, Law and Politics in the European Union*, London, Verso.

Lehmbruch, G. (1979), 'Consociational democracy, class conflict and the new corporatism' in P. Schmitter and G. Lehmbruch, *Trends towards Corporatist Intermediation*, London, Sage.

Levitas, R. (1998), 'The concept of social exclusion and the new "Durkheimian" hegemony', *Critical Social Policy*, spring, 5–20.

Lukes, S. (1973), *Emile Durkheim*, London, Penguin Press.

Nelsen, B. F., and A. Stubb (1994), *The European Union. Readings on the Theory and Practice of European Integration*, London, Lynne Rienner.

Poverty 3 (1992), *The Role of the Two Sides of Industry in the Fight against Economic and Social Exclusion in Europe*, seminar of the Poverty 3 Programme, Aalborg, Denmark, Brussels, European Commission.

Ross, G. (1995), *Jacques Delors and European Integration*, Cambridge, Polity Press.

Schmitter, P. (1979), 'Still the century of corporatism?' in P. Schmitter and G. Lehmbruch, *Trends towards Corporatist Intermediation*, London, Sage.

Slater, M. (1994), 'Political elites, popular indifference and community building' in B. F. Nelsen and A. Stubb (eds), *The European Union*, London, Lynne Rienner.

Smith, D. (1987), 'Women's perspective as a radical critique of sociology' in S. Harding (ed.), *Feminism and Methodology*, Bloomington IN, Indiana University Press.

Stanley, L., ed. (1990), *Feminist Praxis. Research, Theory and Epistemology in Feminist Sociology*, London, Routledge.

Weedon, C. 91987), *Feminist Practice and Poststructuralist Theory*, Oxford, Blackwell.

Wise, M., and Gibb, R. (1993), *Single Market to Social Europe*, Harlow, Longman.

Young, I. (1990), 'The ideal of community and the politics of difference' in L. Nicholson (ed.), *Feminism/Postmodernism*, London, Routledge.

3

Reconciling suprastatism and accountability: a view from Sweden

SVERKER GUSTAVSSON

The reorientation of Sweden's foreign policy in 1990 took place in the aftermath of two major historical events. One was the fall of the Berlin wall. In the new situation Sweden and Finland became less interested in keeping up a buffer zone of non-aligned states in Northern Europe. Thereby the policy of 'non-alignment aiming at neutrality in wartime' became obsolete. The other was the impossibility of fighting unemployment alone. In an international context of established neo-liberalism, the policy of full employment turned into a political impasse (J. Gustavsson 1998).

As a combined effect of these two major developments – the end of the Cold War and the international retrenchment of the welfare state – Sweden entered the European Union (EU) on 1 January 1995, after a referendum on 13 November 1994. Politically this meant that Sweden did not debate membership until the democratic deficit had come to the forefront through the ratification problems related to the Maastricht Treaty. As a consequence, it became hard to convince the Swedish public that the deficit could be handled according to the pre-1989 idea of permissive consensus. The problem of reconciling suprastatism and democratic accountability did not seem to have any obvious practical solution.

Three main questions have been posed in the post-1995 public debate on the EU in Sweden. First, what should be our position as to the principle of *open government*? Should we contribute to a less secretive standard by trying to open up the EU procedures via using the less restrictive practices in Sweden? Second, what should be our position on the principle of *parliamentarianism*? The political system, which was introduced in 1917, meant a fusion between the majority in the Riksdag and the government. These basic institutions started to work in close co-operation with each other on regulatory as well as on fiscal matters. After we joined the EU, important parts of the legislative competences are pooled in the Council of Ministers at the EU level. Should the individual ministers in Stockholm then keep working together with their opposite numbers in the Riksdag? Or should they restrict themselves to a purely informative role in relation to their political base in the Riksdag? Third, what should be our position as to whether the democratic deficit in the EU should be *preserved* or *abolished*?

This third question – on which I am going to concentrate in this chapter – is the core constitutional policy problem within the general problematique of democracy and sovereignty (Newman 1996). In sum, and in my own view, there are two normatively defensible solutions – the German Constitutional Court's option of *autonomy-compatible provisionalism* on the one hand and the idea of *democratizing suprastatism* on the other.

When the Swedish people said yes to the EU in 1994, the majority in the referendum was based on the German idea of the provisional character of European suprastatism. As a consequence, the current Swedish discussion on joining the EMU and giving more weight to the more populous member states in the Council is very much influenced by the fact that the Swedish public defines the democratic problem at the European level as a matter of autonomy-compatible provisionalism. However, it is easy to consider joining the EMU as *neither* autonomy-compatible *nor* provisional. Likewise, it is hard to accept a demographic adjustment of the weights given to the different member countries in the voting rules of the Council. Why should Britain be given more weight than Sweden, as long as the Union as a whole is a union of states rather than a union of citizens?

One problem, five solutions

The broad and general problem, as I see it, is *whether* and if so *how* suprastatism and democratic accountability can be reconciled. By suprastatism I mean the particular combination of majority voting, direct effect and precedence of federal law that distinguishes a federal from a confederal form of government.

By democratic accountability I mean the principle that it should be possible to replace the holders of political office through general elections founded on universal suffrage and civil rights, and to achieve an alternative set of policies thereby.

My argument is formulated against the backdrop of federal systems being compared historically and worldwide. All such systems face the problem of how to reconcile the two basic principles of suprastatism and accountability. How can decision-making be carried out on a suprastatal basis while maintaining the accountability of office-holders, i.e. ensuring that leaders can be replaced and policies changed through elections?

The most common solution to the problem is to strike a balance between the one-state-one-vote principle, on the one hand, and the one-citizen-one-vote principle, on the other. This is accomplished through a two-chamber system, in which the states are equally represented in the one chamber and the citizens are equally represented in the other. Not only Canada and the US have overcome the opposition in this way, but also Austria, Germany, Spain and Switzerland.

The great and interesting exception is the EU. Its member states are democracies. Governance within the Union as such, however, diverges from the usual pattern by which suprastatism and accountability are combined. Within the framework of the first pillar, decision-making is suprastatal in character, at the same time as it is beyond the reach of collective judgement and review.

There are two main main lines of argument concerning this exception from the main rule. One view holds the asymmetry of the EU to be normatively unacceptable. Those who take this position wish to *abolish* the democratic deficit and to establish a symmetrical relationship between power and responsibility at the national as well as at the European level of governance. Abolitionism divides into two sub-options. Both aim to set the asymmetry at naught, either by abandoning suprastatism or by introducing democratic accountability at the European level.

The other main argument considers the Union to constitute progress, at any rate as compared with being forced to choose between two undesirable alternatives – the abandonment of suprastatism on the one hand, and its democratization on the other. Those preferring to uphold the imbalance between power and accountability choose, then, to *preserve* the democratic deficit. Preservationism divides into three sub-options, which

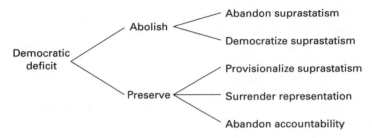

Figure 3.1 Five recommendations concerning the democratic deficit

are the subject of this chapter. These are to provisionalize suprastatism, to surrender representation or to abandon accountability. All are designed to reconcile suprastatism and accountability, but in a manner different from the way in which the two abolitionist alternatives do this.

In this chapter I leave the two abolitionist options aside.[1] After presenting an overall view of the alternatives, I remind the reader of the proposal to provisionalize suprastatism. The main focus will then be on the second and third variants of preservationism. The first of the latter two arguments seeks to defend suprastatism without accountability by arguing that a transnational separation of powers is more important than individual representation. The second defends the democratic deficit by pleading the increased need for independent rather than accountable government. In conclusion, I return to evaluating the three preservationist options as compared both with each other and with the two abolitionist options.

Provisionalize suprastatism

The defence of the democratic deficit which has been most frequently argued is the one set forth in the 1993 verdict (*BVerfGE*, 17, 155–213) of the German Constitutional Court. The question facing the court was whether the Law of Accession to the Treaty on European Union – which the Bundestag had passed by a large majority in December 1992 – could be reconciled with the demands for democratic accountability enshrined in the German Basic Law. Not until the court had answered that question in the affirmative could the Maastricht Treaty be ratified.

The German Constitutional Court argued as follows. The

suprastatism established in the first pillar of the Union Treaty is *provisional*. Sovereignties are delegated rather than surrendered. Such a delegation of sovereignties is acceptable, according to the court, as long as the criteria of the Basic Law are upheld. According to those criteria, the use of competences in common must be *marginal* in relation to the functioning of German democracy as a whole, and the uses to which those competences are put at the European level must be *predictable*. The delegation of German sovereignty must also be *revocable*; that is, the German authorities must retain the prerogative of reassuming the powers delegated if the criteria of marginality and predictability are not met. The German Constitutional Court deemed these three criteria to have been met, and so concluded that the ratification of the treaty was consistent with the demands for democratic accountability laid down in the Basic Law.

A relevant critical observation, it appears to me, is that the provisional character of suprastatism has never been demonstrated in practice. Besides its lack of realism, moreover, the argument presented by the court is inconsistent. For the court defends the democratic deficit in terms of marginality, predictability and revocability, leading one to expect the court would be disinclined to view the EMU as democratically acceptable. Yet the converse actually obtains. In adducing the position of the constitutionally independent and guarded Bundesbank, the court makes a European virtue out of a German exception from the general rule of popular sovereignty and democratic accountability.

Notwithstanding its vulnerability to such criticisms, however, the preservationist position, as argued by the German Constitutional Court, is in fact widely embraced. It can be examined in one of its most elaborated versions in the work of Fritz W. Scharpf. He calls for an overall European arrangement which is compatible *both* with the demands for autonomy put by the member states *and* with the advantages associated with collective action arising from the principle of provisional suprastatism (1994: 131 ff.). As a reformist and piecemeal constitutional engineer, Scharpf argues that we should attempt to achieve as much democracy as possible. If our purpose is to defend the principle of democratic governance in Europe, in the twenty-first century, we must proceed on the basis of a realistic picture of the political options facing us in view of the completed internal market.

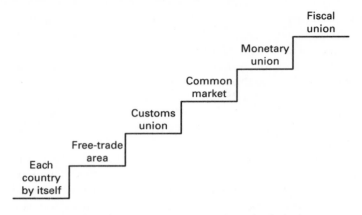

Figure 3.2 Bela Balassa's stairway metaphor of political integration

The implication of Scharpf's general idea becomes clear in the light of Bela Balassa's staircase metaphor of political integration (Figure 3.2). The member states of the EU have now reached the fourth step on the staircase, i.e. the completed Common Market. In the twenty-first century, Scharpf argues, the European system of governance should be based on recognition of the difference between *negative* and *positive* integration as regards the fulfilment of this fourth step. Negative integration is the abolition of barriers to the free movement of capital, goods, services and labour. Positive integration is the building up of welfare state arrangements – of the 'in kind' as well as the 'in cash' type – to compensate for the effects of negative integration.

Regulatory (and negative) policies do not require the same degree of democratic accountability and legitimacy as the *redistributive* (and positive) policies, Scharpf argues. Hence the established asymmetry is double. It is not only an asymmetrical relation between the location of power and and the location of responsibility. There is also a parallel asymmetry as to the *content* of public policies. Deregulation can be forced through by suprastatal means. Positive measures, in contrast, can be achieved only through individual but co-ordinated decisions by fifteen member states according to their constitutions and political structures.

This means – translated to the context of the Maastricht

Treaty – that the move from Common Market to monetary (and thereby probably by implication to fiscal) union is historically critical. If we insist upon going further up the staircase, we risk the introduction of fiscal federalism without a corresponding growth in the powers of the European Parliament. That would mean a far worse constitutional predicament than provisional suprastatism at the present level of mainly deregulatory policies and double asymmetry in non-fiscal matters (Scharpf, 1995: 581 ff., 1996a: 109 ff., b: 15 ff.).

The notion of provisional suprastatism is based on a rejection of two imagined scenarios of a contrary character. That is the thrust of the Scharpfian argument. Neither a system of sovereign nation states nor a completed federation is to be considered a 'historically natural' condition. The choice as to which arrangement is the more suitable should be made, rather, in the same way as the conflict between public and private ownership of the means of production is adjudged in the social democratic tradition, i.e. on a pragmatic and piecemeal basis.

The overriding purpose, from a modern (as distinct from a premodern or postmodern) standpoint, is to preserve the capacity for consciously accomplished and evaluated political change. Such a capacity presumes an argumentation about open alternatives which is based on reason. No course of development is inevitable. Neither the Westphalian system of nation states nor a United States of Europe represents the end of history. The democratic deficit is thus defended on the basis of the claim that the established suprastatism in Europe is provisional – and thus within the reach of democratic accountability still.

Those arguing for the provisional character of European suprastatism consider themselves limited in their thinking by two important restrictions: representative government and democratic accountability. Both these principles should be maintained, in the view of the German Constitutional Court. The desire for a partially suprastatal order may not be fulfilled at the expense of the member states as political entities with their own identity and capacity for action. Similarly, national electorates must continue to be able to hold their leaders accountable. Rather than give up these two restrictions, champions of provisional suprastatism abandon the principle that the citizens of the member states should not delegate their right of decision.

Surrender representation

One of the two restrictions considered here – representative government – is not respected if the representation of individuals belonging to a particular state is surrendered. The word 'state' here does not refer to an ethnically based political unit but rather to a territorally bounded constitutional community. The citizens of Switzerland count up the votes cast everywhere in their country equally, without regard to the fact that French, German, Italian and Romansh are spoken there.

The distinctive mark of a state, as that word is here employed, is the equal counting of votes within the constitutionally delimited community. *Verfassungspatriotismus* is the word used in German. It is the state which presents – under democratic conditions – the outer preconditions of public discussion and, thereby, willingness on the part of the minority to accept the decisions of the majority. For such decisions appear possible to influence. The Swedish-speaking citizens of Finland, for example, as a permanent minority have their rights guaranteed in the Finnish constitution. In this way a foundation is laid – through the procedure of a simple majority – for the use not merely of the regulatory norm-giving power, but of the redistributive fiscal power too.

According to the historically established form of normative democratic theory, there is a solution to the problem of the permanent minority. It is the provision of constitutionally stipulated rights. According to the fourth and fifth recommendations regarding the democratic deficit, however, this solution is insufficient, on account of the cultural, economic and social heterogeneity characterizing twenty-first-century Europe.

Those championing the fourth position consider it unsatisfactory, as a matter of principle, to present the suprastatism of the EU as provisional in nature. The deficit ought, in their view, to be defended more aggressively. They argue that the notion of representation for individual citizens must be abandoned. Otherwise, no effective defence of the prevailing constitutional asymmetry can be mounted against the onslaught of those wishing to abolish it.

According to those recommending the surrender of representative government, suprastatism and accountability should be reconciled in a manner different from that proposed by those embracing the first three recommendations mentioned. Instead of accountability on the basis of the representative-democratic principles of individual suffrage and of mediation through the agency of parties and elected representatives, they put the emphasis on the following two principles: separation of powers within the structure as a whole, and holding referendums in which all Europeans are asked to give their opinion.

The argument for surrendering representative government – as the best way of reconciling the presence of suprastatism with the absence of accountability – begins with objections to each of the other possibilities:

- *Abandon suprastatism.* Correct in principle, but the Common Market would disappear.
- *Democratize suprastatism.* Correct in principle, but there is no European demos. 'The great jump' is too risky.
- *Provisionalize suprastatism.* There is no satisfactory normative theory behind such an idea of a federal balance.

Edgar Grande may serve, in this review, as an exemplar of the position that representative government should be surrendered. He formulates this standpoint by presenting it against the background of a widely accepted critique. Wholly irrespective of European integration, he avers, there is cause to criticize representative government. Such a system does not succeed in actively forming popular opinion through an interplay between electors and elected. It is, likewise, far from admirable as regards the effective control by citizens over the policies actually pursued (Grande 1996: 347 ff.).

It is not with the ideal of popular government within a framework of national democracy, in other words, that Grande's recommendations should be compared. They should be assessed, rather, against the actual functioning of existing representative systems. He thus warns against the so-called Nirvana approach, which so easily appears in all political analysis. The ideal should compared with the ideal, and actual systems with actual systems. If one compares ideals with actual systems, one runs the risk of serious misjudgement.

Let us turn now to Grande's two proposals. One of his practical suggestions is *transnational referendums.* By such means, he suggests, a sufficient degree of legitimacy can be attained to make possible the maintenance of a structure marked by suprastatism without a corresponding mechanism for holding the European tier of government accountable. This is accomplished through having the European population as a whole adjudicate the conflicts arising from the confrontation of different constellations of Union organs and member states.

The point of these transnational referendums would not be simply, he writes, to grant immediate legitimation to the changes in the Maastricht Treaty then in session. All-Europe referendums would be able – in the long term, too, and with permanent effect – to work in a community-building manner. The word 'immediate' is of central importance here. All-Europe referendums would work in a Europeanizing direction. They would establish, as a *fait accompli*, a constituent power. A European *demos* with its own competence to establish its own competences would already be established thereby.

To this political effect may be added the establishment of a constitutional weapon on behalf of European citizens. In this way the possibilities are enhanced, at the margins, that the all-European system of decision-making will become responsive, if not responsible, to the 300 million Europeans who constitute the electorates of the member states (Grande 1996: 355).

Grande's second proposal for solving the problem of suprastatism without a corresponding mechanism for holding the European office-holders accountable is by establishing a *transnational separation of powers*. Given the material and institutional complexity of suprastatism in today's Europe, he argues, the responsibility of individual citizens and of parties, mass media and political organizations would simply be too much, even under the most favourable conditions. Effective control of the norm-giving and fiscal powers could be achieved at the European level only by consciously changing from the principle of individual control to that of institutional control, and achieving thereby the optimization of institutional control in the political system of the EU (Grande 1996: 355).

Grande cites one of the eighteenth-century American Federalist Papers, No. 51, according to which the different powers will 'control each other, at the same time that each will be controlled by itself' (Madison *et al.* 1787: 321). This idea is yet more relevant in the present European context, he argues. In twenty-first-century Europe, still more than in the eighteenth-century US, the effective control of political power can be secured only through strong institutions, rather than through procedures by which individual citizens within states have their say in general elections.

On the basis of this general approach, Grande recommends

that we go further – with both a stronger European Parliament and a two-chamber system at the European level, complete with the use of concurrent majorities. There is a risk, certainly, that increasing complexity will reduce the possibility of European-level decision-making. On this point, however, we are fortunate to have the European Commission as a possible institutional arbiter and mediator. Together with transnational referendums the Commission should be enough, according to Grande, to ensure that the separation of powers does not lead in excessive measure to a reduced capacity for action, as far as the use of suprastatism for integrative purposes is concerned.

Grande argues that, as a general matter, there is a dilemma here which must be confronted. The separation of powers should not, on the one hand, be permitted to produce a total decisional blockade. On the other hand, a system of mutual institutional controls – based on the separation-of-powers principle – is needed. According to the conceptual framework embraced by Grande, however, no demand for *democratic* accountability follows from the latter requirement. Such a notion orginates, namely, in the idea that legitimate governance issues from *private individuals* who *are represented* by those they elect. If we surrender this notion, the problem can be solved. In surrendering representation, those disposed to defend the democratic deficit emerge from their quandary more easily than if they cling stubbornly, in Grande's view, to the much more demanding alternative of keeping suprastatism provisional.

Abandon accountability

From the first two preservationist proposals – to provisionalize suprastatism and to surrender the element of individual representation – I turn now to the third such option. This is to abandon democratic accountability – in favour of a system of government which is independent rather than accountable, and which derives its legitimacy from the fact that, instead of being majoritarian in character, it is based on expertise, and is also beyond the reach of public opinion, parliaments and electorates.

The suspicion entertained by adherents of this view towards the idea of democratizing the European suprastate is fundamentally the same as that expressed by those favouring the abandonment of the idea of individual representation. Their practical recommendation, however, is different. The problem is solved not by dividing power between a series of independent institutions but rather by establishing a cluster of technocratic and regulatory regimes released from the need for democratic accountability. On the contrary – and somewhat paradoxically – these regimes assume their own legitimacy, to the extent that they are exempted from the very need for legitimacy in democratic terms.

This notion too functions within a framework of non-majoritarian, Madisonian political theory. The stress in this case lies, however, not on the separation of powers, but on the exercise of the said powers independently of majority preference. The problem to be solved in both cases is 'to carve out an institutional system that will bring a remedy to the current legitimacy crisis of the Community, *without at the same time* [my emphasis] exposing it to the dangers of majoritarian solutions' (Dehousse 1995: 135). The problem can be solved either by separating powers from each other or by rendering their exercise independent of any requirement of accountability.

According to this fifth option, then, *independence* is the key concept. The transnational separation of powers implies checks and balances between institutions. Independence, by contrast, implies not a system of institutional checks and balances, but rather an institutional monopoly for those exercising authority within the particular area in question (e.g. energy, banking, food prices, the environment, competition law).

Otherwise put: Madisonian theorists are of two kinds where the preservation of the democratic deficit is concerned. Some are pluralists; others are technocrats. The bottom line for both groups is the following: democracy is not to be equated with the rule of the majority. Pluralists surrender the notion of representative government. They continue to insist, however, on the need for accountability. This is to be met by checks and balances. Technocrats take the Madisonian argument one step further. In his book *Regulating Europe* Giandomenico Majone avers that majoritarian rule is 'particularly inadequate in the case of the European Union'. This is so, he argues, because 'The Union is not, and may never become, a state in the modern sense of the concept' (1996: 287).

There are two types of policy within the constitutional framework of a state 'in the modern sense', Majone argues. One is *regulation*, designed to increase efficiency in the interests of all. The important thing here is obedience – not so much how decisions came about, or what opportunities are available for holding decision-makers accountable.

The other type of policy is *redistribution*, which does *not* lie in the interests of all. In order for the transfer of resources across borders to be possible – recall that the countries in question are democracies – majority decisions must be made. It must be possible to hold decision-makers accountable. This presupposes, in turn, that the Union as a whole constitutes a democratic state. Citizens must be motivated by mutual solidarity and must be able to communicate with each other politically.

The technique for making the market a common one is, in all important respects, regulation. Some marginal subventions and regional support for agriculture and peripheral parts of the Union certainly exist. They are needed for ensuring acceptance of the common rules governing the market. As long, however, as the fee for membership of the EU amounts to no more than 1·27 per cent of GNP – as compared with an overall tax level in the neighbourhood of 40–60 per cent – the institutions of the Union will require no legitimation of their own.

Against this background it is surprising, Majone argues, that the emphasis in the debates of the 1990s was so heavily on strengthening rather than weakening the Union's majoritarian features. Confederalists and federalists, provisionalists and political pluralists – all emphasize the need for democratic accountability (to Europe as a whole, to national electorates and to specific veto groups). This is not, in Majone's view, a rational constitutional policy for the EU. Majoritarianism – especially if combined with the separation of powers – can lead only to deadlock and perhaps even disintegration. As a *de facto* matter, moreover, constitutional reforms in a majoritarian direction would limit the role of the small countries (Majone 1996: 287).

The real question, Majone argues, is how 'agency independence and public accountability can be made complementary and mutually reinforcing rather than antithetical values' (Majone 1996: 300). His own theoretical arguments, as well as the experience of the US in the twentieth century with independendent regulatory commissions (IRCs), indicate that independence and accountability can be reconciled by a combination of control mechanisms, rather than by the exercise of oversight from any fixed place on the political spectrum. Such control mechanisms include:

- clear and limited statutory objectives for providing unambiguous performance standards;
- reason-giving and transparency requirements for faciliating judicial review and public participation;
- due process provisions for ensuring fairness among the inevitable losers from regulatory decisions;
- professionalism for withstanding external interference and reducing the risk of an arbitrary use of agency discretion. (Majone 1996: 300)

With a system of multiple rather than concentrated controls, 'no one controls an agency, yet the agency is "under control". At that point the problem of regulatory legitimacy will have been largely solved'. Majoritarian democratic accountability, in this argument, is reduced to 'oversight exercised from any fixed place in the political spectrum' (Majone 1996: 300).

The drawback of allowing public opinion, ordinary citizens, political parties and interest organizations to have an ultimate say in the choice of policies and office-holders is that it does not 'ensure consistency in regulatory policy-making by insulating the regulators from the potentially destabilizing effects of the electoral cycle' (Majone 1996: 289). When seeking re-election, 'legislators engage in advertising and position-taking rather than in serious policy-making, or they design laws with numerous opportunities to help particular constituences. In either case, re-election pressures have serious consequences for the quality of legislation' (Majone 1996: 291).

The core of Majone's argument lies in his positive evaluation of regulatory independence together with his negative attitude towards government by elected politicians. Along with Susan Rose-Ackerman, in her book *Rethinking the Progressive Agenda* (1992), Majone asks himself rhetorically: 'if the courts require the regulatory process to be open to public input and scrutiny and to act on the basis of competent analyses, are the regulators necessarily less accountable than elected politicians?' (Majone 1996: 291). Independence, in this view, means not insulation from the surrounding society, but integrity.

The reason Majone considers advocates of democratic suprastatism to be naive in their federalism is historical. Federalists take their point of departure, he claims, in a presumed analogy with the integrative role of social policy in the growth and establishment of the nation state in nineteenth-century Europe. Historically, social policy made an essential contribution to the process of nation-building by bridging the gap between state and society. 'National insurance, social security, education, health and welfare services and housing policy were, and to a large extent remain, powerful symbols of national solidarity' (Majone 1996: 296). When today's federalists believe that a European welfare state would provide an equally impressive demonstration of Europe-wide solidarity, they embrace unrealistic expectations. The redistribution actually taking place within the Common Agricultural Policy and the system of cohesion funds should be interpreted as 'a side-payment to induce all member states to accept certain efficiency-enhancing measures' rather than as an instrument of social policy (Majone 1996: 298).

The delicate value judgements social policies express concerning the appropriate balance of efficiency and equity can be legitimately made, Majone argues, only in fairly homogeneous communities. He considers this a decisive argument in favour of his particular brand of preservationism:

> It is difficult to see how generally acceptable levels of income redistribution can be determined centrally in a community of nations where levels of economic development and political and legal traditions are still so different, and where majoritarian principles can play only a limited role. Thus, a more active role of the European Union in income redistribution would not reduce the Union's democratic deficit, as many people would seem to think, but would on the contrary, aggravate it. (1996: 298 f)

The point concerns the difference between the norm-giving and fiscal powers. The former are more easily used in concert with other states than the latter. Rules promulgated on a suprastatal basis meet with less opposition than does redistribution conducted at such a level. The art of preserving the democratic deficit thus means avoiding a regulatory policy that calls forth a need for economic redistribution across borders.

Criteria of evaluation

When it comes to evaluating these three preservationist options – as compared both with each other and with the two abolitionist approaches – we require some basic criteria of a more general kind. There are, as far as I can see, two ways of approaching this question. One is to compare the options in terms of end result, the other is to compare them in terms of process.

If one selects the end-result method, a checklist approach may be suitable. To my mind, Michael Zürn's suggestion of a fourfold checklist has moved the debate on the democratic deficit a large step forward. At the top of his list comes *congruence*. In principle, those who are affected by decisions (as objects) should also be those responsible for them (as mandators). If the degree of congruence is too small, the persons affected will consider the system of governance to be alien, in the same way that the law was alien under feudalism. There is a lack of fit, under such conditions, between the range over which democratically legitimated decisions apply, on the one hand, and the range of relevant social and economic relations, on the other. This lack of fit creates a new form of alienation and non-decision-making (Zürn 1996: 39).

The second criterion with which Zürn presents us is *identity*. Of course, a *demos* need not be an *ethnos* as well. However, the members of a *demos* must be 'identical' in the sense of recognizing each other as members of the 'same' political community. In practice, this means preparedness to accept the use of the majority principle and of revenue-sharing, I would like to add. Weiler *et al.* (1995: 13 f.) provide a good example. They suggest, as an intellectual experiment, the entry of the kingdom of Denmark – with its 4 million citizens – into the Federal Republic of Germany as a seventeenth *Land*. How would the Danes then be different from the 4 million Germans who vote for the Greens (and who form something of a permanent minority within the political system of Germany as a whole)? Accepting the majority principle presupposes, in other words, the existence of a community of communication, of memory and of experience. The countries of Western Europe do not, taken as a whole, constitute a community of communication. Nor do they form a community of memory, and only to a very limited extent are they a community of experience (Kielmannsegg 1996: 57).

The third criterion in Zürn's fourfold scheme is *reversibility*. Democratic theory rests on the epistemological notion that decisions are not eternal truths. They should be seen, rather, as the result of an interplay between interests and convictions. We must therefore accept that future decisions on any given issue may differ from past ones, i.e. new decisions may proceed in a different and even contrary direction. This is an important, if largely implicit, reason for accepting majority rule in a democracy (Zürn 1996: 41). Under modern conditions, it is true, reversibility is hard to achieve, for two reasons. One has to do with the empirical character of technologies like nuclear power. The use of simple majority rule is difficult in such cases, for technologies of that type have irreversible consequences as to their substance. The second reason derives from the phenomenon here discussed, i.e. a system of procedural and substantive policy asymmetry which tends to render decisions irreversible. For neither in the public discourse nor (still less) in an election campaign is the actual majority on any specific question confronted, in such a system, with a potential majority for an alternative policy.

Michael Zürn's fourth criterion is *accountability*. Democracy is not preferable to other forms of governance just because the majority is entitled to rule. A still more critical reason is that democracy makes it possible to dismiss bad or incompetent rulers. Not only decisions but the holding of political office too should be reversible. For an electorate *vis-à-vis* its parliament, and for a parliament *vis-à-vis* its government, this is an imperative demand. Its effective execution requires, moreover, a minimum of accurate information, and a general grasp of the achievements of the political system as a whole (Zürn 1996: 41 f.).

I would propose here that we use Zürn's four criteria as a normative guide for deciding whether to abandon suprastatism, to democratize it or to preserve it. The last-mentioned can be accomplished by provisionalizing suprastatism, surrendering representation or abandoning accountability.

Abandoning suprastatism entails establishing a confederation. In an association of states of this sort, all four criteria are satisfied. Citizens decide for themselves, and they have no difficulty in accepting the majority principle within their own state. As far as the element of multi-level decision-making is concerned, policies can be easily reversed. The power of citizens to force governments and legislative majorities from office for political reasons, moreover, is in no way threatened, for decisions in a confederal system are taken in each member state singly. Common decisions in a confederation are not binding until they are ratified by each and every member state in accordance with its own constitutional provisions.

Democratizing suprastatism means founding a federation. If the EU were transformed into a multi-level state of that kind, the European Parliament would be made the ultimate repository of the legislative and – indirectly – the executive suprastatal powers. A federation would work in the same way as member countries such as Austria, Belgium and Germany, all of which are federal in character. The criterion of accountability would then be satisfied. The same could be said of the criteria of congruence and identity.

The matter is trickier in the case of the reversibility criterion, which is difficult to satisfy in *any* federation. Reversibility is satisfied far better, however, in an outright federation than in the present system of double asymmetry and provisional suprastatism. If the EU were a federation, central political issues would be the stuff of a Europe-wide discourse and will-formation, and the composition of the European Parliament would be the decisive factor in resolving conflicts between the member states and the suprastate.

Provisional suprastatism represents the maintenance of the *status quo*. This is preferable, I would argue, to the other options available. Double asymmetry based on provisional suprastatism perhaps can be said – at a stretch – to fulfil the criteria of congruence and identity, but it certainly cannot be deemed satisfactory in the case of reversibility and accountability. Avoiding majority decisions and making as few decisions as possible at the suprastatal level is a pragmatic way to avoid violating the criteria of identity and congruence more than is absolutely 'necessary' to defend the four freedoms.

However, a multi-level decisional system which is not federal – in the sense that governance at its suprastatal level is not founded in direct and general elections – cannot be accepted from the standpoint of reversibility and accountability. As long as elections to the European Parliament do not carry significant political weight, policy alternatives and policy openings are not being confronted according to the principle of majoritarian rule at the European level. The result is that important policies are made by the European governments in common and, thereby, on an unaccountable basis, and with irreversible effect (Zürn 1996: 47).

Surrendering representation, according to Edgar Grande's theory, violates all four of Michael Zürn's criteria. The political structure of European suprastatism would then be turned into a system marked by a transnational separation of powers. Each single element in the system of countervailing powers would be released from its inherent element of individual representation. The Commission, the Parliament, the Court and the Council of Ministers would continue to exist, alongside a system of transnational referendums. The important thing here is checks and balances, not identity, congruence, reversibility and accountability.

Abandoning accountability, according to Giandomenico Majone's theory of technocratic rule, violates the criteria of reversibility and accountability, but not necessarily those of identity and congruence. The last two criteria could be upheld even in a political machine without mandators, in which citizens could change neither policies nor office-holders. In such a system the governing elite will hold referendums. People will identify themselves with the state, but they will have no influence.

From an end-state point of view, provisional suprastatism does not seem an especially good solution. As seen from the standpoint, however, of piecemeal constitutional engineering (Popper 1945: ch. 9), it might be thought preferable to its abolitionist and preservationist alternatives:

> [Utopian] principles, if applied to the realm of political activity, demand that we must determine our ultimate political aim, or the Ideal State, before taking any practical action. Only when this ultimate aim is determined, in rough outlines at least, only when we are in the possession of something like a blueprint of the society at which we aim, only then can we begin to consider the best ways and means for its realization, and to draw up a plan for practical action. (Popper 1945: 138)

The politician who adopts the piecemeal method, in contrast, may or may not hope that mankind will one day realize an ideal state, and achieve happiness and perfection on earth. However, she or he will

> be aware that perfection, if at all attainable, is far distant, and that every generation of men, and therefore also the living, have a claim; perhaps not so much a claim to be made happy, for there are no institutional means of making a man happy, but a claim not to be made unhappy, where it can be avoided. The piecemeal engineer will, accordingly, adopt the method of searching for, and fighting against, the greatest and most urgent evils of society, rather than searching for, and fighting for, its greatest ultimate good. (Popper 1945: 139)

Scharpf, for his part, argues implicitly in such terms when presenting the provisionalizing version of the preservationist position. Economic interdependence is nowadays so far-reaching, he avers, that it would be irresponsible to adopt a strategy of abandonment. The reintroduction of member state self-determination into the negatively integrated single market – the confederal solution – would not simply violate the treaty: 'Escalating national protectionisms would not just mean the end of the Union, it would also plunge the European economy into catastrophic straits' (Scharpf 1995: 582).

Nor, in Scharpf's view, should the suprastatal order be democratized. The legitimacy of the suprastate is admittedly weak. In practice, however, a strategy of democratizing suprastatism – in accordance with the federal solution – would lead to unacceptable results. For it would mean that, during a transitional period of uncertain length, the more legitimate law would be superseded by the less – all in order to achieve a better state of affairs in a distant future. This would mean, in practice, that the legitimacy of member-state democracies would decline, without a corresponding growth in the democratic legitimacy of the suprastate.

Much is therefore at stake if politics at the European level remains weak while politics at the national level has lost its effectiveness. The only way to avoid this horror scenario is to employ the limited opportunities of action present at both levels – national and European – in such a way that the existing opportunities for effective policy are exploited, and predictable frustrations are sidestepped. This has important implications for the relationship between European and national policy (Scharpf 1995: 583 f.).

The thrust of my argument may be summed up as follows. Comparing different options in terms of piecemeal constitutional engineering means that we must identify, specify and try to falsify our premises. A piecemeal approach should not be thought, however, to imply a defence of the *status quo*, i.e. in this context a preservationist position. The point is that the premises underlying each and every step in the development of our constitutional policy should be rendered clear and falsifiable. Premises supporting the *status quo* are quite as important to clarify and to corroborate as premises underlying policies of change.

Virtually all of us have, at the very root of our thinking on the democratic deficit, a psychological tendency to let ourselves be

inspired (consciously or not) by a well known three-stage metaphor. I have in mind the threefold tale of Paradise, Fall and
Resurrection. From the medieval Paradise the Renaissance and
Reformation were sprung, and the system of sovereign states
replaced the indivisible Universal Community in sacred union
with the Holy Church. Yet the modern system of sovereign
states in Europe has never lost its *telos*, according to this
implicit and idealistic creed. Through its *re*unification Europe
shall be resurrected from the consequences of the Fall of Man.
At present, it is true, divisions, splits and schisms prevail. In the
future, however, Europe shall return to its true self, as once it
existed under Pope and Emperor.

According to the principle of piecemeal engineering,
however, policies should be formulated in small, clearly stated
stages so that their premises can be tested. If, furthermore, we
refuse to accept *telos* as an argument, it becomes urgent to criticize what is often said in the current political debate on the
process of European integration. For criticism is in fact called
for, and should be delivered along two different lines.

My first point – and an elementary one it is indeed – is that
there *is* no immanent goal called 'united Europe'. Events and
developments in the area of European integration are not the
servants of some underlying purpose or cunning of history. Only
individuals exist – individual people who actively prefer certain
steps to be taken or not taken. The surrender of congruence,
identity, reversibility and accountability cannot be justified by
reference to 'integration' as an historical 'process' aimed at
bringing Europe back to its 'true self'. The democratic deficit
cannot be defended on the grounds that it is a 'necessary'
element whereby the 'natural' development of things is accelerated. The double asymmetry – of power and responsibility *and*
of positive and negative integration – can only be discussed, and
should only be discussed, in terms of *falsifiable* propositions.
These propositions should relate to the intended and unin-
tended consequences that the double asymmetry brings – in
terms of employment, economic growth, social improvement,
the loss of democracy, the risk of war, etc.

Second, more 'integration' should not be considered, by
definition, to be 'better' than less. The outcome one prefers –
as regards congruence, identity, reversibility and accountability – must be argued for in terms of falsifiable propositions
concerning the anticipated consequences of accepting double

asymmetry *v.* not accepting it. The question is, which option is preferable to the available alternatives at any particular time? Which is considered better must be allowed, moreover, to change over time and in the light of experience. A step in the direction of more integration is not *a priori* better; it should not be equated automatically with progress. Such a step may indeed take the member states one step higher, in terms of the integration staircase metaphor. However, taking one step up the stair does not by definition mean an improvement. The step is higher but not necessarily better.

One can say, as Bela Balassa did when presenting his metaphor in 1961, that the various steps represent varying *degrees* of integration.

> In a free trade area, tariffs (and quantitative restrictions) between the participating countries are abolished, but each country retains its own tariffs against non-members. The establishment of a customs union involves, besides the suppression of discrimination in the field of commodity movements within the union, the creation of a common tariff wall against non-member countries. A higher form of economic integration is attained in a common market, where not only trade restrictions but also restrictions on factor movements are abolished. An economic union, as distinct from a common market, combines the removal of restrictions on commodity and factor movements with a degree of harmonisation of economic, monetary, fiscal, social and countercyclical policies. (Balassa 1961: 5 f.)

A political union – or what Belassa calls 'total economic integration' – involves 'the unification of economic, fiscal etc. policies and requires the setting up of a supranational authority whose decisions are binding for the member-states' (Balassa 1961: 5 f.). Whether this will work or not obviously has something to do with how realistic it is to reconcile suprastatism with the absence of accountability. This can be done more easily at the lower stages of the staircase. The Common Market is the last step which does not imply more than regulatory policies. Monetary union may imply fiscal union and thereby indirectly the need to make federal taxation and spending policies accountable to the European Parliament.

In the light of the staircase metaphor, a terminology for describing varying degrees of integration is not the same as a theory of European federalism as a predetermined process of ever closer union. As an acceptable theory such a notion would have something falsifiable to say in three respects. First, is it an accurate *description* to say that the various steps of the staircase are being reached in accordance with an inherent logic? Second, is it a plausible *explanation* that the process of integration is determined by its immanent purpose? Third, is it a reasonable *prescription* to recommend that the steps should be ascended one after the other, in accordance with a given logic?

My answers to these three questions are all decidedly in the negative. No other ultimate criterion is possible, in my view, than the reformist one stated by Karl Popper, to the effect that we should 'be aware that perfection, if at all attainable, is far distant, and that every generation of men, and therefore also the living, have a claim'. This means that the perfectionist solutions – whether they entail abandoning suprastatism or democratizing it – are unavailable in practice. This notwithstanding the fact that they may be perfect according to the checklist approach.

The proposals to surrender representation or to abandon accountability may be reconcilable with some scheme of Madisonian democracy. Yet, however reconcilable in such terms, they have great difficulty meeting the Zürnian criteria. In conclusion – and this is decisive in my view – they are normatively unacceptable. I cannot accept a political theory not built on the principles of representing individuals and open to the possibility of changing policies and office-holders as a result of general elections.

From the standpoint of piecemeal constitutional engineering, in sum, it would appear that provisional suprastatism remains the best available option, and preferable to both its two preservationist and two abolitionist competitors – surrendering representation or abandoning accountability.

Under the auspices of the Stability Pact

The aim of this chapter has been to consider provisional suprastatism, in theoretical perspective. That raises an additional question. To what extent are the four alternative options actually advocated?

They are in fact proposed by individuals who are either strongly against the democratic deficit or strongly in favour of limiting the reach of democracy through transnational separation of powers or irreversibly technocratic rule. In particular, there are influential protagonists in favour of abandoning accountability. That position is needed in order to defend the idea of the European Central Bank being irreversibly beyond any possible influence from electoral change or shifts in public opinion. Governments have changed in Great Britain, France and Germany during 1997 and 1998. However, when it comes to the Central Bank being unreachable, they are all advocating technocratic rule.

Apart from the important exception of defending the irreversibility, rather than the reversibility, of monetary union, provisional suprastatism dominates the picture. However uncomfortable politicians and political commentators may feel, they tend to defend the democratic deficit. That is done by referring to national sovereignty being delegated rather than surrendered. Accepting the restrictions of marginality, predictability and revocability, they see no better alternative than sticking to democratic accountability within each single country.

Hopefully, this concentration on democratic accountability in the member states will have a practical consequence. The EMU should vitalize the system of nation-wide political parties, popular movements and open government. Otherwise national political life inside a monetary union without fiscal union – in periods and areas of recession and deflation – will have to face a very hard choice. A breakdown of nation-wide political parties and trade unions would force the member states to choose between taking the step up to fiscal union or giving up political rights and free elections in order to prevent social unrest and populist political parties getting dominant. In order to make the stability pact work – meaning that fiscal union and abandoning basic human rights should be avoided at every conceivable price – the member states will need *more* rather than *less* democracy (S. Gustavsson 1998a: 204 ff.).

Pinning our hopes on democratic renewal under the auspices of the Stability Pact may seem too hazardous. In my view, however, there is no better idea than the Stability Pact when it comes to revitalizing national democracy in order to make twenty-first-century Europe a better union of states than the one we have experienced since 1914. My analysis seems to show that the alternatives are even more risky.

Notes

1 In a previous book (S. Gustavsson 1996) I have tried to clarify the two abolitionist options. On two subsequent occasions (S. Gustavsson 1997, 1998b), I have
sought to elucidate the concept of provisional suprastatism. I tried to do so by
explaining how the German Constitutional Court reasoned when, in October
1993, it found the Maastricht Treaty to be in accordance with the demand for
democratic accountability enshrined in the German Basic Law. The present
chapter brings all five alternatives together. In my earlier publications in English
I did not include the alternatives 'surrender representation 'and 'abandon accountability' in my comparison. S. Gustavsson (1998a) gives a broader presentation in
Swedish.

References

Balassa, Bela (1961), 'Towards a theory of economic integration', *Kyklos* 16, 1–17.

BverfGE (Entscheidungen des Bundesverfassungsgerichts), 89, 17, 155–213. The complete text of the Maastricht verdict is available in English, German and French in
Winkelmann (1994), pp. 697–799.

Dehousse, Renaud (1995), 'Constitutional reform in the EC. Are there alternatives to
the majority avenue?' in Jack Hayward (ed.), *The Crisis of Representation in
Europe*, London, Frank Cass, pp. 118–36.

Grande, Edgar (1996), 'Demokratische Legitimation und europäische Integration',
Leviathan 24, 339–60.

Gustavsson, Jakob (1998), *The Politics of Foreign Policy Change. Explaining the
Swedish Reorientation on EU Membership*, Lund, Lund University Press.

Gustavsson, Sverker (1996), 'Preserve or abolish the democratic deficit?' in Eivind
Smith (ed.), *National Parliaments as Cornerstones of European Integration*,
London, Kluwer, pp. 100–23.

Gustavsson, Sverker (1997), 'Double asymmetry as normative challenge' in Andreas
Føllesdal and Peter Koslowski (eds), *Democracy and the European Union*, Berlin,
Springer, pp. 108–31.

Gustavsson, Sverker (1998a), 'Sökandet efter en tredje möjlighet' in Ulf Bernitz *et al.*,
EU i dag, Stockholm, SNS, pp. 172–218.

Gustavsson, Sverker (1998b), 'Defending the democratic deficit' in Michael Nentwich
and Albert Weale (eds), *Political Theory and the European Union*, London,
Routledge, pp. 63–79.

Kielmansegg, Peter Graf (1996), 'Integration und Demokratie' in Markus Jachtenfuchs
and Beate Kohler-Koch (eds), *Europäische Integration*, Opladen, Leske & Budrich,
pp. 47–71.

Madison, James, Alexander Hamilton and John Jay (1788), *The Federalist Papers*,
reprinted London, 1987, Penguin Classics.

Majone, Giandomenico (1996), *Regulating Europe*, London, Routledge.

Newman, Michael (1996), *Democracy, Sovereignty and the European Union*, London,
Hurst.

Popper, Karl (1945), *The Open Society and its Enemies* I, London, Routledge.

Rose-Ackerman, Susan (1992), *Rethinking the Progressive Agenda. The Reform of the
American Regulatory State*, New York, Free Press.

Scharpf, Fritz W. (1994), *Optionen des Föderalismus in Deutschland und Europa*, Frankfurt, Campus.

Scharpf, Fritz W. (1995), 'Demokratische Politik in Europa', *Staatswissenschaften und Staatspraxis* 6, 565–91.

Scharpf, Fritz W. (1996a), 'Politische Optionen im vollendeten Binnenmarkt' in Markus Jachtenfuchs and Beate Kohler-Koch (eds), *Europäische Integration*, Opladen, Leske & Budrich, pp. 109–40.

Scharpf, Fritz W. (1996b), 'Negative and positive integration in the political economy of European welfare states' in Gary Marks, Fritz W. Scharpf, Philippe C. Schmitter and Wolfgang Streeck, *Governance in the European Union*, London, Sage, pp. 15–39.

Weiler, Joseph H. H., Ulrich R. Haltern and Franz C. Mayer (1995), 'European democracy and its critique' in Jack Hayward (ed.), *The Crisis of Representation in Europe*, London, Frank Cass.

Winkelmann, Ingo (1994), *Das Maastricht-Urteil des Bundesverfassungsgerichts vom 12. Oktober 1993. Dokumentation des Verfahrens mit Einführung*, Berlin, Dunckler & Humblot.

Zürn, Michael (1996), 'Über den Staat und die Demokratie im europäischen Mehrebenensystem', *Politische Vierteljahresschrift* 37, 27–55.

4

A Europe of the peoples? – New Labour and democratizing the EU

STEFANO FELLA

The intention of this chapter is to provide an assessment of the Labour Party's attitude to the question of European Union (EU) democratization in the context of both the Party's agenda of democratizing Britain's political institutions and of the evolution of the Party's position on European integration. Labour entered government in May 1997 committed to a wide-ranging reform of the British constitution, justified in terms of rendering it more modern and democratic. The extent to which there exists a thread linking Labour's democratic agenda in relation to the British constitution and its attitude to the European sphere of political decision-making is worthy of examination.

It appears that the traditional 'old Labour' centralist conception of the apparatus of the British nation state was supplanted in the 1980s, in reaction to (and in desperation at) the Thatcher governments' parliamentary absolutism, by a more plural approach to the political process which held that power was best dispersed among a broad range of institutions at the regional, national and European levels. The 'old Labour' conception of democratic government was embedded in the notion of capturing the 'absolutist' levers of the British nation state, based as it is on the absolute sovereignty of Parliament, in order to secure its 'socialist' objectives. Labour was forced to change its approach in the 1980s as the Conservative governments employed these self-same 'absolutist' levers to reverse many of the social democratic gains of 1945–79. In order to both secure its objectives and ensure their maintenance in the future, the Labour Party turned its attention to a more plural model of power. Such a model would have to acknowledge that democracy amounted to more than just 'majority rule', but involved developing institutions which guaranteed the rights of all citizens and social groups and gave due recognition to the diverse regions and nations that make up the UK. It would also have to take into account the growing internationalization of a number of policy issues, with the consequence that the fulfilment of certain policy objectives would require the increased 'pooling' of national sovereignties in international regimes such as the EU. The new Labour Party conception of the British constitution (and the need to reform it), and of the role of the European institutions in the new distribution of political power, could be interpreted as two complementary pieces in the modernizing jigsaw.

Although the long period of impotent opposition to the exercise of untrammelled constitutional power by the Thatcher governments forced the Labour Party to rethink its attitude to the distribution and exercise of power and democracy in Britain, the international context of this attitudinal transformation should not be underestimated. In particular, the traditional role of the nation state was changing, as a consequence of the increasing internationalization of national economies and the development of international political institutions, such as the EU. The growing demand for constitutional reform in Britain, as in other parts of Europe, could therefore, in part, be attributed to the shifting conceptions of political power engendered by globalization and by membership of the EU. It could be argued that the increasing importance of such transnational institutions was causing nation states to reexamine their internal apparatus of decision-making in order to maximize the efficiency of their diminishing spheres of political authority.

In relation to this, the creation by the Maastricht Treaty of a European Committee of the Regions, giving regional governments a voice in EU affairs, boosted the demands of the Scots and the Welsh, together with some of the English regions, for autonomous government, to provide themselves with an effective voice in Brussels. Such bodies would also be better placed to lobby for the regional funds provided by the EU. Furthermore, the principle of subsidiarity, which had been employed by Conservative governments in Britain to justify returning powers from the EU to the national level, could equally be used to justify devolution to the nations and regions of the UK. Subsidiarity in effect required different areas of policy to be delivered at the most appropriate level: local, regional, national or European. While Euro-enthusiasts could use the principle of subsidiarity to justify Monetary Union or a Common Defence

Policy, proponents of devolution have seized on the principle to justify their own cause.

In recent years the Labour Party's pronouncements on Europe, both in opposition up to May 1997, and in government thereafter, have paid lip service to the desirability of democratizing the EU. Indeed, the Labour Party document presented to its annual conference in 1995 (Labour Party 1995) called for a Europe that had the wholehearted consent of its peoples, more accountable to democratic structures such as national parliaments and the European Parliament. This is in keeping with the Party's general discourse on democratization, as applied to domestic constitutional reform. But is the Party's rhetoric on democratization of the EU derived in any way from a more precise conception of how the EU should develop, and does this bring with it particular policy prescriptions, in terms of political reforms to achieve a more democratic EU? While Labour's domestic agenda of constitutional reform is reasonably clear-cut in terms of the changes it is seeking to introduce, the agenda for democratizing the EU is more ambiguous and is fraught with difficulty, given the unique nature of the EU as an international organization resting uneasily between intergovernmentalism and supranationalism. These characteristics pose a number of difficulties for those who seek to find solutions to the EU's democratic deficit through the replication of traditional conceptions of representative democracy as associated with the nation state, at the European level.

Nevertheless, the Labour Party, after reconciling itself to British membership of the then European Community (EC) in the mid-1980s, sought, to a limited extent, to tie the national and European agendas of democratization together, and made a number of proposals to increase the involvement of both the European Parliament and the national parliaments in European decision-making. This chapter will examine the development of the Party's attitude to European democratization in this period, in order to shed some light on the extent of linkage between the national and European agendas and the extent to which convincing policy prescriptions were put forward. In particular, Party policy formation and positioning, in opposition and in government, during the 1996–97 intergovernmental conference (IGC), will be explored. The intergovernmental conference culminated in the treaty agreed in Amsterdam in June 1997, when, for the first time in the short history of the EC/EU, a Labour government represented Britain in the negotiation of major amendments of the Treaty of Rome, and moreover, agreed to a number of treaty changes designed to enhance the EU's democratic character and improve the accountability of decision-making.

Yet pragmatic considerations still tend to dominate the Labour Party's thinking on the EU. This was illustrated by the refusal, based on domestic political realities, of the Labour government to sign Britain up to the new border-free 'area of security, freedom and justice' agreed by the other member states at Amsterdam. Similarly, certain pragmatic considerations affected Labour's programme of constitutional reform in its first year of government as the expediencies of power began to exert greater pressure. Hence there were delays in bringing forward the promised Freedom of Information Act, and in formulating clear proposals for the reform of the House of Lords. While the Labour Party did appear to engage in a serious re-evaluation of its attitude to the distribution of democratic power in Britain and the EU, it is likely that some of the policy prescriptions that emerged from this rethink will fall by the wayside as the pragmatic realities of power replace the aspirations of opposition.

Despite this pragmatism, democratization continues to be a recurring theme in the 'New Labour' agenda, and has been intrinsically linked with the modernization process. The slogan 'New Labour, new Britain' symbolized the link between modernization of the party itself and the political fabric of the nation. Democratization of the UK constitution and the reform of the constitution of the party could be interpreted as part of an all-encompassing modernization project. The continued references by the Labour government to a 'people's Europe' (in which the EU would be brought closer to the citizen) during the UK presidency of the EU in the first half of 1998 suggested a similar desire to create a 'new Europe'. However, the substance of the UK presidency fell short of this rhetoric. In any case the references to a 'people's Europe' were based more on a desire to focus on issues relevant to the 'ordinary' people's concerns such as unemployment, action against international crime and environmental protection than on proposals for further democratic reforms. Moreover, attempts to link democratic reform of the EU with the modernization of Britain and the party itself have also served to highlight the paradox of Labour's constitutional reform programme simultaneously proposing a switch to proportional representation (PR) for European elections and increasing the centralization of leadership control over the selection of party election candidates. This chapter will provide an exploration of how democratization of the EU fits into the new politics of the Labour Party: a new politics characterized by modernizing zeal and new pluralist attitudes to democracy, tempered and sometimes overshadowed by a pragmatic realism, based on a fear of alienating 'middle England' and/or losing control of Party discipline, shaped by the long experience in opposition.

A new agenda for democracy

Labour's programme of reform, formulated during the long years of opposition under the leadership of Neil Kinnock and John Smith, and refined under Tony Blair's leadership, has been justified primarily in terms of improving the fabric of Britain's democracy. This programme involved reform of the House of Lords, devolution to Scotland and Wales, a new Greater London Authority, incorporation of the European Convention on Human Rights into UK law and a Freedom of Information Act. While some on the left of the party argued that this programme represented the last vestige of left-wing radicalism in its programme, it actually represented a departure from the centralizing tendencies of past Labour governments. This rather conservative attitude to the constitution was, however, transformed by the years spent in opposition, in the 1980s in particular. As David Marquand has written:

> old Labour was as committed to the doctrines and practices of Westminster absolutism as were the Conservatives. But in the Thatcher years, when Labour found itself on the receiving end of a ferocious centralism, far exceeding anything it had ever attempted itself, it underwent a death-bed conversion. (1998: 20)

Among the constitutional atrocities committed by the Thatcher governments, perhaps the most brutal was the abolition of the Greater London Council (GLC), which was foolhardy enough under Ken Livingstone's leadership to espouse a political philosophy diametrically opposed to Margaret Thatcher's. This action, reflective as it was of Thatcher's style of government, made painfully transparent to many on the left and the centre-left the deficiencies of a constitutional apparatus which allows the majority party in Parliament (though elected by a minority of the electorate) to abolish a tier of government without any form of constitutional check. The abolition of the GLC came within a general emasculation of local government and an unprecedented degree of centralization of political power, which fuelled demands for devolution, freedom of information and a Bill of Rights. Indeed, the argument for devolution grew stronger and perhaps more convincing in the 1980s as resentment in both Scotland and Wales accelerated at the imposition of Thatcher's distinct brand of social and economic policies, despite both countries electing only a handful of Conservative MPs.

The case for reform of the House of Lords, based as it was on the hereditary principle, was quite straightforward, although differences remained over how a reformed second chamber should be selected. However, the 1980s also witnessed increased calls for reform of elections to the House of Commons. Advocates of PR pointed to the distortions created by the first-past-the-post system, which allowed Mrs Thatcher to accrue such power, based on large majorities despite commanding the support of only 40–5 per cent of the electorate. The demands for PR came mainly from the Social Democratic Party (SDP), formed by former Labour MPs disillusioned by Labour's leftward shift in 1981, and from the Liberal Party, with which it would merge to form the Liberal Democrats in 1987. However, support for PR also came from significant sections of the Labour Party.[1] As with many of Labour's proposed constitutional reforms, Blair inherited John Smith's pledge to stage a referendum on the voting system for national elections, while remaining officially 'unconvinced' of the case for change.[2] While the party remained divided on this issue, in its first year in government, Labour did fulfil its pledge to introduce PR for elections to the new assemblies proposed for Scotland, Wales and London and also introduced legislation to establish PR for elections to the European Parliament.

The fullest exposition of Labour's constitutional reform programme, and of its new approach to Britain's democracy, came in its 1993 policy document *A new Agenda for Democracy* (Labour Party 1993a). Produced under John Smith's leadership, the document presented the reforms together as 'the basis of a new constitutional settlement'. The document painted a picture of a British constitution 'urgently in need of radical change and modernisation', a 'flawed democracy'. The document cited as evidence the most centralized system of government in Europe, the undermining of local government, a swathe of unelected quangos, an outdated legal system and an opaque and secretive system of government: 'If democracy is about content as well as form, the form of our constitution is imperfect and the content of our democracy even more seriously at fault'. The document argued that the issue of 'the constitution' was 'one in which all people have a direct interest. It is about power; where it is located and how it is made accountable.' Despite being written only four years before the 1997 election victory, and presumably with Blair's direct involvement as home affairs spokesman, it employed a form of words which would appear rather out of place with 'new Labour' discourse:

> We seek, therefore, to retrieve the true ideological basis of democratic socialism – action by the community for the benefit of the individual – and set it to work for the modern age . . . This requires . . . a new constitutional settlement . . . which establishes a just relationship between society and individual, one which above all, fundamentally redresses power in favour of the citizen from the state.

Labour's new approach to democracy therefore provided for the relocation of power among a diffuse set of political institutions, balanced in favour of the citizen and away from the parliamentary absolutism of the existing constitutional settlement. Moreover, the document recognized that this new distribution of political power would have to accommodate the major impact of the EC on the traditional power of Britain's political institutions. It referred to an EC which had 'a major impact on all our domestic institutions, including the executive', with laws which 'have a direct effect', reaching into nearly 'all areas of national life'. Accordingly, it noted that the transfer of power to the EC had not come with an equal transfer of public accountability. This deficit in accountability had contributed to Britain's increasingly flawed democracy. Labour's 'constitutional settlement' would therefore have to take steps to remedy the problem of European institutions 'perceived as unresponsive, unaccountable . . . [and] . . . centralising', a perception which had fuelled popular distrust of the European integration process.

The document was produced while the Maastricht Treaty was undertaking its gruelling eight-month passage through the House of Commons, at a time of intense political debate about the direction of European integration and, in particular, about the lack of accountability and transparency in the decision-making process. It was in this context, therefore, that a number of quite radical proposals were put forward to enhance democracy and accountability at the European level. These proposals included giving powers of legislative initiative to the European Parliament as well as the Commission and the Council of Ministers. It was also suggested that all EC legislation should be subject to scrutiny, and a vote of approval, by the European Parliament. These proposals would be within the context of strengthened national scrutiny of EC legislation, and more effective co-ordination of scrutiny between national parliaments and the European Parliament, for example through joint committees of national MPs and MEPs which would meet to discuss proposals for new European legislation. The document also proposed democratic scrutiny of commissioners by the European Parliament, and greater transparency through public meetings of the Council of Ministers.

Capitalist club or guardian of European social democracy?

The 1993 document was produced at a time when Labour's pro-Europeanism, new found under Kinnock in the 1980s, was at its highest point under John Smith's leadership. Smith was undoubtedly the most pro-European of all Labour's leaders, having been among the sixty-nine MPs who had rebelled against the party leadership in 1971, voting with Heath's Conservative government to ensure British entry to the then EEC. The split in 1971 was illustrative of the tortuous divisions and twists and turns in official policy that characterized the Labour Party's attitude to European integration until the late 1980s. Although much of the party remained opposed, the Labour government of Harold Wilson launched an unsuccessful application for British entry in 1967,[3] as a means of addressing Britain's diminishing political and economic influence in Europe and the wider world. Labour reverted to official opposition to the successful application made by the Heath government, then changed tack again by staging a referendum on 'renegotiated' terms of membership in 1975, following its return to government under Wilson in 1974. The referendum was a thinly disguised attempt to paper over the division in Labour's ranks on the issue of EEC membership, with Wilson and much of the Cabinet in favour of membership and the majority of the party at large opposed. Following Labour's election defeat in 1979, the demand for withdrawal from the EEC was central to the demands of the Labour left as it successfully captured the party agenda. Labour went into the 1983 election under Michael Foot's leadership, promising British withdrawal from the EEC, which it portrayed as an elitist capitalist club, membership of which would be incompatible with its programme of socialist regeneration in Britain, a positioning instrumental in persuading a number of Labour MPs to leave to form the SDP in 1981 (Anderson and Mann 1997).

Following the election disaster of 1983, in which Labour was run close for second place by the SDP, Neil Kinnock took over the leadership and carefully began to distance the party from its anti-Europeanism. The 1984 European elections were fought on a platform of developing a pan-European reflation strategy. While many on the left continued to attack the EEC for seeking to institutionalize a certain form of free-market, deregulatory policies, others began to view the European institutions as a possible vehicle for developing the kind of interventionist policies at a European level which had proved unsustainable at the national level owing to the power of international capital. The increasing difficulty of pursuing such policies at the national level had been demonstrated in France following the election of its first socialist President, François Mitterrand, in 1981. His government had been forced to abandon its programme of nationalization, state intervention in the economy and labour market reforms, in the face of a balance of payments crisis. Similarly, many on the left in Britain had not forgotten the image in the 1970s of a Labour Chancellor of the Exchequer, Denis Healey, having to secure a loan from the International Monetary Fund, and adapt the government's programme at its behest, in order to rescue the country's finances. The limited room for manoeuvre that national governments had in relation to economic policy had become increasingly apparent. Joint action at the European level was therefore mooted by Labour MPs such as Stuart Holland,[4] as a possible method of balancing the international strength of capital. It appears that the party may have been won over by this kind of argument, as much as by *Realpolitik*, in dropping its previous antagonism to the EC, and Labour went into the 1987 general election promising to work constructively with Britain's European partners in promoting economic expansion and combating unemployment.

Just as the Labour Party's re-evaluation of the traditional apparatus of the British nation state was shaped by the long experience of opposition to Thatcherism, its new positioning on Europe could also be partly attributed to the impotence it felt as the Thatcher governments dismantled the post-war social democratic consensus. This, coupled with Mitterrand's experience in seeking to pursue 'socialist' policies in international isolation, led to a re-evaluation of the nation state as an effective tool in securing and safeguarding Labour's political objectives. A progressive British government of the future would need to work constructively with its European partners, and could use the EC institutions to secure and safeguard its objectives. The EC could be used to develop and maintain a basic framework of social rights which, given the superiority of EC law over national law, could not be overturned by a national government of a Thatcherite persuasion.

The development of a stronger social dimension to EC policy following the adoption of the Single European Act in 1985 was instrumental in solidifying support for European integration across the Labour movement. Initiatives such as the Community Charter of the Fundamental Social Rights of Workers were championed by the European Commission president, Jacques Delors, and met with outright hostility by the Thatcher government. Indeed, Britain was alone among the EC member states in its refusal to sign the charter. However, the Labour Party's affiliated trade unions were particularly attracted by the notion that they could win back at the European level some of the employment rights they had lost at the national level under Thatcher. This sea change in attitude was demonstrated by the standing ovation bestowed upon Delors at the TUC conference in Bournemouth in September 1988.

John Smith's brief leadership of the party between 1992 and 1994 saw a further cementing of Labour's pro-European credentials, although he faced a number of rebellions from a significant body of Labour backbench MPs, during the long-drawn-out ratification of the Maastricht Treaty. However, the divisions in the party over Maastricht differed from those of the Conservatives, in that many of the Labour opponents of the treaty did not oppose the principle of European integration itself, but rather its undemocratic character. Traditional Labour opponents of integration, such as Tony Benn and Peter Shore, were joined in parliamentary opposition by others such as Peter Hain who, while supportive of European integration, were critical of the absence of democratic accountability in decision-making. This absence of democracy had been exacerbated by Maastricht and by the provisions of the treaty establishing Economic and Monetary Union (EMU), which would grant powers related to the management of a single currency to an independent, and consequently unaccountable, European Central Bank (ECB). While the Labour leadership generally shared this disquiet over the EU's growing democratic deficit, Smith was not willing to use it as a reason to oppose the treaty. However, the policy document *Prosperity through Co-operation* (Labour Party 1993b), approved by the party conference in 1993, did suggest that the whole issue of accountability in the EMU process should be reviewed at the 1996 intergovernmental conference, and that the ECB should be obliged to ensure that the EC's growth and employment objectives were adhered to. It also restated the demand for a pan-European economic recovery strategy.

While John Smith's pro-European credentials were impeccable, those of his successor, Tony Blair, appeared rather ambiguous in comparison, at least after he became leader. In a Charter 88 debate in 1992, two years before assuming the leadership, Blair did reveal some interesting thoughts about the need to link democratization of Britain's political institutions with a parallel process at the European level (Charter 88 1992). He argued: 'We cannot divorce the concept of greater democracy at a European level from the push for greater democracy at the domestic level.' During the debate Blair referred to the need to develop a 'new and democratic agenda' to address the inadequacy of the EC's democratic procedures, adding that such democracy would 'have to be argued and developed from below. You cannot simply impose from above.' What he meant by this was unclear. On a practical level, he suggested a vast improvement in the scrutiny of European legislation by the UK Parliament. However he was sceptical about enhancing the role of the European Parliament as a means to address the democratic deficit, arguing that there would 'have to be a much greater awareness of the European Parliament and what it does, and a much greater linkage between ordinary people and the European Parliament before it can become an institution capable of conducting the democratic will, because at the moment it isn't.' He did not believe that such a linkage could develop simply by giving more power to the Parliament.

Blair also sought to link European democracy with measures to balance EMU with greater social rights and improved economic cohesion: 'This is part of democracy too: you do not divorce the concept of measures assisting the process of monetary union from the concept of greater democracy within the European Community.' Moreover, he appeared to acknowledge worries about the unaccountable nature of EMU. Thus the debate about democracy could not 'proceed accurately unless it proceeds in tandem with the debate about how you ensure that the economic process of integration runs along much more democratic lines and has within it the idea of basic social justice'. Many people would feel 'not merely excluded from that process but positively hostile to it unless the political and economic sides come together'. In terms of seeking to make the process of EMU more accountable, Blair seemed to be reflecting the party line under the Smith leadership. However, in these utterances he appeared to be rather more sceptical of some of the proposals to enhance European democracy espoused in the party's policy documents under Smith's leadership, particularly in relation to developing the role of the European Parliament.

Blair and the intergovernmental conference of 1996–97

Upon becoming leader following the sudden death of Smith in 1994, Blair was immediately aware that Europe would be one of the key, and perhaps most politically sensitive, policy areas for the party as it sought to project itself as a party of government. This was especially the case, given that the intergovernmental conference to review the provisions of the Maastricht Treaty was due to take place in 1996, and would more than likely coincide with a general election campaign. The party's immediate concern was to avoid being portrayed as being 'soft' on Europe by a Conservative Party likely to wrap itself in the union jack in a general election campaign. Policy-making in relation to the intergovernmental conference would thus become dominated by this pragmatic concern. Blair established a policy working group, responsible to himself, to prepare Labour's position should it enter government during the intergovernmental conference. Significantly, together with key members of the

Shadow Cabinet the group would involve a number of Labour MEPs who held key posts in the European Parliament, including David Martin, vice-president of the Parliament and Pauline Green, leader of the Socialist Group (of which the Labour group was the largest component). The inclusion of Martin and Green would ensure that the views of the European Parliament as a whole, and the Socialist Group in particular, would be inputted directly into policy-making. Their inclusion was also useful for the leadership in ensuring that the party line, as it became formulated, would be fully understood and accepted by its representatives in Parliament. This was important given that the Parliament as a whole, and the Socialist Group in particular, was likely to adopt a position considerably more 'federalist' than the party would want to be associated with. A number of Labour MEPs were supportive of such a 'federalist' line, including Martin, who had written a number of pamphlets advocating a federal union, and had been *rapporteur* for a number of federalist-orientated Parliament reports on the future of the EU.[5]

Nevertheless, the European Parliament representatives within the working group would act as key interlocutors between the policy positions of the Labour Party, the European Parliament and those of the Labour Party's sister parties with whom it worked in the Socialist Group of the Parliament. In formulating policy there was also an unprecedented degree of communication between the Labour Party and its sister parties in the 'Party of European Socialists' (PES), in the form of leaders' meetings, meetings of the PES bureau (in which the Labour Party was represented by deputy-leader John Prescott) and bilateral contacts between individual parties. Many of these parties were in government and were thus able to keep the Labour Party informed of intergovernmental conference developments when Labour was still in opposition, and of possible points of agreement should Labour enter government before the end of the intergovernmental conference. Indeed, although the intergovernmental conference was launched in 1996, the intransigence of the British Conservative government made it apparent that serious negotiations would not take place until after the general election in Britain. Furthermore, many EU member governments, not just those of the centre-left, were quietly hoping for a Labour victory and a more constructive approach to the negotiations.

The report to the 1995 Labour Party conference, *The Future of the European Union*, emerged out of the deliberations of the intergovernmental conference working group (although it continued to meet until the end of 1996). The report suggested a more positive approach to EMU and reiterated the Labour pledge to reverse the social policy opt-out negotiated by the Conservative government at Maastricht. The document continued to advocate a Europe-wide strategy for co-ordinated action on growth and employment creation. This would involve a European Recovery Fund with a credit facility which could operate 'at a deficit in periods of recession and in surplus in periods of growth'. The Shadow Foreign Secretary, Robin Cook, who wrote the document, was likely to be sympathetic to such a strategy, while remaining sceptical of the EMU process. Nevertheless, it was surprising that Blair and his Shadow Chancellor, Gordon Brown, had sanctioned the inclusion of a classical Keynesian strategy in this key document. In relation to the intergovernmental conference agenda and improving the accountability of decision-making, the document advocated a generalized simplified European Parliament co-decision procedure in all areas where qualified majority voting applied in the Council. The demand for all legislative proceedings of the Council to be public was also reiterated. The document also recommended granting the Parliament the right of approval over the nominations for the Commission and its president. In addition to these proposals, the document advocated the drafting of a clear and understandable consolidated treaty text to replace the complex tangle of overlapping treaties which existed without any form of explanation as to purpose or meaning.

In all these proposals to enhance democracy and transparency the Labour Party was very close to the positions advocated by the European Parliament (although the Parliament demanded the right to elect the Commission president). The positions were also similar to those advocated by the European Commission and the majority of the member states (as illustrated by the report of the reflection group of member states' representatives which examined proposals for the intergovernmental conference in 1995).[6] Such similarities were particularly interesting given the degree of communication between the Labour Party, its representatives in the European Parliament and its sister parties in other member states. The Conservative government, on the other hand, was oblivious to any such engagement with the European agenda, and opposed all such proposals. This was illustrated by its isolation in the reflection group, and by the negative content of the government White Paper on the intergovernmental conference published in March 1996 (FCO 1996).

Labour also differed from the Conservatives in its support for a limited extension of qualified majority voting in the areas of social, industrial, regional and environmental policy (excluding taxation), and in advocating a consultative role for the Parliament in the CFSP and JHA pillars. Labour also suggested that the Parliament should have the power to oblige the Commission to propose legislation to the Council of Ministers. At the national level, the document advocated improving the scrutiny of European legislation at Westminster, and the development of closer co-operation between committees of the European Parliament and national parliaments in the preparation and consideration of European legislation. Labour remained closer to the Conservative position in rejecting the integration of the CFSP and JHA pillars into the EC decision-making framework, and in rejecting moves to establish a common European defence.

The Treaty of Amsterdam

Labour's more positive approach did facilitate the agreement by the EU member states to a number of improvements to the EU's democratic character at the Amsterdam summit in June 1997, a month after Labour's return to power (Chapter 1). Though limited, all these measures represented progress in addressing the EU's democratic deficit. While the Labour Party acquiesced in, and in some cases actively promoted, all these changes, it is unlikely that its Conservative predecessors would have allowed any such improvements through without a fight. Indeed, if it had stayed consistent to its previous statements and positions during the reflection group and the early stages of the intergovernmental conference, the Conservative government would have blocked all the changes had it remained in office. While the Labour government held similar positions to the Conservatives in certain areas, for example in vetoing attempts to establish a Common European Defence Policy and in negotiating an opt-out from the newly communitarized 'area of freedom, security and justice', its attitude to democratic improvements to the

EU's character differed markedly. This represented one of the major differences in approach between Labour and the Conservatives at the intergovernmental conference.

Labour also differed from the Conservatives in its willingness to accept an extension of qualified majority voting in certain areas and, more predictably, in relation to the social chapter and the new employment chapter. However, although Blair supported the principle of an employment chapter, he sided with the German Chancellor Helmut Kohl in warding off proposals from the new French Prime Minister, Lionel Jospin,[7] to revive the proposals for a European employment strategy put forward by Delors in 1993. Jospin hoped that interest could be reawakened in these proposals, which had been sidelined by the centre-right governments which held sway in 1993, as the centre-left had since won power in Italy in 1996 and Britain and France in 1997. However, Blair punctured hopes of a new centre-left alliance in his lecture to the PES congress in Malmö on 6 June, when he urged European socialist parties to ditch the dogmas of old-style interventionism and unnecessary regulation.

Despite Labour's advocacy of a European recovery programme based on counter-cyclical measures, as recently as the 1995 conference document, Blair distanced himself from Jospin's Keynesianism in the run-up to the intergovernmental conference. This episode demonstrated New Labour's apparent antipathy to the European social model. As David Marquand commented:

> The paradox is that, as the Thatcherites correctly spotted, part of the purpose of the EU is to Europeanise a solidaristic model of society and the economy, drawn partly from the continental social tradition and partly from the (also continental) tradition of catholic social thought. By the same token, part of the purpose of monetary union is to defend that model against the pressures of the global marketplace to create a supranational space in which to protect the European social market from creeping Americanisation. (1998: 20)

Yet New Labour under Blair appeared not to recognize the protection of the European social model as the most convincing rationale for the EU for a party of the left, although the party had shown signs of doing so under Smith and Kinnock. Despite Blair's support for the social and employment chapters, he appeared to prefer the deregulatory model favoured by the US Democrats on matters relating to the labour market.

The Amsterdam Treaty was also a disappointment for those

who had hoped that it would introduce the necessary reforms for the EU to proceed with enlargement while avoiding institutional paralysis, as was the initial objective of the intergovernmental conference. The member states failed to agree on the significant extension of qualified majority voting, restructuring of voting strengths in the Council of Ministers and streamlining of Commission size deemed necessary to facilitate expansion. However, for once Britain could plead 'not guilty' to being the major obstacle to progress. Indeed, the Labour government would later claim that it had been willing to move further in increasing Parliament co-decision than the French, and further in extending qualified majority voting than the Germans.[8] This did not quite compensate for the fact that the previous opt-out on social policy had been swapped for a new one from the newly communitarized 'area of freedom, security and justice'.

A third way for Europe?

Labour's approach to the 1996–97 intergovernmental conference and to Europe in general under Blair's leadership can best be summarized as one of pragmatic engagement. The Blair government has displayed willingness to accept progress in European integration provided that change is, in its perception, in Britain's interests and, more important, is acceptable to the British people. The government was thus able to present the democratic improvements agreed at Amsterdam as a victory for the Labour vision of a 'people's Europe', as were the reversal of the opt-out on social policy and the agreement on action to combat unemployment. Similarly, the opt-out from the 'area of freedom, security and justice' was portrayed as a successful defence of Britain's borders. What set the Labour government apart from its predecessors was willingness to engage with the European agenda (in certain areas), as demonstrated by the lines of communication established with the European Parliament and Labour's sister parties in the PES. It was surely no coincidence that many of Labour's proposals to improve democracy coincided with those of the European Parliament. Indeed, the Parliament, representative as it is of all Europe's major political parties, was able to play an agenda-setting role throughout the EU. Consequently, many of its suggestions were adopted by the member states and agreed at Amsterdam, notably in relation to the simplification of decision-making procedures and the consolidation of the treaties.

Despite the democratic improvements made at Amsterdam, concern still persists about the lack of accountability in EC decision-making, particularly in the swathe of policy areas in which the European Parliament has at best a consultative role. Philip Allot has commented that the central problem of the EC is the Council: 'The Council has virtually no political legitimacy. It is accountable to no-one. Its relationship to the Commission is irretrievably obscure. It is more of a cabal than a cabinet, more of a permanent diplomatic conference than a senate. And yet it legislates profusely' (House of Commons 1992–93: xxvii). While the national Ministers that make up the Council can argue that they get their political legitimacy from their respective national elections, in many cases the European treaties have transferred policy-making powers to the Council, and away from national parliaments, without a parallel transfer of accountability to the European Parliament. Thus the European treaties have reinforced the powers of government Ministers over their parliaments by allowing them to develop policies at a European level without having to subject them to the same rigours of parliamentary scrutiny that would have been necessary had policy remained the sole preserve of the national authorities.

Many pro-Europeans would argue that the solution to this is to make the European Parliament and the Council legislative partners in all areas of EU policy. This, indeed, is the position of the Parliament itself, and appeared to be what Labour's 1993 documents under John Smith's leadership were saying. However, many Labour Euro-sceptics view such attempts to replicate conventional conceptions of democratic government at the European level as impracticable and politically unacceptable. The Labour Euro-safeguards Campaign, which gathers together many of the veteran Labour anti-EC campaigners, has argued that the Council of Ministers 'is only indirectly elected' and therefore 'not truly accountable'. It derides the European Parliament for providing a 'visible but largely spurious veneer to the EU', arguing that it 'has little effective authority'. Furthermore, the campaign contends that any reform of the Parliament to make it perform the same function as a national parliament would be not only unlikely to occur but unworkable: 'Unless and until the different people of Europe feel that they are European more than they are French, German, British etc., no European Parliament whatever its powers, could obtain legitimacy and authority for decision' (Labour Euro-safeguards Campaign 1998).[9] This interpretation of European integration is illustrative of a conception of democracy which views the nation state as the optimum vehicle for representing the popular will. However, as already noted, this traditional view of democracy does not take into account the increasing power of multinational companies, the growing interdependence of international economies and the strength of international capital, which severely curtail the ability of national states to pursue independent political pathways.

In the light of such restrictions on political power at the national level, traditional conceptions of political power, which bind democracy intrinsically to the nation state, lose their meaning. Consequently, European states have 'pooled sovereignty' in order to exercise political power jointly at a supranational or intergovernmental level. Accordingly, the pro-European left sees such pan-European political co-ordination as a means to counter the power of the international economy. The challenge remains, however, to devise methods to ensure that this power is exercised democratically. It is true that the absence of a sense of European identity or a European political culture does make the development of a sense of political legitimacy at the European level difficult. A decentralized political framework which recognizes Europe's diversity therefore needs to be developed to overcome the obstacle.

Labour has made continued reference to increasing scrutiny by national parliaments, and in its first year of office a select committee on the modernization of the House of Commons made a number of recommendations for improving scrutiny by the select committees and standing committees on European legislation. These were approved by the government and were adopted by the House of Commons in November 1998 (House of Commons 1997–98). The Amsterdam Treaty included a protocol on national parliaments, which contained a commitment to provide national parliaments with more time to scrutinize proposed European legislation, and a recognition of the role of COSAC, the conference of European affairs committees of the national parliaments. According to this protocol, COSAC can 'comment' on European legislation as it sees fit. This is hardly revolutionary. In any case, while national parliaments can play a crucial role in ensuring their own Ministerial representatives in the Council are held to account, it is unrealistic to suggest that national parliaments, acting through their European affairs committees or otherwise, can act in unison to hold the Council to account. This is unfeasible, given the differences between national parliaments and their procedures for scrutinizing European legislation, and the difficulty of co-ordinating scrutiny among fifteen or more member states. Moreover, the European committees of national parliaments are unlikely to be able to provide the range of technical and policy expertise necessary, or the amount of time and effort required, to scrutinize in an effective manner the large volume and diversity of legislation which emanates from the Commission and Council. The European Parliament, with its range of specialist committees, appears a far more appropriate body for performing such a function.

It is difficult to see how the debate about democracy and the EU can move beyond such traditional approaches to institutional change. One of New Labour's chief architects, Peter Mandelson, has referred to the need to supersede traditional conceptions of representation, perhaps hinting at more direct forms of democracy. This is possibly linked with the New Labour espousal of a 'third way', a new form of politics which transcends ideologies and traditional political cleavages.[10] Whether this has any relevance to the European level of politics is open to question. Serious discussion of it would require a clearer explanation of what the 'third way' is. Both Blair and US President Bill Clinton addressed a conference to launch the 'third way' on the international stage in New York, in September 1998. The involvement of Clinton demonstrated the closer ideological affinity that New Labour appeared to feel with the US Democrats. That French Prime Minister Jospin did not appear to be on the guest list equally demonstrated New Labour's apparent distance from the more traditional commitment of the major European centre-left parties to the European social model. Despite this distancing, Blair was invited to make a speech to the French National Assembly in March 1998, in which he called on Europeans to embrace the 'third way'. In his speech, delivered in French, Blair referred to a political deficit in Europe, which required 'courage to reform': 'We have an economic framework for the EU. We now need a political framework that is dramatically more relevant, more in touch than the present one' (White 1998).

Foreign Secretary Robin Cook also invoked the notion of a 'third way', in an article in the *New Statesman* in August 1998 (Lloyd 1998). Cook sought to take the initiative on EU policy, proposing that a code on subsidiarity should be developed to ensure that decisions are taken at the appropriate level, giving a clearer definition of the division of powers between the EU and the member states. Accordingly, the EU would concentrate on setting a framework of standards, rather than detailed directives. Furthermore, Cook suggested that a forum of national parliamentarians should be created to ensure the correct application of these new principles. Cook was, in essence, advocating a new European second chamber, made up of members of the national parliaments, to ensure the correct exercise of Europe's jurisdiction, arguing that the only way to tackle the democratic deficit would be through the involvement of 'democratic institutions in which the public have confidence and with which they identify', i.e. the national parliaments and not the European Parliament. Although Cook conceded that the European Parliament did a very useful job, the implicit suggestion was that it lacked the public confidence and the political legitimacy necessary to hold the other European institutions to account.

Understandably, these comments caused some consternation among some Labour MEPs, although they at least reawakened the debate about Europe's democratic deficit, and the need for further institutional reform. However, the suggestion that the European Commission should concentrate on setting a framework of standards did not quite take into account the fact that much of the detailed legislation to which Cook referred concerned measures to enforce the Single Market, of which British governments, both Conservative and Labour, had been fervent champions. Moreover, the suggestion of some kind of second chamber of national parliamentarians had been floating around for a while, and had been proposed by successive French governments. It had also been suggested by Michael Heseltine in the 1980s, and by the London-based centre-right European Policy Forum.[11] While it may be desirable to give national parliaments some kind of collective role in ensuring that principles of subsidiarity are applied (leaving aside the difficulty of translating the principle into agreed practice), Europe-wide accountability is best served by making the European Parliament a legislative partner to the Council of Ministers. This would require it to have the capacity not only to scrutinize the proposals of the Commission but also to amend, remould and ultimately approve or reject all legislation.

Cook's proposal of a code defining the EU's political powers could be interpreted as a nod towards some kind of constitutional document for the EU. Indeed, Cook did suggest that his proposals could form part of 'a programme of reform that will lead Europe to a new constitutional settlement' (Cook 1998). The proposal for a political code best makes sense in this context. One could argue that such a code would be most effective as part of a broader European constitution. This would define the EU's political powers and provide a clear political framework for EU action. Paddy Ashdown, close to Blair on constitutional issues, called for the creation of a European constitution in a speech in July 1998.[12] It has also been a constant demand of the European Movement and the European Parliament and has had many advocates on the Continent in recent years, but it has not gained much credence in Britain, probably because Britain lacks a written constitution. Labour rejected the idea of a European constitution in its 1995 conference document. Fearful that it would bestow a form of federal statehood, the Labour document argued that the EU should remain 'a treaty between independent nations that pool sovereignty rather than the constitution of a European superstate'. This failure to recognize that the EU displays certain aspects of statehood made it all the more difficult for the Labour Party to address its democratic deficiencies.

A European constitution would not only clarify the EU's powers and procedures, together with the rights the EU confers on its citizens but would also provide a political counterweight to the powerful economic constitution entrenched in the EU treaties. This might strike a chord with Tony Blair, given the reference in his French National Assembly speech to the need to establish a political framework to match the economic one. Cook's proposals also overlooked the political consequences of the European single currency, which will increase the need to develop a strong pan-European political counterweight to a powerful set of economic rules constitutionally entrenched in the European treaties. The EU appears all the more undemocratic to many because it entrenches a framework of economic rules which could arguably be described as containing an ideological bias in favour of free-market deregulation and untrammelled competition, for example in restricting the power of national governments to aid ailing industries. The only way to overturn these powerful economic rules is via treaty changes requiring the support of all the member state governments and approval by their parliaments. A European constitution could establish a clearer, and decidedly more democratic, political framework for defining the EU's economic orientation.

The campaign to reassert effective political control over the EU's economic and monetary direction was given powerful impetus following the election of a Social Democrat (SPD)-Green government in Germany in October 1998. This, combined with the appointment of a centre-left Prime Minister, Massimo D'Alema, in Italy shortly after, meant that eleven of the fifteen EU governments were PES-led, including, for the first time, the four biggest member states. While the new German Chancellor, Gerhard Schröder, was seen as ideologically close to Blair, he ceded considerable power to his Finance Minister, Oskar Lafontaine, who shared the Keynesian predilections of the French socialists and with their support sought to revive the plans for a European employment strategy and to promote a more interventionist political approach towards the activities of the ECB. However, Lafontaine's ascendency was short-lived. His resignation in March 1999, following complaints from Schröder and the ECB that his blunt diplomacy was undermining the single currency, came as a relief to advocates of the third way, Blair and Schröder included, but disappointed those on the left who saw the new centre-left ascendency as a unique opportunity to reshape the European project and develop a co-ordinated approach to the social and political imbalances in the EMU process.

Independent of these political changes, the European Parliament was seeking, on its own initiative, to enhance its role in the EMU process and give further impetus to the campaign for greater political control of the ECB. In November 1998 the European Parliament's monetary affairs committee and the representatives of the finance committees of the EU national parliaments agreed to hold joint sessions twice-yearly to monitor the ECB. Accordingly, representatives of the ECB would be invited to explain its policy and interest-rate decisions and to discuss its annual report with the joint committee. This represented an important step, both in improving ECB accountability and in developing new forms of co-operation in the scrutiny of EU activity between national parliaments and the European Parliament.

The European Parliament had increasingly sought to enhance its capacity to hold the European institutions to account, taking full advantage of its rules of procedure and the limited powers bestowed upon it by the European treaties. This was further illustrated when the Parliament's refusal to approve the European Commission's handling of the 1996 budget[13] led first to an (unsuccesful) vote of censure of the Commission and then to the appointment of a 'committee of wise men' which produced a damning report on corruption and mismanagement in the Commission, leading to the voluntary resignation of the entire Commission in March 1999. While this was widely portrayed as a 'coming of age' of the European Parliament, it also provided the opportunity for the Blair government to take the initiative (previously lost to Lafontaine) by launching plans to improve the management and accountability of the Commission. However, these plans related to the internal organization of the Commission rather than to any institutional innovations.

Whether or not the Labour government would produce substantive proposals for democratic reform outside the traditional remedies of increasing transparency in decision-making and developing the role of the European Parliament and national parliaments, and co-operation between the two, remained to be seen. Labour's democratic credentials were in any case coming under increasing criticism as it entered its second year of office. Although the Bills to establish Scottish and Welsh assemblies were carried, Blair had seemed less certain of that part of Labour's constitutional package than his predecessors. Hence his decision to stage referendums in Scotland and Wales to make sure of public support, and his references before the general election to a Scottish Parliament having similar powers to a parish council (Anderson and Mann 1997: 283–7). In addition, the Labour government continued to remain vague about its preferred options for reforming the House of Lords, fuelling fears that Labour would go no further than removing the right of hereditary peers to vote, leaving the Lords as a 'super-quango' of political appointees. Stalling also continued on the implementation of the party's promise to introduce a Freedom of Information Act.

Criticism of the government intensified when it put forward

a closed-list system of PR for elections to the European Parliament, a system denounced as undemocratic by many critics.[14] The closed system was criticized for denying electors a choice between individual candidates (the elector would be asked only to vote for a particular party list) and for centralizing power in the party machines. Each party would have considerable discretion in the selection and ranking of candidates. In the case of the Labour Party the selection and ranking of candidates were undertaken by a selection board appointed by the party leadership, leading to increasing criticism of the 'control freak' tendencies of the leadership, as potentially troublesome candidates, including sitting MEPs, were placed low down on the lists, making their election unlikely. Similar criticisms were levelled at the leadership for its exercise of control over the selection of candidates to the new Scottish and Welsh assemblies and for the new post of mayor of London. Many commentators pointed to the paradox of a Labour Party committed to democratic and pluralist reforms of the constitution while simultaneously centralizing control of its own internal apparatus and denying pluralism to its own membership.

The centralizing tendency of the party leadership reflected impatience with the sizeable collection of individuals who did not share the modernizing zeal of Blair and his acolytes, and their particular vision of the 'third way'. It did not quite square with the focus on pluralism which characterized the party's rhetoric on renewing Britain's democratic fabric. The Labour government appeared to be haunted by the nightmare of division and the lurch to the left which had, in its perception, made Labour unelectable in the 1980s. The attitude of the leadership to internal party democracy was in part a reflection of the desire to avoid a repetition. It would sometimes verge on paranoia about any statements by candidates, MPs or Ministers which appeared to be 'off-message'. This was not surprising, given the hostility of the press to 'old Labour'.

It is this fear of a return to the past that tempers all Labour policies, often suppressing its remaining radical tendencies. A hard-edged pragmatism, based on what is and what is not realistically achievable and acceptable to the public, pervades much of Labour's agenda. While the commitment to modernize Britain's political institutions remains genuine, it is tempered by this pragmatic realism. Similarly, the Labour Party has demonstrated a desire to engage with the European agenda but remains constrained by domestic political concerns. Such pragmatic realism is likely to prevent the party from advocating some kind of all-encompassing vision which places a revitalized British democracy at the heart of a new democratic settlement at the European level. This pragmatism also prevented the government from taking part in the first wave of the single currency, although there were strong indications that it would seek to secure British entry once it felt it could win its promised referendum on the issue. The launch of the single currency in January 1999 heightened the imperative of a new constitutional settlement at the European level. Given Britain's exclusion, a meaningful contribution from the Labour Party in shaping this settlement would be all the more unlikely.

Notes

1 The leading advocate of PR in the party is the Foreign Secretary, Robin Cook, who chairs the Labour Campaign for Electoral Reform.

2 As a first stage Blair appointed a commission on electoral reform, chaired by Roy Jenkins, following Labour's election victory in 1997. The Jenkins commission published its report in October 1998, advocating an 'alternative vote' system with a proportional 'top-up' element. Jenkins hinted that Blair had been won over by his proposals. Nevertheless, the majority of the Cabinet, as with the party at large, opposed the proposals, and it seemed likely that any referendum on them would be delayed until after the following general election.

3 This was Britain's second application for membership of the EC. Like the first application, made by the Conservative government of Macmillan (1961–63), it was vetoed by the French President, Charles De Gaulle.

4 Stuart Holland was formerly an economist and adviser to Harold Wilson. He later resigned his seat to take up a professorship at the European University Institute in Florence, while working on a European Recovery Programme with Jacques Delors.

5 Martin had been *rapporteur* for the report delivering the Parliament's proposals for the Maastricht intergovernmental conference, and co-*rapporteur* of its initial report on the 1996 intergovernmental conference.

6 The reflection group was chaired by the Spanish Foreign Minister, Carlos Westendorp, and comprised representatives of each of the member states' Foreign Ministries, the European Commission and the European Parliament, with a remit to examine reform proposals.

7 Jospin's socialists had come to power in France at the beginning of June 1997 following a disastrous gamble by Gaullist President Jacques Chirac to stage early elections, in order to win a mandate for EMU-inspired austerity measures.

8 Labour's European co-ordinator, Larry Whitty, made this suggestion in a speech to the European Parliamentary Labour Party fringe meeting at the Labour Party Conference, Brighton, 28 September 1997.

9 The campaign is chaired by Peter Shore, a Labour Cabinet Minister in the 1970s and veteran anti-EC campaigner.

10 Mandelson made these comments in a private seminar on 'European Integration and National Sovereignty' staged in March 1998 by the Bertelsmann foundation in co-operation with the UK embassy in Germany, with the participation of key British and German politicians and opinion-formers. Mandelson was forced to resign as Secretary of State for Trade and Industry in December 1998 following revelations concerning a substantial loan received from fellow Minister Geoffrey Robinson, whose financial affairs were the subject of an investigation by Mandelson's department. Although this was interpreted as a severe blow to the 'New Labour' project, Mandelson was likely to remain a major influence on Blair's thinking.

11 Heseltine suggested this in his evidence to the House of Commons Foreign Affairs Committee during its consideration of the Single European Act (House of Commons 1989–90: xxii). The European Policy Forum proposed a chamber of national parliamentarians with the same role as that proposed by Cook (European Policy Forum 1993).

12 Ashdown suggested this in a speech to the Centre for European Reform, in London, on 16 July 1998. Ashdown announced his intention to step down as Liberal Democrat leader in January 1999. This was widely interpreted as a blow to the Blair project of establishing a grand anti-Conservative coalition, with closer ties with the Liberal Democrats a first stage. Some pundits went so far as to suggest that Mandelson's resignation may have precipitated Ashdown's, given that he was the only major member of the Cabinet to share Blair's enthusiasm for closer ties.

13 The European Parliament has the power under the EU treaties to retrospectively refuse to discharge (i.e. approve) the European Commission's implementation of the EU budget.

14 The closed-list system provided for political parties to each put a list of candidates forward to elections to large, multi-candidate regional constituencies, in a fixed order of ranking (in an open-list system the ranking would be undertaken by the voter.) Accordingly, if a party garnered 40 per cent of the vote in a ten-member constituency, the candidates occupying the first four places on the party list would be elected. The House of Lords had rejected the European Parliament elections Bill five times by November 1998, forcing the government to reintroduce the Bill in the 1998–99 legislative session. That the Conservative opposition in the Lords had been reliant on the hereditary peers to defeat the government also served to deepen the government's resolve to pass the necessary legislation to remove the hereditaries' voting power in the 1998–99 session.

References

Anderson, Paul, and Mann, Nytta (1997), *Safety First. The Making of New Labour*, London, Granta Books.

Charter 88 (1992), 'Report of third Sovereignty lecture', 15 June.

Cook, Robin (1998), 'Full steam ahead', *Guardian*, 14 August.

European Policy Forum (1993), *Proposal for a European Constitution*, Report of the European Constitutional Group, London, EPF.

Foreign and Commonwealth Office (1996), *Partnership of Nations. The British Approach to the European Union Intergovernmental Conference 1996*, London, HMSO.

House of Commons (1989–90), *The Operation of the Single European Act*, Foreign Affairs Committee, Second Report, Session 1989–90, HC82–I.

House of Commons (1992–93), *Europe after Maastricht*, Foreign Affairs Committee, Second Report, Session 1992–93, HC642–I.

House of Commons (1997–98), *The Scrutiny of European Business*, Select Committee on Modernization, Seventh Report, HC799.

Labour Party (1993a), *A new Agenda for Democracy. Labour's Proposals for Constitutional Reform*, London, Labour Party.

Labour Party (1993b), *Prosperity through Co-operation. A new European Future*, London, Labour Party.

Labour Party (1995), *The Future of the European Union. Report on Labour's Position in Preparation for the Intergovernmental Conference 1996*, London, Labour Party.

Labour Euro-safeguards Campaign (1998), *Questions and Answers on Democracy and the European Union*, bulletin, March.

Lloyd, John (1998), 'Interview: Robin Cook', *New Statesman*, 14 August.

Marquand, David (1998), 'The Blair paradox', *Prospect*, May.

White, Michael (1998), 'EU must change, Blair tells French', *Guardian*, 25 March.

5

How democratic is the European Parliament?

JOHN LAMBERT AND CATHERINE HOSKYNS

In the early 1990s, one of us (Lambert) depicted the European Parliament as a luxury cruise liner, whose passengers and crew were involved in complex activities and rituals about which the outside world knew little and cared less. Occasionally the 'floating palace' returned to port, but once it set sail again its existence was forgotten. Well, the liner is now permanently berthed and the passengers and crew have moved into the gigantic, fortress-like *espace Léopold* building in the European quarter of Brussels. Far from representing an airy, open public space, the building glowers across at the equally massive Council of Ministers building on the next block. Herein lies the dilemma for the Parliament: should it, can it, represent an alternative style of politics, while at the same time 'acting tough' and gaining a presence in the undemocratic and intimidating power structures through which the EU is at present governed?

The question 'How democratic is the European Parliament?' is thus an important one. It involves two aspects: first, how democratic is the Parliament as regards its internal procedures and politics, and second, how democratic is the position it has achieved/been given in the overall policy process of the EU? Finally, it is important also to ask in what sense the Parliament is contributing to new ideas about how democracy could be strengthened in the evolving EU.

In answering these questions, the test of democracy which we shall use is whether the people of Europe are gaining some say in and some control of the following three areas of European decision-making:

- major economic policy;
- the protection of the environment;
- the social contract.

This test puts the emphasis on content and outcome rather than procedure, and we accept that there may be many different ways of achieving the above objectives. The degree of open debate about political alternatives in these areas can be seen as markers of democratization. In contrast to the economic sphere, the member states appear to have no goals for the EU in a political sense. Their attitude to political reform is: 'if the boat leaks, mend it'.

The structure of the European Parliament as it stands is broadly democratic, although as with most parliaments activities may take place within its walls which are not democratic at all. However, its place in the decision-making process and its powers are very different from those normally accorded to parliaments in Western democracies. In essence, it is one actor in the bargaining process rather than being itself the main legislator. On top of this, although Members of the European Parliament (MEPs) are elected by and in theory represent the people of Europe, the Parliament itself as an institution is not well known or trusted by the public. Thus the Parliament if it is to be effective has to increase both its institutional power and its broader credibility.

Two models

The progress of the European Parliament in recent years can be understood in terms of two models: 'the shuttle' and 'the tug-of-war'. The shuttle represents the bit-by-bit increase in the power of the Parliament within the system of decision-making dominated by the Council of Ministers. It has led to a situation where in certain fields decisions are 'shuttled' between the two institutions and where the Parliament has blocking powers, or 'negative assent'. This kind of relationship, which in effect builds the Parliament into the Council system, has gained broader significance and become central to the workings of the EU.

The other model is the tug-of-war. This assumes an inherent conflict between the Parliament on the one hand and the Council on the other, so that an increase in the power of one is perceived as involving a decrease in that of the other. Within this conflict, the European Commission, with its crucial power to initiate and implement proposals, can act either to moderate the conflict or tip the balance to one side or the other. If this model predominates, outcomes are likely to involve either deadlock or an abrupt shift of power from one institution to another.

It is the argument of this chapter that both these models have substance, and that at the moment the shuttle model is serving to blur the reality of the tug-of-war. At the same time, the shuttle process has the capacity to create opportunities for the Parliament which if grasped to the full can make the tug-of-war more equal. The relation between the models is all the more complex because the European Parliament is a highly diverse organization, within which political groups, issue-based committees, individual MEPs and their staffs, lobbyists and experts gyrate and spin. A hierarchy of Members and the Parliament's own staff are appointed to keep order. While attempts are made to impose conformity, diversity and dissonance still break through.

The shuttle

The significance of the shuttle lies in the attempt to graft onto the basic system of European Community (EC) decision-making an intensified dialogue between the Council and the Parliament. This is the essence of the change which is taking place, with the Commission playing a key role between the two. Given this influence, control of the Commission (how its members are appointed, who it is accountable to) becomes extremely important. The transition in the decision-making process has happened gradually, moving from consultation to co-operation, to 'co-decision'.[1] All of these descriptive names refer to the role of the Parliament.

The consultation phase

The Parliament (then called the Assembly) started off in the 1950s as a largely cosmetic body, ancillary to the real centres of EC decision-making. Under certain articles of the Treaty of Rome, the Council was obliged to consult it on pieces of legislation being prepared by the Commission. The opinions of the Parliament were advisory only; there was no requirement for them to be incorporated into legislation or even taken seriously. As a result the Parliament was active but marginal, and most of its members retained seats in their national parliaments. The 'visionary' element within it, those who believed in a federal Europe with Parliament at its centre, campaigned to expand the scope of consultation, to implement the treaty commitment to direct elections and to strengthen social policy within the remit of the Community. They were for the most part sidelined, and the Parliament as a whole had difficulty in participating effectively in the burgeoning economic concerns of the Community.

During the 1970s, in a new political atmosphere, the scope of consultation was increased and the Parliament gained more status, and with it important new budgetary powers. This was the start of the shuttle, with the Council and the Parliament forming the twin arms of the budgetary authority, and becoming involved in quite intense face-to-face negotiations. This gave the Parliament some powers to encourage particular aspects of policy but always within a very restricted scope. The Parliament was also required to 'discharge' the Commission's accounts for each financial year: its familiarity with laxity and irregularities in Commission procedures derives from this.

In 1979 elections to the Parliament were finally held on direct universal suffrage, but through a separate process in each of the member states. The resulting Parliament was energetic and more 'full-time'. It was also more diverse. Immediately after the elections the 'old guard' of politicians tried to raise the threshold for forming a political group in the Parliament, a status which was advantageous in terms of financial and other support. The smaller groups and independent members on the left opposed the move by joint action and filibuster, and managed to ensure the important principle that the Parliament should encourage and support smaller transnational groupings. The links made at this time laid the basis for the formation of the Rainbow Group, a transnational alliance of Red/Green MEPs which was active in the Parliament in the 1980s.

This early confrontation illustrates an important strand in the politics of the European Parliament, that is, the struggle between control and efficiency, on the one hand, and diversity and debate on the other. The Parliament needs to be professional and to show discipline – but it also needs to represent as wide a political spectrum as possible, encourage transnational contacts and engage the public. Sometimes these roles conflict, as an account of the further development of the shuttle system suggests.

How to co-operate

From 1979 on, pressure grew to increase the Parliament's role in the decision-making process. This was partly achieved with the adoption of the co-operation procedure in the Single European Act of 1986. Basically, the co-operation procedure adds a second reading to the consultation process. Instead of the Council being able to adopt a measure once the Parliament's opinion has been received, it has to approve a 'common position' (which may or may not contain amendments suggested by the Parliament) and return the proposal to the Parliament. The Parliament then has the opportunity to reject or amend the Council draft – if it can muster an absolute majority of its members. In the 1989–94 session such a majority required a positive vote of 260 out of the 518 members, a high hurdle. The Council can reinstate its position only by unanimity.

In order to have a chance of obtaining this high vote, amendments have to be proposed in the Parliament which are acceptable to a wide range of members. In 1994, out of the total of 518 MEPs, 197 were European socialists (PES) while 162 belonged to the (mainly Christian Democrat) European People's Party (EPP). Rather than attempt to build up majorities by winning over the 'further left' or 'further right', the two big political groups have often chosen to negotiate and compromise between themselves. If they can reach agreement they have a good chance of achieving the absolute majority. This strategy, however, tends to lead to secret deals rather than open politics and to reduce debate and the discussion of alternatives. It is not unknown for particular committees to become aware that such a deal has been done and to realize that there is little point in further discussion.

On the other hand, there is no doubt that the new powers have had the effect of making the Parliament more serious and more professional and have increased the demands on individual MEPs. In the process, and via the co-operation procedure, some important amendments of Community legislation have been adopted, including higher exhaust emission standards for small cars, improving consumer protection in package holidays and banning hormones in beef.

In institutional terms, co-operation increased the interaction of the Parliament with the Commission, which had to pay more attention to the likely views of Parliament when drafting its proposals. The Council, however, under this procedure remains aloof and uninvolved, although some of its decisions have been affected.

Co-decision?

Co-operation is now little used, having been gradually replaced by the co-decision procedure since the Maastricht Treaty came into effect in November 1993. However, many of the underlying characteristics and effects discussed above remain the same. Under co-decision, the Commission's initial proposal goes to the Parliament at the same time as it goes to the Council. The Parliament can also at second reading amend the Council's common position. If the Council does not accept the amendments a Conciliation Committee is set up, consisting of equal representatives from the Council and the Parliament and usually with a representative of the Commission present. If agreement is reached, both institutions approve the measure. If it is not, the Parliament can reject the measure but not get its own version adopted: the procedure is still therefore one of negative assent. Agreed measures are designated as 'Acts of the Council and the Parliament' and are signed jointly.

This procedure represents a considerable increase in the Parliament's power and involves direct contact and direct negotiation between representatives of the Parliament and the Council. This had previously happened only over the budget. Interesting by-plays now occur whereby countries which are in a minority in the Council – perhaps because they want a higher level of standards than those being proposed – may look to the Parliament for support. The Commission still plays an important role, and where it throws its weight significantly alters the outcome.

However, the extent of change should not be exaggerated. The initiation of this procedure came at a time when the bulk of Single Market legislation had been adopted, and when the emphasis was on the application of 'subsidiarity' and the reduction in general of legislative activity at the European level. The scope of the legislation to which co-decision initially applied was also fairly narrow although it did include further internal market provisions and measures on public health, consumer protection and environmental programmes. Co-decision did not apply to 'comitology', the term invented to describe the large number of committees set up between the Commission and the Council to implement and regulate measures already taken. As will be discussed later, this has become a major bone of conten-tion between the Parliament and the Council and is a key area to watch for progress in democratization.

The main recipient in the Parliament of co-decision meas-ures has been the Committee on the Environment, Public Health and Consumer Protection (the Environment Committee). During the 1990s this changed from a 'cinderella' committee, not much favoured by aspiring MEPs, to a rigorous and professional negotiating chamber for some highly conten-tious measures. The change took place under the effective and sometimes rough chairmanship of the British Labour MEP, Ken Collins. The committee sessions are open and the extent to which they are packed with smart-suited visitors is evidence of its growing importance. Business and industry lobbying around the committee is intense, as is the interest of consumer bodies and environment NGOs. The difference is that while the former have permanent advisers monitoring the committee, the latter on the whole attend for specific issues and campaigns. Despite this interest in its proceedings, and the crucial nature of some of its decisions, even the Environment Committee has not so far been able to attract extensive media coverage of its activities.

The overriding problem for a committee of this kind, faced with a heavy load of legislative measures coming through from the Commission and Council, is to generate sufficient indepen-dent expertise and establish a core of committed MEPs with influence in their broader party groups. Given the degree of interest in the outcomes, what seems like a solid agreement in committee can melt away in the plenary session where the crucial votes are taken. As under co-operation, the easiest way to achieve and sustain an absolute majority in the Parliament as a whole is for agreement to be reached between the two major party groups on the broad outlines of the Parliament's position. Inevitably, this involves compromise on the content and tends to push policy towards the middle ground.

Co-decision represents the shuttle at its most intense. Decisions go from the Council to the Parliament and back and the presumption is that this produces efficient and 'justifiable' outcomes. The effect of the absolute majority threshold is to push the Parliament into a single negotiating position and to play down debate and alternative views. The procedure does, however, bring a different element into the negotiations, and the amendments proposed by the Parliament usually at least start from a more pro-citizen/pro-consumer point of view. In terms of our original 'test of democracy' this undoubtedly represents an improvement – but at the moment it is one which may either be built upon or contained. In present circumstances the way the Parliament operates makes the latter more likely. The Amsterdam Treaty which came into force on 1 May 1999 replaces co-operation with co-decision in most areas except those concerned with EMU.

As with the Environment Committee, the Parliament's greater power now makes it subject to intensive lobbying. Here as elsewhere in the EU this is overwhelmingly conducted by business and industry representatives and their advisers. The Parliament's 'other' role of giving greater access and influence to civil society groups and social NGOs, and in the process extending its constituency and establishing its own legitimacy, has not so far been sufficient to correct this.

The tug-of-war

The Council in its various manifestations has generally shown itself over the years to be hostile to the Parliament and what it stands for. The term 'Council' is used here as a shorthand for the many and different occasions when combinations of member state politicians and their officials, even including heads of state, meet together in what are basically intergovernmental forums. This is not to say that all governments and officials oppose the Parliament on all issues all the time. Rather it is that the structures and working practices of intergovernmentalism contradict those of parliamentary democracy, even in the weak form in which this exists at European level.

Thus it is often member state officials, who have to make the system work, who are most dismissive of MEPs and of the capacities of Parliament as a whole. The requirements of a Parliament are hard to accommodate with the normal practices of interstate bargaining, based as these are on secrecy and package deals. This situation is made more complex by the fact that basic decisions about the Parliament (the way it is elected and its location as well as any change in its formal powers) have to be agreed unanimously by member state governments – in just such forums.

This generalized and rather fundamental hostility of the

Council to the Parliament goes back a long way and was indicated in the early days of the EC by the Council's attitude to the issue of direct elections. The Treaty of Rome laid down that the Assembly (as it then was) should be elected 'by direct universal suffrage using a uniform procedure in all member states' (Article 138). However, when proposals were put forward by the Assembly to implement this the Council delayed and prevaricated for more than a decade, querying in particular what the uniform procedure might involve. In the course of this it became clear that the majority of governments were reluctant to allow elections which carried with them an element of transnationalism.

In the end, when the Parliament threatened to bring a case before the European Court of Justice, new proposals were put forward in the mid-1970s. These involved a compromise whereby the elections would go forward but the issue of the uniform procedure would be left to be decided at a later date. Thus the elections of 1979 were organized separately in each member state, using whatever procedure was seen as appropriate. For a variety of reasons, despite proposals from the Parliament, no further move on the uniform procedure was made during the 1980s.

The reluctance of politicians to undermine the national political space is understandable. However, the decision and particularly the delay prevented the framework being laid at an early stage for a European public politics, and deprived the Parliament of the legitimacy which such a process might have brought. Although the uniform procedure issue looks like being partially resolved as a result of decisions taken at Amsterdam, it is in a context where assumptions about the weakness of the Parliament and the essential 'nationalness' of European elections are now solidly implanted in the public mind.[2]

The split site

The issue of where the Parliament should be located is another example of Council hostility – although indifference may be nearer the mark. While the Council and the Commission are located in Brussels, under a 'provisional' agreement reached in 1965 the Parliament's activities were split between Luxembourg (the secretariat) and Strasbourg (plenary sessions). This located the Parliament away from the main centre of power, prevented it from developing a concentrated presence, and made socialization among its far-flung MEPs more difficult. The Parliament's answer has been to establish itself nonetheless in Brussels, occupying bigger and bigger buildings, including a chamber large enough for plenaries. For some time now, all parliamentary committee meetings have been held in Brussels – essential for co-decision – and much of the secretariat is based there also.

After Maastricht, it was agreed that a permanent decision had to be reached on the location of institutions. The Parliament made strong submissions to be located in Brussels alongside the other two policy-making bodies. Perhaps the most telling observation about the negotiations which followed is that they showed that no state really cared about the outcome except the countries (and particularly France) which had or might have institutions on their territory. The result was to confirm the 1965 agreement, while allowing the Parliament to continue to hold its committee meetings and additional plenaries in Brussels. The decision was the result of a national 'deal', with little attention being paid to the needs either of the Parliament or of the political process as a whole. The Parliament has stated that it does not accept the decision.

These two examples – and others could be cited – demonstrate the basis of the tug-of-war. The governments as a collectivity feel threatened by the Parliament and use their control either to ignore it or to restrain its influence. It is only when there are compelling 'other' reasons, usually in terms of the governments' own legitimacy or the 'efficiency' of decision-making, that concessions are made. When such issues are raised, and the governmental consensus breaks up, a more varied politics begins to emerge. It is in the Parliament's overall interest to try and produce such situations. It can normally do so only by adopting a stance of 'moderate confrontation' and by recognizing the reality of the tug-of-war. It is the concessions which governments have made in these circumstances that have produced the shuttle.

The draft treaty

One of the best and earliest examples of moderate confrontation was the drawing up by the Parliament in the early 1980s of the draft Treaty on European Union. This was a project which arose out of the disappointment felt by many MEPs elected in 1979 at the Parliament's lack of power and the refusal of the Council to take its new status seriously. Members were particularly con-cerned that the unanimity rule in the Council meant that one country could effectively veto all institutional developments. The catalyst of the draft treaty was the Italian MEP Altiero Spinelli, a former communist, resistance fighter and European Commissioner, and an imaginative and realistic thinker about the role of the Parliament. Spinelli felt that treaty revision was necessary if the position of the directly elected Parliament was to be improved, and that rather than try to persuade the Council to take action the Parliament should draft its own proposals. The aim was to turn the Parliament into its own constituent assembly.

Spinelli was anxious to get as broad an involvement as pos-sible across the political groups in the Parliament and at the same time to generate public debate. The achievement of the former led to an emphasis on structure rather than policy and reduced the political content. The draft treaty was adopted by the Parliament on 14 February 1984 by 237 to thirty-one votes, with forty-three abstentions – not an absolute majority of the total number of MEPs. In the end, the EPP supported it fully but a number of socialists abstained. Attempts were made to involve national parliaments and a wide spectrum of organizations but despite many efforts interest remained confined to elite circles.

The text of the draft treaty accepted the existing structure of the Community but sought to build on it in ways that, it was hoped, would enhance both efficiency and democracy. It encom-passed many ideas which have since become EU practice: joint decision-making between Council and Parliament, a role for the latter in appointing the Commission, a hierarchy of Community Acts with differences in the way each should be adopted, and an expansion of scope towards foreign and secur-ity policy. One proposal which has not been adopted was that treaty revision should be able to go ahead without the agree-ment of all member states.

The confrontational element in the draft treaty lay in its provenance and the way in which the different groups in the Parliament had worked together to produce the text. The actual proposals were moderate and carefully judged to increase the powers of Parliament in ways that might be acceptable in certain circumstances to at least some of the member states. Its value was that it provided a text and drafted proposals in areas where very little concrete thinking had so far been carried out.

Its weakness was that despite all efforts it did not spark off a public debate and in the end had little in it to attract the general public.

The draft treaty was adopted at a time when moves were being made to 'relaunch' the Community with the creation of the Single Market. The strength of the Parliament's view, together with the fact that efficiency was seen as requiring a streamlining of the decision-making process, meant that treaty revision was in the air. The Parliament's proposals were sucked into the intergovernmental process which led up to the Single European Act. However, the continuing requirement that all states must agree led to considerable dilution of the proposals. The co-operation procedure, already discussed, was the result.

Parliament has never repeated this particular confrontation, though it has continued to demand a say in and a presence at intergovernmental meetings, especially those which have a constitutive role. So far they have been unsuccessful. Parliament was excluded from the Maastricht Treaty negotiations and was able only to submit proposals and organize hearings. The Amsterdam procedure was intended to be more open. Parliament had two members on the preliminary Reflection Group but they were permitted only to be observers of the final negotiations. This was seen by some as an important concession, but to others it was an insult which the Parliament should not have gone along with. Spinelli's precedent of drafting a separate treaty was not followed.

Accountability, mismanagement and fraud

The Parliament is given certain scrutiny and supervisory powers in the Treaty of Rome and the intention was that this should be one of its main roles. Over the years it has attempted to increase those powers, *de facto* if not *de jure*, and more recently this has become a major area of confrontation. It is all the more important since there has been a tendency for powers to be devolved to unaccountable forums and agencies as the EU's competences have increased The small size of the Commission and its under-funding mean that it has little choice but to contract out not just administrative tasks but also key areas of policy. It is in this context that the issues of openness and transparency have come to the fore, and the Parliament is playing an important role in pressing for new procedures and guidelines.

Gradually during the 1980s concern about fraud in the Common Agricultural Policy grew and this reflected upon the EC's management and funding programmes more generally. The Parliament pressed at the time of Maastricht for increased powers in this area and as a result was accorded in the treaty the right on the one hand to establish an Ombudsman to receive complaints from citizens and residents about maladministration in Community institutions and bodies, and on the other to set up its own temporary committees of inquiry into allegations of maladministration in the implementation of Community law.

The Ombudsman, Jacob Söderman, was appointed by the Parliament in September 1995 and has been gradually defining his role and getting his office and presence known. Though for the moment complaints are mainly from those 'in the know' (and to a large extent about recruitment to Community institutions) he has been helpful to those attempting to use the new 'access to documents' provisions and is starting to develop 'own initiative' investigations. The proceedings are virtually free, relatively quick and admirably uncomplicated. The post of Ombudsman undoubtedly helps to create unthreatening channels between the EU and its public but depends in turn upon the EU itself becoming better known and understood.

Rules of procedure for the committees of inquiry proved hard to draw up, involving as they did crucial issues about the right to see documents and to compel witnesses (including senior politicians) to attend. In particular, the Council has shown itself reluctant to submit to such accountability. So far, two committees of inquiry of this new kind have been held. The first, on the so-called 'fraud at the frontiers' issue, dealt with tax evasion in the Community transport system. The second was concerned with the way in which the BSE crisis (involving the ban on British beef to the rest of the EU) had been managed. In the latter case, the British Minister of Agriculture, Douglas Hogg, refused to attend the hearings, demonstrating clearly his scorn for the Parliament and his unwillingness to accept that it should have powers of investigation. Both committees reported in 1997 and received considerable publicity.[3] Both were critical of the Commission. The strategy of 'attacking the weak gazelle' (in this case the Commission) suggested that the Parliament was flexing its muscles – and beginning to challenge the Council over who should control the Commission and its operations.

The March crisis

This strategy appeared to be being carried further in March 1999, when the entire Commission resigned over allegations from the Parliament concerning fraud. However, strategy is probably too grand a word for what was in fact a set of *ad hoc* decisions and uncontrolled events. The crisis began at the end of 1998 with the refusal of the Parliament's Committee on Budgetary Control to discharge the Community budget because of what it saw as the arrogance of the Commission in refusing to answer queries over apparent mismanagement. The question was then posed as to whether such refusal amounted to a formal censure of the Commission. This issue became tangled up in broader accusations which specifically targeted the French commissioner, Edith Cresson, and the Spanish commissioner, Manuel Marin. Since both were social democrats, it seemed to some that an attempt was being made to discredit social democrat parties and governments in the run-up to the European elections due to be held in June 1999. This suspicion helps to explain divisions and hesitations among the Socialist Group (PES) leaders at this point. Whistleblowers and investigative journalists weighed in at various points to substantiate and expand the charges.

Amid complex game-playing, which involved some national governments attempting to pressurize their MEPs, the Parliament eventually adopted a resolution on financial management in the Commission in its plenary session of January 1999. Among other things, this called for the setting up of a committee of independent experts to examine the allegations against the Commission. The Commission president, Jacques Santer, agreed to 'respond' to its findings. By that time it seems to have occurred to some at least of the leaders of the political groups that mounting a challenge to the Commission might gain useful publicity for the Parliament as the elections approached.

If publicity was the aim, it was certainly achieved. The committee of independent experts was appointed quickly and consisted of high-ranking individuals with relevant expertise and independence. Its first report (delivered in March) targeted both individual commissioners, including Jacques Santer, and the overall procedures of the Commission.[4] Since Santer was a Christian Democrat, the report appeared evenhanded in terms of the political affiliations of those accused. Unusually for EU documents, it was written in an accessible manner and with obvious 'sound bites'. The result was extensive press coverage which led in the end to the resignations. If this dramatic outcome was to a considerable extent the result of mishandling on the part of the Commission, it also revealed the anomaly that neither the Parliament nor the Commission president could sack an individual commissioner – commissioners could only be 'recalled' by the government which appointed them. This the French government obdurately refused to do in the case of Cresson.

This was a rare occasion where EU politics appeared dramatic and serious and were accorded appropriate publicity. Although the governments stepped in swiftly to take hold of the situation and agree on a proposal for a new Commission president, it was acknowledged from the start that he/she must be acceptable to Parliament. The Parliament had shown its teeth.

However, raising the issues of fraud in such an up-front way may in the end rebound on the Parliament unless it tightens up its own procedures and controls. As the Parliament demonstrates power, and is directly involved in the decision-making of the EU, the attentions of lobbyists are becoming more focused on its activities. Despite the fact that there has been a 'register of members' interests' in the European Parliament since 1990, there has been opposition from MEPs to its being made widely available or to there being a requirement to submit entries. At the moment the register is not published and is available in single copies only in Brussels, Luxembourg and Strasbourg. It is not translated and each entry remains in the member's own language. There are no sanctions against refusal to submit an entry.

The reluctance here appears to be due in part to different traditions in these matters. German and British members are used, for example, to fairly rigorous controls, while in other countries such scrutiny is regarded as 'insulting'. At the same time, many MEPs genuinely do not see the need for controls and believe that they are perfectly able to resist being influenced by lobbyists and experts even if they accept help from them. There is growing evidence that business groups do offer MEPs 'help' – including fees for advice, hospitality, trips abroad, research support and expertise. Sometimes this extends to the point of assisting with drafts of reports.[5] Since access to the Parliament is still grossly unbalanced, this remains an anomaly. Transparency and accountability (which the Parliament insists on elsewhere) would seem to require that such help be registered – and more precise criteria established for what is and what is not permitted. In May 1999 the situation was compounded when the plenary of the Parliament rejected a resolution which would have required MEPs to submit receipts when claiming their expenses. All this suggests that an internal clean-up operation is needed before the Parliament presses too hard on fraud and unaccountability elsewhere.

Comitology

The final point of confrontation under this general head concerns the 'comitology' committees discussed earlier. The setting up of consultative, management and regulatory committees to carry out important tasks of implementation was first extensively used under the Common Agricultural Policy and expanded with the introduction of the Single Market. These committees, usually consisting of 'experts' and member state officials, can play a significant role in adapting and pursuing policy. In June 1998 the Commission produced its proposal to the Council for a new decision on the issue and the Parliament has drafted its opinion and amendments.[6] The Parliament is pressing, not for direct involvement in the process, but for full information on meetings, agendas, minutes and results, and to be given powers to 'return' decisions made by the committees which it finds unacceptable.

At the time of writing, it is not clear whether the Parliament in the negotiations which are to follow will insist on public access to documents, as agreed at Amsterdam, applying to these committees. Nor has it, as far as we know, raised questions about the membership of committees, or pressed either for broader participation in them or for a 'declaration of interests' from those who are members. At the moment, on this issue the Parliament seems more concerned to establish its formal position and its right to be treated as a full partner with the Council than to insist on broader democratic values and procedures.

This is typical of the tug-of-war. The Parliament started its moderate confrontation with treaty revision, but having achieved a certain amount in that respect is now firmly focused on accountability. Sometimes the commitment to use the

Parliament's status and resources to increase direct links with the public and to broaden access to EU processes – in other words, to enhance participation in democracy – seems to be lost.

The Parliament's 'other' role

As we said at the beginning, the Parliament has needed to increase both its institutional power and its credibility with the public. It has certainly made gains on the first count, although it is still on sufferance as far as governments are concerned. On the second, the outcome is less clear. Some would argue that if the Parliament does become a serious player in European decision-making it will automatically gain credibility; others that much more is needed to erase its image of weakness and irrelevance. As far as democracy is concerned, some believe that the Parliament's new status ensures greater democracy; others remain to be convinced.

Whatever the truth of the above, there has always been an element within the Parliament which has looked beyond the strict decision-making process towards other roles which the Parliament might play. These MEPs and officials have seen it as part of their function to foster transnationalism and debate, to raise issues outside the strict EC/EU remit, and to encourage networking among and access for groups not normally represented at European level. The virtue of this attitude is that it goes beyond representation and enables social groups to attain visibility and speak for themselves. It has always been a contested view within the Parliament itself.

One group which decided early on to use the potential of Parliament in this way was the Green Alternative European Link (GRAEL). GRAEL formed part of the Rainbow Group which was active in the 1984–89 Parliament. A decision of principle was taken by GRAEL MEPs that as much time should be given to civil society work as to work within the Parliament itself, and staff were recruited with that in mind. All political groups in the Parliament have the right to meeting rooms with interpretation for five days each month. GRAEL regularly used two of these days to bring together civil society groups from across the member states and to encourage the exposure of new issues at European level. Some of the work on violence against women and on racism began here.

Another way in which Parliament itself during the same period attempted to raise issues outside existing Community competence was through committees of inquiry, mandated by the Parliament as a whole. Two of the most important of these from the perspective of civil society were the 1986 Evrigenis report on the rise of fascism and racism and the 1990 Ford report on racism and xenophobia.[7] Both inquiries were based on hearings and written submissions and amassed telling evidence. They exposed the cross-Europe links of the far right and gave voice and visibility to previously marginalized groups. They also laid the framework for Community work on these issues.

This kind of activity has continued, though in a more sporadic and less grass-roots fashion. It is also more likely now to be directly related to Community policy and legislation. To give a recent example, in April 1999 a one-day meeting was held in the Parliament, sponsored by Green MEPs, for all organizations and individuals working on or interested in issues to do with transparency and openness in Community institutions. It was addressed by officials as well as activists and alerted a wide range of groups to the current situation and how to use the new powers granted under the Amsterdam Treaty. The aim was to open up debate and dialogue and enable outside groups to exert pressure on the institutions and encourage the broadest possible interpretation of the new mandate.

The parliamentary committees

The parliamentary committees can also play a role in this opening-up process. In addition to their scrutiny function in the legislative procedure, they serve as unique forums within which certain types of transnational politics are played out. Depending on the type of issue and the views of those in charge, access can be made more or less easy for interest groups and for the public. Publicity is also variable.

Of all the committees in the Parliament, the one that most obviously engages a specific external constituency is the Committee on Women's Rights. The committee was set up in 1984 after a hard-fought resolution had enumerated the many ways in which women were disadvantaged in the EC and within its institutions. Since then it has helped to process the legislation on equal treatment for women which the EC/EU has adopted, and has commented on much else from the perspective of women. It has also encouraged and supported transnational lobbying around its activities and has adopted 'own initiative' reports on issues it sees as important. On the whole, MEPs from different parties have been able to reach a broad measure of agreement.

The Committee on Development and Co-operation also takes a firm line in this respect. It deals with matters concerning EU relations with developing countries and, in addition to scrutinizing legislation and aid and trade measures, it invites visitors from the countries concerned, encourages debate on development issues and endeavours in every way possible to open up its proceedings. The committee has built up a close relation and dialogue with development NGOs, which form an active and outgoing constituency.

It is becoming clear, however, that this kind of activity is not particularly valued or given priority by the leaders in the Parliament. At the end of 1998 proposals were made to 'streamline' the committee system, giving priority to the legislative function and the need to act efficiently in the new co-decision environment. This proposal included winding up the Women's Committee and absorbing its functions elsewhere. However, the good external links created by the committee paid off. So many protests were received by the Parliament from women's organizations and others across the EU that the committee was reprieved, and indeed given an extended mandate for the next session.

While increasing the Parliament's efficiency is clearly important, these kinds of developments suggest that the civil society role of Parliament is not being seen as of equal importance. It is also the case that the greater demands being placed on MEPs leave them with less time to make and consolidate such links.

Innovation

One can see in the committee experience some possibilities for new forms of democracy which encourage participation in an evolving system of transnational politics. On the whole, the Parliament has been slow to take up such ideas and encourage experiment. The wholly innovative co-decision procedure is seen as enough for the time being. However, unless greater participation is built in at this stage, and more imaginative forms of democracy envisaged, it may be too late further down the line.

There are two embryonic developments which suggest possibilities in this respect. The first is contained in the Parliament's proposal for its own electoral system, which raises the possibility of 'transnational lists'. This would allow 10 per cent of the total seats to be elected on transnational rather than national lists and add a more genuinely European dimension to the campaign. This would be a recognition that the decision to allow European citizens residing in a member state other than their own to vote and to stand in the European elections has begun to erode the national basis of the elections. This is a proposal for the future, since it would require treaty amendment.[8]

The second concerns the continuing need for some kind of civil society forum to monitor and encourage debate about EU developments. Though the Parliament does to some extent carry out this function, this has never been seen as sufficient. In 1991 left activists in Belgium formed the Charte 1991 movement, the aim of which was to monitor the activities of the Belgian presidency of the EU in 1993. They hoped to pass the task on to groups in other EU countries as the presidency changed hands.

A number of socialist MEPs supported this development and in June 1992 a conference of interested groups was held in the European Parliament. Both the logistics and the politics of such an enterprise proved hard to handle and after the Belgian presidency the movement collapsed. Something similar was attempted with the People's Europe conference held in London during the British presidency in 1998. This had more official support but as a result was subject to considerable restrictions. There is a clear need here for some formal funding for such an enterprise (ideally, free of conditions) which would allow a parallel process to develop, bringing civil society closer to formal decision-making, and increasing accountability. This is unlikely to become a reality unless the Parliament sees it as beneficial and supports both recognition and funding.

The issue of democracy

There is no easy answer to the question posed in the title of this chapter. For many people, the move of the Parliament into a stronger position in the decision-making of the EU is an indication of greater democracy. And, of course, in a sense that is true.

The Parliament is the most democratic of the institutions and its plural and amorphous nature means that it continues to represent a wide range of political views and social trends. However, it has not so far succeeded in engaging the public, or establishing its own legitimacy, although some steps have been taken in this direction.

Perhaps most important, it has not as yet managed to secure for civil society access to and influence in Community procedures equal to that enjoyed for many years by business and expert lobbies. Some believe that this will be automatically achieved by the increased role of the Parliament, and that little further action is necessary. However, exactly the contrary may be true. For unless there is a change in the balance and composition of those with influence at the European level, the Parliament as it becomes more central in the decision-making process will be subject to exactly the same pressures as are currently at work. There is little evidence that it will prove any more able to resist. This is one of the biggest question marks at present over the process of democratization.

The shuttle, in the form of co-decision between Council and Parliament, is now the main form of decision-making and gives the Parliament undoubted new powers. However, the precise way the Parliament is being incorporated into the system has the effect of undermining some at least of its democratic attributes. This is where the tug-of-war reveals itself. Obviously, the Parliament can fight against this type of incorporation, but at the moment there is little indication that it will. On the contrary, the Parliament seems to be gearing up to be the integrated player the present system requires, and in the process is reducing links with the 'awkward squad' outside, who may raise difficult questions and demand participation. In this context, it is significant that the visionary elements in the Parliament, those who dreamed of federalism and more open politics, have almost entirely vanished. Though their dreams were unrealistic, they provided an important counterweight to the pragmatism of the majority.

On the test of democracy which we gave at the beginning of this chapter (the capacity of the people of Europe to begin to participate in/control key aspects of EU decision-making) there is little indication of real advance. In particular, decisions like the adoption of the euro or on the role of NATO are still taken without open debate and outside the public domain. They are then presented as a *fait accompli* for approval. Some would argue that despite or perhaps because of this situation a more 'political' approach to the EU system is developing, and that the appointment of the Ombudsman and the new emphasis on transparency are evidence of this. All that can be said is that these democratic stirrings have as yet made little impact on the intricate forms of inter-elite bargaining which constitute the 'style' of the EU.

European elections

The elections to the European Parliament which took place in June 1999 illustrate many of the themes of this chapter. Except in Ireland, Portugal and Spain, the turn-out was the lowest ever – 24 per cent in the UK, 29 per cent in the Netherlands, 30 per cent in Finland, 46 per cent in France. The overall turnout of 49·9 per cent was inflated by the fact that several countries have compulsory voting. Despite moves in the direction of more common procedures (a proportional system, for example, in the UK) the elections remained stubbornly national. But, in contrast to past years, national governments and parties hardly bothered to campaign. Certainly there was little attempt to convince people even in national terms that it was important to vote and choose effective representatives.

These reactions reveal the salience of the tug-of-war model and provide a further demonstration of the natural, if usually unconscious, hostility which governments customarily show to the Parliament. Having been forced to grant the Parliament more power, national leaders and officials see no reason to hand it legitimacy as well.

Parliament itself – MEPs, political groups and officials – has so far been unable to create this legitimacy itself. Elections pit MEPs against each other, and in career terms the pull of the national is still strong. Evidence suggests that while the March 1999 confrontation did break through the visibility barrier, it has largely been seen by the public as evidence not of a vital and challenging Parliament but of further sleaze in politics, this time at the European level. Equally important, the effort put into gaining a place in the decision-making process *as it is*, and the consequent downplaying of community and other links, has left the Parliament without a real constituency, certainly not one with the power to break through nationally orchestrated apathy.

The tug-of-war, and the in-built and long-lasting confrontation which it represents, remains, we would argue, the essential metaphor for the Council/Parliament relationship. One important strand in this confrontation is the struggle between non-democratic and democratic procedures and values. As a result, any *rapprochement* or bargain between the two institutions (and the new co-decision procedure provides an excellent example) has as much capacity to close off democratic opportunities as it has to enhance them.

This is not to say that such bargains should be opposed. The Parliament clearly needs to make them. However, the dangers for democracy as well as the opportunities have to be acknowledged, and strategies developed to combat and contain them. Only when the Parliament fights equally on both fronts – to ensure its role in decision-making and to enhance the EU's engagement with the public – will it truly deserve the designation 'democratic'.

Notes

1 'Co-decision' was the name the Parliament used in its own submissions before the adoption of the Maastricht Treaty in 1991. The term was not adopted at Maastricht but has been used informally ever since.

2 The history of and current thinking on this issue are set out in the Anastassopoulos report of the Parliament's Committee on Institutional Affairs, A4–0212/98, 2 June 1998.

3 *Committee of Inquiry into the Community Transit System*, 19 February 1997, PE 220.895; *Temporary Committee of Inquiry into BSE*, 7 February 1997, A4–0020/97/A.

4 Committee of Independent Experts, *First Report on Allegations regarding Fraud, Mismanagement and Nepotism in the European Commission*, 15 March 1999.

5 Interesting evidence was presented in the BBC *File on 4* radio programme 'Lobbying in Brussels. Transparency in the European Parliament', 23 March 1999.

6 *Report on the Proposal for a Council Decision laying down the Procedures for the Exercise of Implementing Powers Conferred on the Commission*, Committee on Institutional Affairs, A4–0169/99, 30 March 1999.

7 European Parliament, *Report drawn up on behalf of the Committee of Inquiry into the Rise of Fascism and Racism in Europe* (Evrigenis report), A2–160/85, 1986; European Parliament *Report drawn up on behalf of the Committee of Inquiry into Racism and Xenophobia* (Ford report), A3–195/90, 1990.

8 See Anastassopoulos report, p. 21, n. 2.

Further reading

As a journalist rather than an academic, the main author of this chapter (John Lambert) has relied on documents from the EU institutions, day-to day reporting, and above all his own experience and long years of critical discussion and debate on the meaning of European integration. A fuller treatment is given in J. Lambert (1994), *Solidarity and Survival. A Vision for Europe*, Aldershot, Avebury. More detail about the activities of the European Parliament and its history can be found in:

Burgess, M. (1989), *Federalism and European Union. Political Ideas, Influences and Strategies in the European Community, 1972–1987*, London, Routledge.

Corbett, R., F. Jacobs and M. Shackleton (1995), *The European Parliament*, third edition, London, Cartermill Publishing.

Corbett, R. (1998), *The European Parliament's Role in Closer EU Integration*, Basingstoke, Macmillan.

Westlake, M. (1998), *The European Union beyond Amsterdam*, London, Routledge.

6
Controlling Monetary Union

VALERIO LINTNER

The nature and implications of EMU

After the failed attempt at Economic and Monetary Union (EMU) in the 1970s and despite the successes of the European Monetary System (EMS) in the 1980s, monetary union in the (European Union) EU appeared to be a remote prospect up to the late 1980s. That it moved to the top of the agenda, with the Delors report eventually precipitating the timetables and conditions for full monetary union in the Treaty of European Union (the Maastricht Treaty), is testament to the rapid advance in the integration process in the few years up to late in 1992. Despite the problems that the EMU process has encountered since then, and despite the recent crises in the global economy, the impressive political momentum that developed for actually bringing about this historically momentous development has actually resulted in the launch of a single currency among eleven EU states in 1999, the notes and coins themselves being introduced in 2002. Others, including the UK, are likely to join around that time or soon after.

EMU will have far-reaching implications for the conduct of economic policy in general, and monetary and fiscal policies in particular, for it will involve their being determined and conducted to a large extent at the supranational level. Monetary union will be impossible to achieve and maintain at an acceptable political cost without a considerable degree of economic convergence among EU states, and this in turn is impossible to achieve without a commensurate amount of joint policy-making and implementation. If one does not have an appropriate level of convergence, then it is likely that the union will lead to the rich members benefiting at the expense of poorer participants. Broadly speaking, countries or regions with a relatively high level of competitiveness will tend to attract economic activity and employment at the expense of areas which are less well off. Without a monetary union, countries might hope to bridge competitiveness gaps by devaluation (assuming it actually works in practice in anything but the short run). If there are no different currencies, their values cannot of course change, and, in the absence of devaluation, differences in competitiveness must either be balanced by falls in living standards (if there are flexible labour markets which permit wages to fall in response to a decline in the demand for labour) or by unemployment (supplemented, to the extent that labour is mobile, by migration as workers follow the geographical distribution of jobs) and a decline in the level of economic activity and hence in material prosperity.[1] Thus it will be seen that the costs of the monetary union will tend to fall disproportionately on weaker areas in such a scenario.[2]

It is important to note that there are different definitions of what should constitute convergence. As we shall see, the Maastricht model of EMU has adopted a definition which is based almost exclusively on financial variables. It will be argued in this chapter that this definition is an excessively narrow one, and that it would be more appropriate to include 'real' variables such as the level of employment, social variables and living standards in the definition of what constitutes convergence. The inclusion of real variables in the definition of convergence would imply different economic policy targets and would therefore significantly alter the type of policies adopted by the EU in the economic arena.

Of necessity EMU will also have a huge bearing on the myriad of policy areas that are financed from the public purse in EU countries. For example, the Maastricht model of EMU, and in particular the Stability Pact which now forms part of it, would entail public finances operating under constraints that are determined at the supranational level. And of course interest rate and other monetary variables would be determined outside the nation state, with obvious implications for inflation, growth and employment. This throws up a number of important issues, many of which are associated with basic principles of democracy. It is these that this chapter sets out to explore.

In this context we will adopt a fairly general definition of democracy as a basis for the analysis of the current EMU proposals. It concentrates on two dimensions of democracy:

- *inclusiveness*, the extent to which developments and policies work for the benefit of the entire community of European citizens rather than just for some;
- *accountability*, the extent to which citizens can exert an influence over policies and events through the various democratic processes.[3]

Clearly, what is of the most basic importance to the debate here is the very nature of the EMU model to be adopted: that is, what policy stances are actually to be adopted at the supranational level and how they are to be determined. Yet the debate about EMU has largely ignored these questions, concentrating instead on somewhat more populist issues. The aim of this chapter is also to make a small contribution to redressing this imbalance, and to promote debate on these fundamental points. The chapter will examine whether the Maastricht Treaty and the Stability Pact can be considered an appropriate and democratic model for EMU, and it goes on to debate how it might be amended to promote greater overall economic welfare and greater involvement of the citizens of Europe in the determination of economic policies.

The chapter starts from the assumption that some form of EMU, although not necessarily one based on the Maastricht model, is fundamentally desirable, basically because it offers the possibility of increasing the effectiveness of economic policy-making in the context of the decreasing national control over macroeconomic policy that has resulted from globalization, and in particular from the emergence of vastly powerful and deregulated international capital markets. In other words, EMU represents a necessary response on the part of European nation states to the process of globalization. The experience of the 1992 crisis of the exchange rate mechanism (ERM), of the first Mitterrand presidency in France between 1981 and 1983, the inability of the Conservative government to control the money supply in the early 1980s, and even the experience of the Labour government with the IMF in the 1970s, provide evidence of the declining macroeconomic sovereignty of individual medium-size nation states. The more recent crises in the Far East and in Russia sharply emphasize the point. Global capitalism is becoming more and more out of democratic control, and EMU and the centralization of macroeconomic policy-making that goes with it offer at least the possibility of recapturing some of this lost control on a 'unity is strength' principle. The euro bloc, when it in fact emerges, will be a powerful actor on the international economic stage and will afford its participants collective policy options not open to individual states.

In addition, EMU may also offer vulnerable states the advantage of adopting some of the stability and credibility that have been enjoyed by Germany and others over recent years, thus instantly providing a credible anchor for the economy. EMU offers a number of other potential advantages mainly associated with making the Common Market work better, but the view taken here is that the issue of national economic (and political) sovereignty is paramount in this context.[4] Needless to say, this is a controversial area which throws up many issues which are not testable from a rigidly empirical point of view,[5] but it is important to note that sovereignty fundamentally involves an issue of democracy, for loss of economic sovereignty to international capital markets means that citizens are deprived of the possibility of having their choices on economic policy implemented. The determination of important aspects of economic policy has effectively been transferred to capital markets, which are of course not democratically accountable. The experience of Italy and the UK during the ERM crisis of September 1992 represents a particularly good case study of this. It should be remembered that during the period between the UK's entry into the ERM in October 1990[6] and its ejection on 16 September 1992 there was almost complete consensus in the UK on ERM membership. It was the central anchor of the government's economic policy, it was supported by the official opposition, the Liberal Democratic Party, the CBI and the TUC. Furthermore, the full weight of the government's exchange market and macroeconomic policy levers and of the additional means of intervention provided by the EU were employed to attempt to keep sterling within the ERM. In Italy the situation was very similar, ERM membership and participation in EMU being a matter of almost universal consensus. None of this availed in the face of the power of global deregulated capital markets.[7] It should furthermore be noted that this is not merely an issue of currency speculation, as has often been claimed in the media.[8] If we consider the UK, the investments of its financial services industry alone are roughly equivalent to 100 per cent of the

country's GDP, and a mere 5 per cent shift of these holdings out
of sterling would effectively neutralize the whole of the UK's
foreign exchange reserves – the front-line means of intervention
to support the currency. Even in the absence of speculation,
prudent portfolio adjustment alone can thus affect the government's ability to control the economy and pursue its economic
objectives.

On the other hand, critics of EMU have argued that participation in the project and the consequent transfer of policy-
making powers to the supranational level erodes national
sovereignty. This claim is based on belief in the effectiveness of
the residual economic powers still retained by nation states.
Others also point out that the proposed EMU might increase
regional disparities, and would be certain to carry substantial
risks, especially in its initial stages. However, it is argued here
that these potential problems are likely to be outweighed by the
counter-arguments discussed above, and some form of monetary union in the EU is basically necessary and desirable.

Maastricht: an appropriate and democratic model for EMU?

We now turn to an examination of the model that has been
chosen by the EU for its monetary union, the so-called
Maastricht model. This fundamentally consists of the EMU provisions of the Maastricht Treaty and of the set of agreements
and arrangements that have been agreed since then, the most
important of which is the Stability Pact on fiscal policy. The
proposals for EMU contained in the Treaty of European Union
arose from proposals contained in the report of the Delors
Committee in April 1989. The latter had been established to
examine the way forward for the EMS. They have remained
largely unaffected by the Treaty of Amsterdam in 1997. The
specific Maastricht proposals and timetable are summarized
below.

First of all, EMU was to be achieved in three stages. Stage 1
consisted of the completion of the Single Market, increased co-
ordination and co-operation in the economic and monetary
fields, a strengthening of the EMS, an extended role for the
European Currency Unit (ECU) and an enhanced profile for the
Committee of Governors of EU members' central banks. This
stage began in 1990 and should have been completed by January

1993. In fact it was thrown into disarray by the currency crisis of late 1992. Stage 2 involved the groundwork for the single currency: all members were to be included in the narrow band of the ERM, and the European Monetary Institute (EMI) was to be set up to promote the co-ordination necessary for EMU. This stage began in January 1994, but turmoil in the ERM meant that it was arguably never really completed. Finally, stage 3 consists of complete monetary union, with the introduction of what has now been named the euro as the single currency of the EU, or most of it. A specific agenda was developed for this, with deadlines and convergence criteria to be met.

The timetable for stage 3 involved, by December 1996, and if the Council of Finance Ministers decided by a qualified majority that a critical mass of seven states (six with the UK opt-out) had met the convergence criteria, a date being set for introducing the euro in qualifying states. Failing that by December 1997, there should be the start of an automatic process leading to complete monetary union among a minimum of five states by January 1999. Additionally, 1998 was to see the start of the creation of the European Central Bank (ECB), which replaces the Monetary Institute and is seen as the independent issuer of currency, and of the European System of Central Banks (ESCB), the independent body responsible for the conduct of monetary policy and foreign exchange operations. National central banks had to become independent by this time. The Maastricht convergence criteria are set out.

- a maximum annual *budget deficit* of 3 per cent of GDP;
- a maximum *total public sector debt* of 60 per cent of GDP;
- *no realignments* within the ERM;
- a rate of *inflation* not more than 1·5 per cent above the average of the three lowest-inflation countries in the year before decision; this rate to be judged 'sustainable';
- *long-term* (government bond) *interest rates* to be no more than 2 per cent above the average of those in the three lowest-rate countries.

The Maastricht proposals can be seen as being half-way between the 'gradualist' and 'shock' theory approaches to EMU which have dominated the debate on how best to achieve EMU within the EU/EC:[9] there are provisions for promoting a certain type of convergence between EU countries, but there is also a very definite and tight timetable within Maastricht. The driving force behind EMU may be (partly) economic, but the establishment of

EMU under Maastricht involves a definite political choice. Under the Major government Britain negotiated an 'opt-out' from the Monetary Union provisions of Maastricht. Under Blair the rhetoric is infinitely more positive, and the Labour government has committed itself to joining EMU subject to a referendum vote. Nevertheless the decision to join has been put off until the next Parliament. There are plausible economic reasons for this delay in joining, including the famous lack of synchronicity between the economic cycles of the UK and those of other EU states, and the advantages of avoiding early problems with the new arrangements.[10] But one suspects the real motivation is political. First of all, the Labour government must nurture some uncertainties about whether it could actually win the promised referendum on UK entry into EMU without a sustained campaign of persuasion.[11] Second, early entry would probably have dominated the parliamentary agenda, crowding out legislation in other areas.[12]

The Maastricht proposals have had a distinctly bumpy ride since their inception. The 1992 currency crisis blew the ERM apart and it has arguably never been fully restored, despite the fact that currencies have remained largely within the original bands. Above all, meeting the convergence criteria was rendered very problematic by German unification and by the early 1990s recession in the European economy. German unification meant high Continental interest rates, and this exacerbated the European recession, which would probably have happened regardless. The consequent downturn in economic activity cut government tax receipts and increased expenditure on welfare. In this context, meeting strict public debt and borrowing criteria meant bringing further deflationary bias into economies by big tax increases and severe cuts in public spending, further exacerbating the recession.[13] The net result has been record European unemployment of 17 million in 1997, which will prove very hard to reduce, especially in the context of the current technological revolution.[14]

The original Maastricht proposals have been supplemented in the overall EMU model by a number of agreements, the most notable of which is the Stability Pact,[15] which seeks to control post-EMU fiscal policy by projecting the Maasticht fiscal limits into the future.

The essential features of the Stability Pact were agreed at the Dublin summit of December 1996, and its final version was included in the Amsterdam Treaty of 1997. It basically aims to ensure fiscal rectitude in EMU by codifying the 'excessive deficit procedure' in the Maastricht Treaty. Countries will be free to conduct their own fiscal policy, but national budgets are to be controlled by limiting government borrowing to the Maastricht level of 3 per cent of GDP per annum, with a maximum public debt of 60 per cent of GDP, 'national rate capping' as Michie (1996) calls it.[16] Countries will be free to spend more, but will have to raise taxes to do so, *de facto* severely limiting public spending in the context of a common market with its free movement of labour and capital. There will be quasi-automatic fines for those who deviate from this position, and furthermore the potential restrictions on national fiscal stances are exacerbated by the 'gross' definition of debt in Maastricht, which ignores all assets in calculating government balance sheets. The key provisions of what may turn out to be a most significant development are summarized by Artis and Winkler (1997):

Member States
1 commit themselves to respect the medium-term budgetary position of *close to balance or in surplus* set out in their stability or convergence programmes [. . .];
5 will correct excessive deficits as quickly as possible after their emergence; this *correction* should be *completed in the year following its identification*, unless there are special circumstances;
7 commit themselves not to invoke the benefit of Article 2 paragraph 3 of the Council Regulation on speeding up and clarifying the excessive deficit procedure unless they are in *severe recession*; in evaluating whether the economic downturn is severe, the Member States will, as a rule, take as a reference point an *annual fall in real GDP of at least 0·75%*.

The Commission
3 commits itself to *prepare a report* under Article 104c(3) whenever there is the risk of an excessive deficit or *whenever* the planned or actual government *deficit exceeds* the 3% of GDP reference value, thereby triggering the procedure under Article 104c(3);
4 commits itself, in the event that the Commission considers that a deficit exceeding 3% is not excessive and this opinion differs from that of the Economic and Financial Committee, to *present* in writing to the Council the *reasons for its position*;
5 commits itself, following a *request from the Council* under Article 109d, *to make*, as a rule, *a recommendation* for a Council decision on whether an excessive deficit exists under Article 104c(6);

The Council

3 is *invited to impose sanctions* if a participating Member State fails to take the necessary steps to bring the excessive deficit situation to an end as recommended by the Council;

4 is urged to always require a *non-interest bearing deposit,* whenever the Council decides to impose sanctions on a participating Member State in accordance with Article 104c(11);

5 is urged always to *convert* a deposit *into a fine after two years* [. . .], unless the excessive deficit has in the view of the Council been corrected.

Nevertheless there has been a substantial amount of political will to make this project work, no doubt reinforced by the amount of personal political capital invested in it by former Chancellor Kohl, and at the time of writing the project has been launched and is heading full steam for the complete introduction of the euro in 2002 in the eleven willing countries which have been deemed to have met the convergence criteria. There are many risks still involved, not least as a result of developments in Russia, in Brazil and in the Far East, but the Maastricht model does seem likely to succeed in introducing EMU. This in itself is a momentous achievement. Below is the planned sequence of events involved in the introduction of the single currency.

Phase A. Launch of EMU (one year maximum)

Start of the phase:
- List of participating member states.
- Date of start of EMU to be announced (or confirmed).
- Deadline for the final change-over to the single currency.
- Setting up of the ESCB and the Central Bank.
- Start of production of notes and coins.

Throughout the phase:
- Stepping up of preparations and implementation of measures that will, if possible, have been adopted beforehand.
- Legal framework.
- National steering structure.
- Banking and financial community change-over plan.

Phase B. Start of EMU (three years maximum)

Start of the phase:
- Fixing of conversion rates.
- ECU becomes a currency in its own right.
- Monetary and exchange rate policy in ECU.

- Inter-bank, monetary, capital and exchange markets in ECU.
- New government debt issued in ECU.
- Corresponding wholesale payment systems in ECU.

Throughout the phase:
- Banks and financial institutions continue the change-over institutions.
- Public and private operators other than banks proceed with the change-over, circumstances permitting.

Phase C. Single currency fully introduced (several weeks)

Start of the phase:
- ECU notes and coins introduced.
- Banks have completed the change-over (retail business payment systems).
- Notes and coins denominated in national currency are withdrawn.
- Public and private operators complete the change-over.
- Only the ECU is used.

(EC Commission 1995)

Having said that, we must now examine the appropriateness of the Maastricht model to successful and inclusive EMU and to the needs of the European economy into the new millennium. The view taken here is that the Maastricht model suffers from a number of fundamental flaws, which have resulted in considerable costs up to now and which may pose serious problems in the future. Above all, it substantially fails to meet the criteria of inclusiveness and accountability discussed above. The problems associated with 'Maastricht' are summarized below.

First, the convergence criteria are very narrow in nature. One might claim that they are ideologically loaded to the extent that they are clearly the product of the economic orthodoxy of the 1980s and early 1990s, based largely on the neo-liberal tenets of free markets, control over inflation as the main objective of economic policy, and tight fiscal and (above all) monetary policy as means of achieving it. As a result the convergence criteria are exclusively financial, with no regard to real variables such as the level of employment, social factors or regional disparities. Furthermore, we have seen how it is intended to project the Maastricht convergence into the future by means of the Stability Pact. This would seem to reflect a rather partial and incomplete definition of convergence, for surely a more far-reaching convergence in real variables must be of fundamental importance within the new economic order which is being created. It may be argued that the process by which this definition of convergence was arrived at is dubious from the point of view of democracy. How democratically accountable was the Delors Committee, or even the process of Maastricht ratification? The narrowness of this definition of convergence certainly works against the establishment of an inclusive society within the EU, prioritizing, as it does, financial rectitude above welfare and employment.

Second, perhaps also because of their neo-liberal origins, the convergence criteria have been deflationary in their effects. It has been argued above that, along with German unification, they exacerbated the recession of the early 1990s and that they are partially responsible for the huge current level of European unemployment. The fact is that achieving or attempting to achieve the required levels of fiscal and monetary rectitude has resulted in great economic hardship and political fall-out.[17] In Italy, for example, there have been years of tax increases, cuts in public spending and the privatization of welfare.[18] A similar picture is to be found in most EU countries. Even then the public debt criteria have had to be 'interpreted' liberally, and arguably even Germany has had to indulge in creative accounting in order to meet the deficit requirements. Again, all this has increased the degree of exclusion and marginalization in European societies and threatens to continue to do so, as we shall see below.

Third, the proposed structures and operation of EMU are also caught in a similar ideological mind set. The ECB has the exclusive objective of keeping inflation low, regardless of the effect on employment and social variables (Article 3b). There are potentially very serious technical problems involved in changing from national currencies to the euro, which require the successful establishment of the euro as a *bona fide* and strong currency accepted and trusted by international and national capital markets. In this context, there may also be a temptation on the part of the new monetary authorities in the ECB to establish a reputation for financial rectitude, by adopting tighter monetary and fiscal stances than would otherwise be appropriate. This might impart a further deflationary bias on the European economy after EMU. We have also seen how there is also provision in the overall model (via the Stability Pact) for ensuring tight controls over fiscal policy after EMU. National governments in time of recession will be forced to cut public debt in order to keep within the limits, and that will increase the severity of economic downswings. This may suit some countries eager to establish a new reputation for financial propriety (Italy and the British Labour government may fall into this category), but it will also preclude expansionist and interventionist policies in areas such as job creation. Yet again, this is hardly conducive to the maintenance of an inclusive society.

Fourth, inclusiveness requires some provision for redistribution, if nothing else, to compensate the areas and groups of people that are likely to lose out from the process. (We have argued that EMU is likely to increase regional and other inequalities in Europe.) Here the proposed EMU falls short as well. There is only very limited provision for redistribution under Maastricht. The MacDougall report (1977) suggested that a budget of 7 per cent of Community GDP would be needed to eliminate 40 per cent of existing inequalities at the time of the Werner plan. The existing budget of the EU amounts to a mere 1·27 per cent of EU GDP, and even the proposal of a modest increase to 1·38 per cent was rejected at the Edinburgh summit.[19] There are also potential technical problems involved here. A redistribution mechanism is also likely to be required in the future in order to fund a system of transfers between states so as to balance EU economies in the face of asymmetric shocks.[20]

Finally, perhaps the most contentious aspect of the Maastricht model concerns the democratic accountability of economic policy. The Maastricht Treaty and the Stability Pact in fact make very little provision for such democratic control. A central aspect of EMU is how the objectives of economic policy should be determined between a number of countries. This in turn opens a debate on the nature of economic policy-making. There are essentially two positions. Some believe that economic policy is a purely technical issue – the objectives of economic policy are given and unchangeable. Here the solution is simple, for economic policy can be conducted by 'experts' working within the monetary union's economic institutions, and in such a situation there is no need for political involvement in the process. This is largely the position adopted in the Maastricht Treaty, which envisages an independent ECB, run by 'experts' and modelled on the Bundesbank, which is not under political control and has fixed objectives such as low inflation

(Article 3b) enshrined in its statute.[21] The alternative position is that the conduct of economic policy does involve political choices, and that the nature of those choices may change over time. This would imply the need for some political and democratic input into the process of economic policy-making. (It may be that democratic input is not necessary in a world in which economic policy-making is a politically neutral and unchanging process. The reality, however, is that it probably is.) Table 6.1 shows the position of the ECB in contrast to other models of central bank independence.

We have also seen how the Stability Pact constrains fiscal policy within tight parameters and effectively removes the choice of fiscal stance from democratic control. The question is whether the provisions in the Maastricht model are appropriate in the context of a European economy which is currently characterized by mass unemployment, for they imply absolute inability to gear economic policy to tackling unemployment and social problems, as well as to dealing with asymmetric shocks. These provisions will furthermore be very difficult to change in the short run. If a British Chancellor of the Exchequer wished to alter the way in which the Bank of England operates, in order to bring it back under political control, it would be problematic (in terms of the credibility of economic policy with the markets) but in principle it would be possible and technically easy to achieve. To change the statute of the ECB in order to make it more responsive to the needs of the real economy would require unanimity among EU members and probably considerable legal change as well. It could certainly not be achieved within a short time period.

Alternative ways forward

We have discussed some of the doubts and potential dangers surrounding the Maastricht model both as a democratic entity and as the basis of successful EMU. It could be argued that in the mid-1990s the ideal scenario might have been to postpone the introduction of the single currency and to have negotiated a revised Maastricht Treaty, introducing EMU when more meaningful convergence had taken place and when the historical circumstances were more favourable. Nevertheless EMU under the aegis of Maastricht has now commenced, and indeed a

Table 6.1 Different degrees of central bank independence

Aspect	'New' Bank of England	Deutsche Bundesbank	Federal Reserve System (US)	European Central Bank
Framework	Operational independence (set rates but not target)	Statutory independence (set target and rates)	Fully independent but accountable to Congress	Statutory independence (set target and rates)
Objective/targets	Price stability (inflation 2.5% or less), support government growth and jobs policy	'Internal and external price stability', usually 0–2% inflation, firm D-mark	Price stability and maximum employment	Price stability. Support the general economic policies of the Community
Government powers	Can override Bank in emergency	Cannot override without changing law	Cannot override without change in Fed's terms of reference	Instructions or influence from Community bodies and member states prohibited
Supervises banks?	Yes	No	Yes	No
Board/Council	Nine members: five from Bank, four outsiders	Seventeen members: eight from central bank direct, nine from *Länder*	Twelve-member Federal Open Market Committee	Six-member Executive Board plus the governors of EU central banks
Accountability	Parliament	Public	Congress	Public – through Treaty?
Meetings	Monthly, one member, one vote, minutes published after six weeks	Fortnightly, one member, one vote, no minutes	Eight times annually, minutes published	At least ten times a year. Proceedings confidential
Head	Eddie George, five-year renewable term	Hans Tietmeyer, eight-year renewable term	Alan Greenspan, four-year renewable term	Wim Duisenberg (eight-year non-renewable term)

Source: David Smith, 'The Bank's first task is to get the rate right', *Sunday Times*, 11 May 1997, and author.

retreat at this point might scupper the project for ever. Hesitation might also seriously damage the project by reducing its credibility with the financial markets. The best available option would seem to be to make a success of EMU under the Maastricht model while bearing in mind the lacunae it contains.

It is, however, important in this context to suggest alternative ways forward which might form part of a reform agenda designed to influence the evolution of the EMU. A model for a more democratic EMU, more appropriate to the needs of the European economy and of European citizens into the new millennium, might encompass some of the following.[22]

First, real as well as financial criteria for convergence. For example, unemployment, regional variables and social variables such as social security, pensions and even poverty might be included. At the very least this would focus attention on the standards of living and the quality of life of all parts of the European population, and force monetary policy-makers to take them into account.

Second, greater macroeconomic flexibility. This would take the form both of greater flexibility in setting macroeconomic targets within the existing EMU, to take account of differing local conditions, and of a more flexible ERM in the transition period for new entrants. The former would include greater flexibility for national budgets than is at present envisaged in the Stability and Growth Pact. This would have to be subject to some consideration of the impact of the actions of regional authorities on inflation, but again it is highly desirable both on technical and on democratic grounds. From a technical perspective, it would help in coping with the asymmetric shocks discussed above. From a democratic point of view, it would help in accommodating regional preferences in the macroeconomic policy mix, and it would also be of help in tackling specifically regional social problems. A more flexible ERM would reduce the costs of transition and render them more manageable. This may be of particular importance in view of the enlargement of the EU into East and Central Europe, which would inevitably involve absorbing economies which are at substantially different levels of economic development in comparison with existing member states.

Third, a credible redistribution mechanism. It has been argued above that the lack of redistribution is a major problem with the Maastricht model, yet such a mechanism is desirable not only from the point of view of equity but also from a practical perspective, in order to convince potential losers from the process that it is in their interest to participate, and in order to render the macroeconomic management of the euro zone more effective. Increasing redistribution would entail both reducing expenditure on the CAP very significantly and increasing the size of the overall EU budget, both of which are problematic but probably essential in order to create and maintain a workable EMU in the long run.

Fourth, perhaps some controls over speculative capital movements. Over the last few years it has been assumed that the operational difficulties involved in this might in practice render it problematic in the contemporary globalized economy. From a neo-liberal economic perspective it is of course anathema. Recently, however, in the context of problems in the Far East and elsewhere, this orthodoxy has been called into question. We have seen Malaysia impose exchange controls, and the chief economist of the World Bank, Joseph Stiglitz, has been quoted as advocating:

> financial systems that buffer the economy against shocks rather than magnify shocks . . . I think that the time is ripe for an open debate and discussion on the advantages and limitations of a variety of approaches, including some form of taxes, regulation, or restraints on international capital flows.[23]

It therefore seems as if the issue is back under discussion, if at present only in the context of developing economies. There is provision, however, for some sort of control of short-term capital movements within Maastricht, and the prospect of this being invoked has probably been increased by the election of broadly left-of-centre governments in Germany, France, Italy and the UK.[24] It is certainly the case that any increased purchase by the EU on the operation of capital markets is likely to increase democratic control over the conduct of economic policy, to the extent that it would constrain the ability of those markets to subvert democratically expressed preferences in economic policy.

Finally, greater political influence over the ECB. This is clearly a very thorny issue, for the credibility with international capital markets must also be established by the new EMU, and of course the current wisdom is that central banks should be as independent as possible. Nevertheless the issue requires some thought for the reasons outlined above, i.e. for democratic reasons and because exclusive emphasis on the control of inflation is not an appropriate approach to the conduct of economic policy in an era of high unemployment. A first question that arises here is the overall form that any democratic control might take. There is clearly a highly technical side to economic policy-making, and direct political control of the main levers of economic policy would probably prove technically inefficient, and would probably also result in a substantial decline in the credibility of EU economic policy *vis-à-vis* international capital markets. A reasonable compromise may be found in the 'New Zealand model' which has been adopted in the UK, wherein the inflation objectives to be achieved are set by democratically elected authorities while the bank is left to implement a monetary policy designed to achieve them.

Even if one accepts the desirability of greater democratic control of the ECB, the fundamental issue which is immediately encountered concerns the means by which it may be achieved. This of course involves issues and principles that go far wider than even EMU, concerning the basic democratic nature of the EU and its institutions. It is therefore to some extent beyond the scope of this chapter. Nevertheless, some of the more obvious models which might be adopted to enhance democratic control over the ECB are briefly discussed below.

Perhaps the most obvious of these would consist of placing the ECB under some form of direct control by the European Parliament, which might set the ECB's objectives (and thus the principal objectives of macroeconomic policy) and review its effectiveness in implementing them. This would be in line with the New Zealand model mentioned above, and it would open the possibility of the ECB being given wider objectives than those at present envisaged. The model would clearly involve a radical increase in the Parliament's powers, a substantial transfer of power to the supranational level and a fundamental shift in the current approach to EU institutions. The recent operations of the European Parliament's Economic and Monetary Committee would seem to represent a step in that direction. The committee has tried to establish a line of accountability to the bank, and its Single Currency sub-group has also been active on behalf of consumers' interests in the run-up to the adoption of the euro. There has additionally been some debate in the

Dutch parliament on the general issue of accountability within EMU, and this may represent the beginning of attempts on the part of national parliaments in EU member states to gain some influence over supranational economic policy-making. The confrontation between the Parliament and the Commission over the issue of corruption may furthermore signal an increased propensity for the Parliament to exercise whatever powers it actually does possess.

In addition there is the possibility of subjecting the ECB to some sort of control by the European Council. Again, the Council might determine the overall objectives for the bank to pursue, leaving the ECB with the task of meeting the objectives. This option would be the easiest to achieve, to the extent that it least disturbs the current EU institutional balance of power.

Third, there is the option of increasing political representation on the ECB executive. Representatives might be chosen to reflect political representation in national parliaments or even in the European Parliament. It might in principle also afford a greater democratic dimension to the ECB's decision-making.

Fourth, one could act to make the deliberations and processes of the ECB's executive more open, for example by publishing the minutes of meetings soon after they have taken place. This practice, which is employed by the Bank of England's Monetary Committee following the reforms introduced by the Labour government in 1997, would not of course in itself directly affect the policies adopted by the ECB, but it would at least render the ECB's operations more open to scrutiny and would thus make the institution more publicly accountable. That in itself may indirectly influence some of its actions. It is furthermore a measure that seems relatively uncontroversial, at least outside central banking circles, and should be reasonably easy to achieve.

These issues are of fundamental importance not only to EMU but to the very nature of the EU which is being created. Will what emerges consist of a set of technical and economic arrangements, or will it truly reflect the needs of and be democratically controlled by the majority of European citizens? We shall see.

The changes which have recently occurred in the political composition of EU national governments, with the election of left-of-centre governments in the form of the Blair government in the UK, the Schröder SPD government in Germany, the

Jospin government in France, as well as the Ulivo coalition in Italy (led, at the time of writing, by D'Alema from the PDS) are likely to increase tensions between the independent ECB and elected politicians. This is likely to bring the issues discussed in this chapter to the forefront of public debate, and may provide the impetus to change of some kind. There was some evidence of this at the Austrian summit in November 1998, which placed a greater emphasis on employment as an objective of economic policy, and which opened up the prospect of some large EU infrastructure projects.

It is difficult to judge what the best way forward might be. Within the present context of globalization and powerful, deregulated international capital markets it is difficult to envisage a ECB which is not to some extent independent, despite the democratic imperatives discussed in this chapter. The view taken here, at the risk of appearing to adopt an excessively Anglo-Saxon perspective, is that on balance the best and most realistic way forward may well consist of adopting a variant of the UK/New Zealand model in which the objectives of economic policy are determined by elected politicians, probably through the Council of Ministers (principally ECOFIN and the 'summits'), while the implementation of the objectives is left to the 'experts' who run the ECB. The European Parliament will undoubtedly have a role to play in the determination of economic objectives, as well as in monitoring the performance of the ECB. The view taken here is that the role of the Parliament may prove to be significant in the longer term rather than in the immediate future. At the same time it should be remembered that fiscal policy is also an important part of the overall macroeconomic stance, and there would seem to be considerable scope for introducing (always within well defined limits) greater flexibility in this area. Amending the provisions of the Stability and Growth Pact would on the surface seem to be less politically and institutionally problematic than changing the statute under which the ECB operates, and it might also be more acceptable to the international capital markets which will act as arbiters of the credibility of the EMU project.

Notes

1 This may jeopardize the very creation of the monetary union, since potential losers from the process would of course be reluctant to join in the first place.

2 For a fuller treatment of the theory of monetary union see, for example, Lintner and Mazey (1991), Lintner (1997, 1998), Edye and Lintner (1996) and De Grauwe (1996).

3 See Newman (1996, 1997).

4 Here national economic sovereignty is loosely defined as the ability of a state to determine and implement its preferred objectives in economic policy regardless of events and policies elsewhere.

5 For a full treatment of the issue of national sovereignty see Brouwer et al. (1994), Newman (1996), Strange (1996) and Milward et al. (1993).

6 The Conservative government had always refused to join the ERM until the 'time is right'. The irony is, however, that it eventually joined at the time of German unification . It would be difficult to imagine a worse time to join, given that German unification led to higher interest rates than would otherwise have been appropriate, exacerbating or even partially causing the European recession of the early 1990s.

7 Although it is also arguably the case that the UK government of the time mismanaged UK entry into the ERM by joining at an excessive exchange rate for sterling.

8 In which George Soros is often credited with responsibility for the UK devaluation.

9 In the context of the first attempt at EMU, the Werner plan, the gradualists were referred to as 'economists' while the shock theorists were known as 'monetarists'.

10 There are also dangers, such as being excluded from the formulation of the 'rules of the game' of EMU, as well as the effects on sterling of remaining outside. In the short run the latter might result in an overvalued exchange rate for sterling, which may be regarded as a safe hedge against the uncertainties involved in the launch of the euro.

11 A point reinforced by the success, albeit with an extremely low turn-out, of the increasingly anti-European Conservative Party in the 1999 elections to the European Parliament.

12 For a very readable account of the history and development of the UK's relationship with the EEC/EC/EU see Young (1998).

13 As well as what can arguably be regarded as some creative public sector accounting, and some wide interpretation of the public debt rules.

14 The argument is often made that the real problem here is the inflexibility of European labour markets, and that the US has managed to secure high rates of employment within a similar set of parameters. This is to ignore the issue of the quality of the employment that has been created in the US. To a large extent it has been poor. If we are interested in creating 'good' jobs, the US is not a model to follow.

15 Or, more accurately, the Stability and Growth Pact. The word 'growth' was added at the insistence of French Prime Minister Jospin, and this aspect is now being given greater attention.

16 The Stability Pact does include some escape clauses for severe recession, but national governments will have to aim for balanced budgets in the long run, otherwise the 3 per cent deficit limit will hamper the working of fiscal stabilizers in the economic cycle

17 There may be a link with the recent rise of the ultra-right in Europe.

18 For a review of some likely effects of EMU on welfare see European Parliament (1994).

19 Currie (1997) suggests that a budget of 2 per cent of GDP might suffice for this, provided that it was entirely dedicated to redistribution and not to financing policies such as the CAP. This would permit redistribution of 20 per cent at the margin between EMU members. For a fuller treatment of fiscal federalism see Oates (1972).

20 For example, an increase in the price of oil will benefit the UK which still produces some, but will be detrimental to other EU countries.

21 The perhaps more democratically accountable Council of Finance Ministers (ECOFIN) does have a role in setting exchange rate policy in consultation with the ECB, and this may in the future precipitate political conflict with the ECB.

22 What follows is intended as a 'shopping list' of potential reforms, and it is designed to promote discussion.

23 In a speech made in 1998, quoted in the *Guardian*, 7 September 1998.

24 Although there are significant differences in approach to economic policy between these various governments. The Blair government in the UK is more closely associated with neo-liberal economics than the Jospin government in France or the German government led by Schröder, both of which tend to adopt a more traditional and interventionist interpretation of left economics.

References

Artis, M. J., and Winkler, B. (1997), *The Stability Pact. Safeguarding the Credibility of the European Central Bank*, Working Paper RSC 97/54, Florence, European University Institute.

Brouwer, F., V. Lintner and M. Newman, eds (1994), *Economic Policy and the European Union*, London, Federal Trust.

Church, C., and D. Phinnemore (1994), *European Union and European Community*, Hemel Hempstead, Harvester Wheatsheaf.

Commission of the European Communities (1977), *Report of the Study Group on the Role of Public Finance in European Integration*, Economic and Financial Series 13, Luxembourg, Commission of the EC. (The MacDougall Report.)

Commission of the European Communities (1993), *Growth, Competitiveness and Employment. The Challenges and Ways forward into the Twenty-first Century*, Luxembourg, Commission of the EC. (The Delors White Paper.)

Currie, D. (1997), *The Pros and Cons of EMU*, London, HM Treasury.

De Grauwe, P. (1996), *The Economics of Monetary Integration*, second edition, Oxford, Oxford University Press.

Edye, D. M., and V. Lintner (1996), *Contemporary Europe. Economics, Politics and Society*, Hemel Hempstead, Prentice-Hall.

European Commission (1995), *One Currency for Europe*, Green Paper on the practical arrangements for the introduction of the single currency, Brussels, Commission of the EU.

European Parliament (1994), *The Social Consequences of Economic and Monetary Union*, working paper, Social Affairs series, Luxembourg, European Parliament.

Lintner, V. (1997), 'Monetary integration in the EU. Issues and prospects' in V. Symes *et al.* (eds), *The Future of Europe*, Basingstoke, Macmillan.

Lintner, V. (1998), *Alternative Paths to Monetary Union*, UNL European Dossier 45.

Lintner, V., and S. Mazey (1991), *The European Community. Economic and Political Aspects*, Maidenhead, McGraw-Hill.

Michie, J. (1996), 'Economic Consequences of EMU. Implications for Britain', paper presented at UACES conference 'Domestic Consequences of the Single Currency. National Perspectives', London, October.

Michie, J., and J. Grieve-Smith, eds (1994), *Unemployment in Europe*, London, Academic Press.

Milward, A., F. Lynch, F. Romero, R. Ranieri and V. Sørensen (1993), *The Frontiers of National Sovereignty*, London, Routledge.

Myrdal, G. (1957), *Economic Theory and Underdeveloped Regions*, London, Duckworth.

Newman, M. (1996), *Democracy, Sovereignty and the European Union*, London, Hurst.

Newman, M. (1997), 'Democracy and the EU' in V. Symes *et al.* (eds), *The Future of Europe*, Basingstoke, Macmillan.

Oates, W. (1972), *Fiscal Federalism*, New York, Harcourt Brace.

Strange, S. (1996), *The Retreat of the State*, Cambridge, Cambridge University Press.

Symes, V., C. Levy and J. Littlewood, eds (1997), *The Future of Europe. Problems and Issues for the Twenty-first Century*, Basingstoke, Macmillan.

Young, H. (1998), *This Blessed Plot. Britain and Europe from Churchill to Blair*, Basingstoke, Macmillan.

7

Eastern enlargement and democracy

MARY KALDOR

The European project is a political experiment. There is now widespread acknowledgement that the European Union is a new type of political animal, which is neither a superstate in the making nor a traditional type of international institution. Rather it is a new kind of polity constructed, albeit haphazardly, through a complex process of negotiation and compromise, in response to the processes widely known under the rubric of globalization. The character of this new type of polity is still undetermined; how it develops depends upon political decisions. In other words, it is not possible to predict how the European Union will develop simply on the basis of the analysis of past trends. Several possible directions of development may be foreseen, but the outcomes will be dependent on normative choices now being made.

A key determinant of these choices is the process of enlargement. The enlargement to the east marks a turning point in the evolution of the European Union. Some ten Central and East European Countries (CEECs) are slated for membership of the European Union plus Cyprus, Turkey and Malta. Of these, five CEECs (Hungary, Poland, the Czech Republic, Slovenia and Estonia) plus Cyprus have begun accession negotiations which should eventually lead to membership around 2005. Meanwhile, *Agenda 2000* sets out the reforms to the European Union in institutions, structural funds and agricultural policies that will need to be undertaken in order to adapt the European Union to the additional members (European Commission 1997a).

Eastward enlargement is a much greater challenge than any previous enlargement. The CEECs are much poorer than the West European countries and have experienced a traumatic history of violence and repression. The success of enlargement, I would argue, depends to a large extent on the degree to which the Union is able to transform itself and, in particular, on the degree to which it is able to create mechanisms through which the demands of ordinary citizens in both Eastern and Western Europe can be expressed: in other words, the extent to which it is able to enhance democracy in substantive terms and to redistribute power within Europe. Without such mechanisms, the trend towards 'ever closer union' could be reversed and enlargement or the failure to enlarge could mark the beginning of a process of fragmentation or disintegration.

In developing this argument, I shall focus on the CEECs. I will start by describing the transition to democracy in the CEECs, then consider the problems of enlargement; in the last section I will develop the concept of a European democratic space.

Democracy in the CEECs

The political criteria for membership of the EU include democracy, the rule of law and respect for human rights and minority rights. It is possible to draw a distinction between formal or procedural democracy and substantive democracy.[1] Formal democracy refers to the institutions and procedures of democracy. Substantive democracy refers to political equality, to the distribution of power, to a political culture of democratic participation. Substantive democracy is the situation in which the individual citizen is able to influence the decisions that affect his or her life, in which political institutions are responsive to the demands of citizens.

In all the CEECs, the prerequisites of formal democracy have largely been met. These include: inclusive citizenship – nearly all residents can acquire citizenship; the rule of law; the separation of powers between the executive, the legislature and the judiciary; the election of power-holders; regular free and fair elections in which all citizens can vote and through which alternation of government can take place; freedom of expression and the availability of alternative sources of information; associational autonomy; and democratic control of the security services. Moreover, the CEECs have taken seriously various international treaties, such as the European Conventions on

Human Rights, and incorporated them into domestic legislation.

There are, of course, weaknesses. In the CEECs the rule of law is not fully established – ordinary people still feel a sense of insecurity, although the sources of insecurity may have changed since communist times. There has been a big increase in crime everywhere. This is partly for economic reasons and partly because of unfamiliarity with the rules of a market society. In some countries, notably the Baltic states, where police forces had to be built from scratch, there is a problem of law enforcement. In many countries the judiciary is weak and inefficient and the experience of independent courts slow to establish. And in some countries the 'dark forces' of secret security services still seem to persist.

In nearly all the CEECs constitutions define the nation in ethnic terms and, in some countries, this has meant a non-inclusive citizenship. In Estonia and Latvia the large Russian minority have great difficulty in acquiring citizenship. Consequently, they cannot vote in national elections (or in local elections in Latvia) and they have difficulty in obtaining travel documents. Formally, they are eligible for citizenship on the basis of residence but there are many bureaucratic obstacles to naturalization, including the language requirement. Estonians and Latvians were automatically granted citizenship on the basis that they or their parents were citizens before 1940. The fact that Estonia was selected to begin negotiations for membership before Lithuania, which does not have a Russian minority problem on the same scale, does seem to indicate the priorities given to economic criteria in the selection process. A similar situation pertains to the Roma in the Czech Republic; despite easing of the citizenship requirements, there are still many Roma who have not acquired citizenship rights.

In Slovakia before the recent elections, and in Romania before 1996, the separation of powers was questionable because of presidential interference in the legislature.

But if the formal prerequisites of democracy have been more or less met, there is still a considerable deficit in substantive terms. Formal democracy has been imposed from above; acceptance of rules and norms has not followed so quickly. With the exception of the post-communist parties, political parties tend to be small and centred around individual personalities. These parties try to extend control over social life in the way that the

Communist Party used to do, thus limiting the possibility of political participation through parties. The electronic media tend either to be strongly influenced by government or else, in the case of private television and radio, concentrated on popular entertainment, thereby limiting political debate largely to the print media, which reach fewer people. In most CEECs racism, xenophobia and homophobia are widespread, providing a basis for populism which also limits the possibilities of dialogue and deliberation. In particular, in many of the CEECs the situation of the Roma people is getting rapidly worse. A major problem in all CEECs is the lack of a public service ethic and the politicized and clientelistic character of administration, which limits the possibility of public access. Although the autonomy of local government has been established in all the CEECs, there is a tendency to centralization, either through financial control or through political manipulation.

One positive feature of democracy in the CEECs has been the dramatic growth in NGOs, which I will discuss further in the final section. Nevertheless, NGOs are still largely concentrated in major towns and tend to attract only the educated elite. Despite the growth of NGOs there is still widespread political apathy, as expressed in low voter turn-out in elections and in low participation in both parties and NGOs.

In the literature about the transition to democracy in the CEECs these weaknesses are largely explained in terms of the legacy of totalitarianism, and, of course, it is a convincing explanation. Additional explanations focus on the so-called simultaneity problem, the fact that the transition to democracy is combined with the transition to the market, and the weakness of transformative agents (Bozoki 1994; Elster *et al.* 1988). It is argued that, because there was no public space before 1989, there was no opportunity to mobilize popular attitudes around the democratic alternative and to build an entrenched constituency in favour of democracy.

But there is another explanation. Transition, in both economic and political terms, can be viewed as an opening up to the world economy and to global political arrangements – in other words, as the process whereby the CEECs succumb to the pressures of globalization. In this context, the space for manoeuvre within a national context is extremely limited. All mainstream political parties are committed to transition strategies, based on a more or less standard recipe drawn up by Western so-called experts, and that may explain why it is so difficult for a party in power to respond to popular demands. In particular, since the parties of the 'left', which tend to be the post-communist parties, are committed to these strategies, the whole political spectrum is shifted rightwards. Parties which seek a distinctive political stance are likely to do so on the basis of national and religious identity rather than on social issues. Given the constraints of globalization, there is a tendency for governments to press forward with difficult economic decisions on the basis of a presumed formal legitimacy but without consultations or democratic participation. Before 1989 East Europeans experienced politics as purely instrumental or manipulative action by their rulers. To some extent, that experience is reproduced as transition strategies are imposed from above by what appears to be a collusion between national authorities and global institutions: 'We have exchanged Soviet tanks for Western banks,' the Hungarians like to say. Interestingly, the language of mobilization for transition, the promise of better times ahead when capitalism is finally achieved, is very reminiscent of the language relating to the transition to socialism used in the 1950s.

The standard recipes for transition cannot easily be translated into popular ideas which can generate energy and commitment. This is mainly because the benefits of transition are so unevenly distributed – the winners of transition are, on the one hand, former *nomenklatura* who have succeeded in transforming their political positions into economic gain through privatization and, on the other, urban educated generally English-speaking people whose horizons have expanded infinitely through freedom to speak, organize and travel. But equally important is the fact that transition strategies seem to sanction egoism and greed as the underlying attitudes in societies which formerly emphasized communitarian and solidaristic values. What is lacking – and this is implied by the argument about the absence of transformative ideas and agents – is an emancipatory political project around which politics could be mobilized. As the Polish sociologist Marcin Król puts it: 'What . . . really endangers democracy is not weak nationalism but the absence of a common project. Individualist and utilitarian attitudes – which are not dangerous when accompanied by a solid moral vision of society – seem to be overwhelming' (Król 1998).

In fact, it is not altogether true that there were no transformative ideas or agents. On the contrary, there were movements in Central and Eastern Europe before 1989, especially in Poland and Hungary, and they generated ideas about civil society and 'anti-politics' that were to have a global influence. They were ideas about change 'from below', about creating autonomous spaces in society within which public concerns could be articulated, they were about a substantive notion of participation. Moreover, these ideas were always situated in a transnational context. It was the Helsinki Accord of 1975 signed by all the East European countries that gave groups like Charter 77, KOR in Poland or the Democratic Opposition in Hungary an instrument which they could use to raise issues concerning individual rights. It also provided a security framework within which there was greater room for manoeuvre. And it was links with similar movements in the West that provided the support and even a degree of protection needed to be able to play an active public role. In effect, the agents of the 1989 revolutions had developed a set of ideas and indeed a political project which was basically about the radicalization and transnationalization of democracy.

These ideas could not be applied, however, at a purely national level. Paradoxically, the opening up of Eastern Europe to globalization was associated with the imposition of globalization strategies applied at a national level. There was no space for debate or discussion of the kind envisaged by the revolutionaries of 1989. This is not a problem confined to Central and Eastern Europe, of course. The strategies associated with globalization, neo-liberalism and deregulation, are everywhere imposed at a national level and indeed seem to be linked with a tendency to centralization, weak participation and apathy. The question is whether those same ideas of participation and civil society could be applied at a European or global level and could, perhaps, supply the missing political project.

The challenge of enlargement

The goals of the founders of the EU were not so very different from the goals of the 1989 revolutionaries. It was the methods that were different. When Monnet and Schuman launched the European Coal and Steel Community (ECSC) in 1950, their strategy was to use very practical means to secure peace and democracy on the Continent and, as was stated in the preamble to the treaty, 'to create real solidarity'. It was this technique of finding intergovernmental compromises on concrete forms of co-operation, pioneered in the ECSC, that has shaped the EU and its predecessor, the European Community. On the one hand, it has evolved through grand compromises from above. This has tended to lead to an emphasis on the market place (the Common Market, the Single Market, Economic and Monetary Union) especially in the last two decades because that is where agreement is easiest to reach. In the case of the Single Market, for example, Mrs Thatcher agreed to a very considerable pooling of sovereignty, contrary to her proclaimed convictions, in exchange for a far-reaching liberalization of trade. On the other hand, it has also evolved through incremental processes of functional integration resulting from those compromises that have become embedded in both formal and informal institutions (just as the founders envisaged): the Commission itself, sectoral networks, the Court of Justice, the plethora of regulations governing environmental and social standards, and so on.

What has been missing, by and large, from these processes is the underlying involvement of European democratic politics. The grand compromises result from the political relations between governments, which may be responsive to their individual domestic constituencies but are, first and foremost, elite-level bargains. The functional processes of integration give rise to a politics of special interests and generate what some have described as 'issue networks' (Peterson 1995) or even the 'network state' (Castells 1998). There has been no Europe-wide political debate in which European institutions are directly responsive to European citizens and in which the European project can be articulated through a bottom-up process. Hence the loftier goals of European integration can easily be swamped in the politics of intergovernmentalism and particularist interests.

The relationship between the EU and the CEECs has followed a largely similar pattern, with functional links established as a result of intergovernmental agreements (Sedelmeier and Wallace 1996). Association agreements ('Europe Agreements') were signed with ten CEECs between 1991 and 1996. Although these agreements expressed ambitious political goals and include provision for political dialogue, they were basically commitments to open trade asymmetrically over a ten-year period. There were some concessions to special interests, as expressed in the limited concessions made by the EU in the so-called sensitive sectors, and in the provisions for contingent protection for both the EU and the CEECs (Rollo and Smith 1993). A programme of technical assistance, especially the Phare/Tacis programme, was also initiated through which a range of concrete links and networks are being established.

The commitment to eventual membership was made at the Copenhagen European Council in June 1993 (Sedelmeier 1994). In July 1997 *Agenda 2000* was published, which expressed the Commission's opinions on the CEECs' applications. Five CEECs were selected to begin negotiations – the Czech Republic, Estonia, Hungary, Poland and Slovenia. Together with Cyprus, accession negotiations opened formally in March 1998 and began seriously in November 1998. The remaining five CEECs were included in a pre-accession strategy which aimed to help these countries meet the membership criteria and to prepare them to accept the *acquis communautaire* (the accumulated rules and standards, etc., that EU members have adopted). Turkey was initially excluded from the antechamber of accession but was partially reinstated after the Cardiff European Council in June 1998.

Agenda 2000 specified some of the reforms that would need to be adopted by the EU in order to adjust to the new members. Key changes include institutional reform, reform of the Common Agricultural Policy (CAP), reform of structural funds, and external relations. Institutional reform is needed because the increase in the number of members from fifteen to twenty-six will make current arrangements unwieldy – there will need to be adjustments in voting in the Council of Ministers, for example, and in the College of Commissioners. It will no longer be possible to stick to the present number of commissioners per country. CAP and structural funds will have to be reformed because the CEECs are so much poorer than the present members and, under current rules, expenditure on CAP and structural funds would rocket, going well beyond the budget limit of 1·27 per cent of Community GDP which is so important to the neo-liberal consensus. Finally, the borders of the EU will move eastward towards some of Europe's trouble spots; there is concern about how to cope with refugees and asylum seekers and how to manage the relationship between those selected for membership and those who are excluded.

Table 7.1 Impact of successive enlargements on the EU (based on 1995 data)

€	Increase in area (%)	Increase in population (%)	Increase in GDP (%)	Change in per capita GDP (%)	Average per capita GDP (€ =100)
6–9	31	32	29	−3	97
9–12	48	22	15	−6	91
12ᵃ–15	43	11	8	−3	89
15–26	34	29	9	−16	75

Note:
ᵃ Includes East Germany.
Source: European Commission (1997b).

This process of reform of the existing EU is supposed to be completed before enlargement takes place, i.e. without the involvement of the potential members, though they are supposed to be 'consulted'. Up to now there has been very little public debate within the potential new members about whether or not to join the EU – the benefits are taken for granted – and there has been almost no public discussion about the terms of membership. Moreover, despite the growth of the NGO sector, interest representation is very underdeveloped compared with Western countries. In earlier negotiations, especially the most recent round with Sweden, Finland and Austria, the negotiators were under pressure from domestic lobby groups – employers' organizations, unions, farmers, women's groups, etc. This pressure will be much weaker in the case of the CEECs. Since the elites are anxious to join on any terms, the end result is likely to be a form of annexation – membership of the EU on Western terms. A parallel can perhaps be drawn with the fate of the eastern part of Germany after unification.

This could have dangerous consequences for the whole of Europe. The enlargement is quite different from any previous enlargement. Table 7.1, taken from *Agenda 2000*, shows the impact of membership on population and GDP. As *Agenda 2000* points out the most striking feature of the table is the projected reduction in the average *per capita* GDP of the EU as a whole, 'which is unprecedented and greater alone than that resulting from all previous enlargements' (European Commission 1997b: 23).

Table 7.2 Trade between the EU twelve and the CEECs (ECU billion)

	Agricultural		Manufactures	
	1990	1995	1990	1995
EU exports	1·0	2·3	9·6	42·5
EU imports	1·9	1·8	8·4	34·5
EU trade balance	−0·9	0·5	1·2	8·0

Source: Eatwell *et al.* (1997: 34, 36).

Membership of the EU may help to reduce income difference between existing members and potential members but it is likely to increase unemployment and inequality within the new members under the impact of the opening up of markets which is the most important element of membership. Already under the impact of liberalization the trade deficit between the EU and the CEECs has widened, as shown in Table 7.2. In 1996 the trade deficit widened further to 16 billion ECU (European Parliament 1998). Part of the deficit can be explained by EU import controls in sensitive sectors and part by EU dumping. But also it reflects EU competitive advantages. Further trade liberalization is likely to have severe consequences for the economies of the CEECs. As Helmut Schmidt put it: 'If I were a Polish entrepreneur, I would be very alarmed. Within six months of joining the EU, Poland will be wiped out, because in the fields of marketing, productivity and so on, it is far from being able to compete' (Eatwell *et al.* 1997: 28).

The widening trade deficit will be expressed in growing unemployment in the CEECs, much as happened in East Germany. But, unlike East Germany, there will not be the same compensation in financial terms. In East Germany unemployed workers could claim the same welfare benefits as in West Germany; moreover infrastructural and other types of investment did generate jobs and other benefits. Some of this will occur as a result of membership but not on the same scale. Indeed, the reform of CAP and of structural funds is being designed to reduce, not increase, the claims of the CEECs. Estimates based on current criteria for the provision of structural funds, for example, suggest that structural funds would need to double and could amount to 7 per cent of GDP for Slovenia – the lowest level – or as much as 39 per cent of GDP in the case of Bulgaria (Grabbe and Hughes 1997). When Britain, Ireland, Spain, Portugal and

Greece joined the Community, structural funds were greatly increased. But in the case of the present enlargement, where, arguably, an increase in structural funds is more needed than in any previous enlargement, *Agenda 2000* has specified that structural funds should not exceed 4 per cent of GDP. CAP expenditure would also need to increase by 30–50 per cent if it were to be applied to CEECs on the present basis. It is partly in order to avoid this that CAP has to be reformed, although, of course, there are other good reasons for reforming it.

Another expected compensation for the growing trade deficit is foreign direct investment. It has been very low up to now, primarily because of the inadequacy of the infrastructure and fears about stability; this will take time to change.

Thus one can expect more shocks as a consequence of membership. In countries which have already experienced the trauma of transition, and where ordinary people have been used to expect full employment and to value equality, the process will severely test the existing fragility of the new-found democracies.

The economic impact cannot be isolated from the impact on security. In many of the CEECs protest against growing income differentials seeks scapegoats in terms of racism and xenophobia. Discrimination against Russians in Estonia or against Roma in the Czech Republic is particularly severe among the first round of applicants. Since these groups are excluded from national citizenship, they will not be counted as EU citizens, either. Moreover, the growing differential between 'ins' and 'outs' (those who have been excluded from the first round) can contribute to growing insecurity from criminalization and racial or ethnic conflict among the 'outs'. Great emphasis has been placed on the need to strengthen the borders of the 'ins' in order to stem the inflow of refugees and asylum seekers. The new potential members have been, up to now, the first port of call from those fleeing from conflict zones, such as the former Yugoslavia (Slovenia, Hungary and the Czech Republic) or from growing repression in places like Belarus (Poland and Estonia). On the one hand, exclusion could exacerbate the sources of conflict and repression. On the other hand, these phenomena cannot be contained through border controls. Ethnic hatred and criminal networks have a tendency to spread. In this globalized world it is often the negative networks that are most effective in crossing borders.

Thus membership of the EU on Western terms could have the opposite effect from what is intended. Instead of strengthening prosperity and democracy in the CEECs, membership could import material and even physical insecurity into the EU. This is not to suggest that membership is a mistake. Without membership the situation in the CEECs will not improve. Moreover, the argument about borders applies to the West as well. Nowadays it is more and more difficult to isolate wealthy regional enclaves from the poverty and instability outside. The challenge is how to develop an inclusive approach and to expand the European Union in such a way as to address the sources of insecurity.

Towards a European democratic space[2]

When people refer to the 'democratic deficit' in Europe, they usually the mean the deficit in formal terms. Nation states have surrendered part of their sovereignty to European institutions which do not meet the formal criteria of democracy. Elements of sovereignty that used to be the preserve of accountable national parliaments have been abrogated in favour of institutions in which decisions are initiated by an appointed agency, the Commission, often in consultation with special interests and functional networks, and finalized in the relatively secretive environment of the Council of Ministers. The role of the European Parliament, compared with national parliaments, is severely restricted (Dinan 1994).

Undoubtedly, formal democratic reform is of the utmost importance, but the absence of European domestic politics has to be primarily explained in terms of a 'substantive' democratic deficit. What is lacking is not only forms of access for critical individuals and groups at a European level but also a sense of civic belonging to the European polity. The EU is more unpopular than it has been for a decade. Despite the fact that Europe is more integrated than ever before, there is a sense that European institutions have become increasingly detached from ordinary people. Fewer than half the EU population think that membership is a good thing, and support for enlargement is only lukewarm (Leonard 1998).

Yet the most important condition for successful enlargement to the east could be what former Commission president Jacques

Delors called 'active solidarity' between EU citizens and citizens of the CEECs, as distinct from the current system of elite co-operation only (see Ross 1995). If Eastern Europe is not to be annexed on Western terms, if political engineering is not to become a substitute for democracy, and if growing exclusivism is to be confronted, then ordinary people need to be engaged in the process of enlargement.

During the Cold War there could be said to have been an Atlantic public space – an arena for debate not just among elites within the Atlantic area. The shared political project of combating communism provided a basis for a debate around which people could mobilize, both for and against. In the post-Cold War period it is not only people in the CEECs that lack a common political project. Many of the weaknesses of substantive democracy experienced in the CEECs are shared in Western Europe, albeit to a lesser extent. Could a movement for pan-European democracy remobilize political energies and generate a new sense of political identity at a European level?

This is what is meant by a European democratic space. It means that individual Europeans see themselves as part of a common endeavour which could be defined in terms of a deepening of democracy – a commitment to formal and substantive democracy among all member states and the CEECs as a concrete primary goal of the EU. It means a space in which ordinary people, through mutual deliberation and joint action, appear to each other as European citizens, members of a European polity, in an attempt to reach decisions about issues which concern everyone. The EU would be seen as a problem-solving organization, coping with problems that could not be solved at a national level by involving the opinions of ordinary people and providing a forum for negotiation and compromise. In effect, it is a proposal for a political movement for democracy.

A political project of pan-European democracy is a partisan strategy aimed at building support for democrats. Within the CEECs, democracy is viewed both as a procedure and as an inclusive emancipatory project – a political position which is opposed to exclusive nationalism. Such a project would have to encompass debate about concrete policies aimed at enhancing the political position of democrats. Thus 'active solidarity' with democrats would imply inclusive European citizenship, for example, allowing non-national residents of the Union to be European citizens – a radical move that would empower Roma in the Czech Republic, Russians in Estonia and Turks in Germany. It would also imply a more energetic and independent security policy in relation to the conflicts boiling in the Balkans and in post-Soviet countries. In both Bosnia and Kosovo democratic solutions have been impeded by the lack of cohesion among European countries and by the dominance of the US. In both cases democrats, i.e. non-nationalists, advocated active intervention on the gound to protect civilians and to preserve a non-nationalist political space – a new kind of peace-keeping that is somewhere between soldiering and policing. The Americans, who took the key decisions because of European indecisiveness, were unable to envisage any middle way between bombing, which does not risk own casualties, and diplomatic efforts. Both approaches end up strengthening nationalists and weakening democrats. Yet polls show that, in Western Europe, eight out of ten people think that peace-keeping missions should be a priority for the EU (Leonard 1998).

A project for pan-European democracy would have to come to terms with the notion of equality. Substantive democracy is about both political equality and 'active solidarity'. It would have to include demands for inclusion, both social and political, particularly in the light of enlargement strategy. For example, instead of reducing structural funds, it might be necessary to increase the Community budget in order to minimize the inequalities resulting from enlargement. The neo-liberal taboo about increasing the share of Community GDP would need to be challenged. New methods of increasing the Community's 'own resources' would also have to be considered. It might be done, as has been proposed, through issuing bonds but it might also require discussion of another taboo area – introducing new forms of EU-wide taxation. There have been some innovative ideas about new types of taxes relating to the consequences of globalization – a carbon tax, for example, or a transmission tax – which would be a way of redistributing income from information-rich to information-poor sectors of society, or various proposed taxes on currency speculation.

The problem is how to provide a context in which such ideas can be expressed and heard; how to create a medium through which a Europe-wide political debate can be conducted. Pan-European networks do exist, of course, as a result of the 'structured dialogue' and of various academic and cultural exchanges, but they tend to be confined to elites. The question is how to strengthen the existing networks and how to reach out beyond elites to local community organizations, women's groups, young people and so on. There is, for example, a lively youth culture in Europe in which the values of anti-racism, anti-xenophobia, anti-homophobia and transnational solidarity are expressed in music, dance and theatre. Are there ways in which these widespread and strongly felt sentiments, which are currently associated with a tendency towards anti-political attitudes, can be translated into pan-European activism?

As mentioned above, one of the most positive features of democracy in the CEECs has been the dramatic growth of NGOs, facilitated by Western funding. Although many of the new NGOs are concerned with hobbies, sport or culture, there is a significant NGO sector concerned about democracy and human rights. They are the inheritors of the ideas of 1989. Often they form links with similar groups in the West. And sometimes, through access to European institutions, they are able to put pressure on their governments. Slovakia and Romania represent two striking examples of the success of NGOs. Both countries, despite major obstacles to democratization, have had lively NGO sectors which operate through co-operative networks and which extend beyond the capital cities. In both countries NGOs were instrumental in drawing public attention in Western Europe to the weaknesses and abuses of democracy resulting both from repressive and authoritarian leaders – Iliescu in Romania and Meciar in Slovakia – and from a social legacy of racism and xenophobia. In both countries the influence of NGOs on political culture, especially among young people and outside the capital cities, may help to explain the remarkable defeat of Iliescu and Meciar in elections in 1996 and 1998 respectively, despite the control exercised by those leaders over the electronic media and other aspects of public life.

The NGO sector represents an embryo movement for democracy, although, at present, its efforts are often frustrated by the overall economic and political climate, by centralizing tendencies at national level which limit what can be done at the local and European levels, and by financial constraints. Moreover, the national segmentation of the public sphere constitutes a perennial obstacle to moving beyond the current configuration of intergovernmentalism and functionalism. On the one hand, there needs to be an articulation of the democracy project so as to stimulate involvement and, on the other, there need to be new forums through which the project can be articulated. The aim is the institutionalization of pan-European opportunities to raise key concerns about the process of democratization in a sustained and public way.

The British presidency pioneered the idea of People's Europe – a civil society meeting which parallels the European Council and which has access to the Council. What was new about People's Europe was not the civil society meeting, *per se*, but the fact that it was able to report back to the presidency and to feed recommendations directly into the Council. The Cardiff European Council recommended that future presidencies should organize similar events, thus institutionalizing a parallel civic process. Consultations with NGOs and other civil society groups could be built into a range of official EU activities. Proposals could also be developed for accessible shared media debates or regular European television news time so as to expand pan-European media coverage. Assistance for young people wanting to take part in a democracy mission, partnerships among NGOs, municipalities, women's groups, etc., are also avenues to be explored.

A European democratic space would involve two aspects which ought to mutually reinforce each other. It means a pan-European project for democracy defined in the widest sense to mean equality and active solidarity. It also means a set of mechanisms – the creation of various networks and forums – through which the project can be expressed. In other words, the challenge of enlargement is how to democratize Europe as a whole. This is what has to be faced if the European process is to be sustained and not reversed.

Notes

1 This section draws heavily on my article written together with Ivan Vejvoda and a report undertaken for the European Commission on the evaluation of Phare democracy assistance (Kaldor and Vejvoda 1997, 1998).

2 This concept was developed as part of a project undertaken for the European Commission and the Council of Europe aimed at developing a methodology for assessing democracy (Kaldor and Vejvoda 1998, especially the concluding chapter).

References

Bozóki, A., ed. (1994), *Democratic Legitimacy in post-Communist Societies*, Budapest, T Twins.

Castells, M. (1996), *The Rise of the Network Society* I, *The Information Age: Economy, Society and Culture*, Oxford, Blackwell.

Dinan, D. (1994), *Ever Closer Union? An Introduction to the European Community*, London, Macmillan.

Eatwell, J., M. Ellman, M. Karlsson, M. Nuti and J. Shapiro (1997), *Not 'Just another Accession'. The Political Economy of Enlargement to the East*, London, IPPR.

Elster, J. (1998), 'The necessity and impossibility of simultaneous economic and political reform', in D. Greenberg *et al.* (eds), *Constitutionalism and Democracy*, Oxford, Oxford University Press.

Elster, J., C. Offe and U. Preuss (1998), *Institutional Design in post-Communist Societies. Rebuilding the Ship at Sea*, Cambridge, Cambridge University Press.

European Commission (1997a) *Agenda 2000*, Com (97) 2000 final, Brussels, European Commission.

European Commission (1997b), *Agenda 2000. For a Stronger, Wider Union*, Brussels, European Commission.

European Parliament (1998), Briefing No. 22, Statistical Annex on Enlargement, PE 167.614/rev. 1 Or EN.

Grabbe, H., and K. Hughes (1997), *Eastward Enlargement of the European Union*, London, Royal Institute of International Affairs.

Kaldor, M., and I. Vejvoda (1997a), 'Building democracy in Central and Eastern Europe', *International Affairs*, January, 59–82.

Kaldor, M., and I. Vejvoda (1997b), *Final Report. Evaluation of the Phare and Tacis Democracy Programme, 1992–97*, prepared by ISA Consult, Brighton, European Institute, University of Sussex/Hamburg, GJW Europe.

Kaldor, M., and I. Vejvoda, eds (1998), *Democratization in Central and Eastern Europe*, London, Cassell/Pinter.

Król, M. (1998), 'Democracy in Poland', in M. Kaldor and I. Vejvoda (eds), *Democratization in Central and Eastern Europe*, London, Cassell/Pinter.

Leonard, M. (1998), *Rediscovering Europe*, London, Demos.

Peterson, J. (1995), 'Decision-making in the European Union. Towards a framework for analysis', *Journal of European Policy* 2 (1), 69–93.

Rollo, J., and A. Smith (1993), 'The political economy of Eastern European trade with the European Community. Why so sensitive?', *Economic Policy* 16, 139–81.

Ross, G. (1995), *Jacques Delors and European Integration*, Oxford, Oxford University Press.

Sedelmeier, U. (1994), *The European Union's Association Policy towards Central and Eastern Europe. Political and Economic Rationales in Conflict*, SEI Working Paper 7, Falmer, European Institute, University of Sussex.

Sedelmeier, U., and H. Wallace (1996), 'Policies towards Central and Eastern Europe', in H. Wallace and W. Wallace (eds), *Policy-making in the European Union*, third edition, Oxford, Oxford University Press.

8

Democratization: a constitutionalizing process

RICHARD KUPER

It is generally agreed that the European Union is a peculiar animal, defying any simple attempts to label it. The problem of making sense of this unique international organization is highlighted by the fact that interpreters cannot even agree as to whether it has a constitution at all, let alone whether or not it needs one.

Some argue that the founding treaties and their various amendments in fact amount to a constitution. Others believe that the EU neither has nor needs a constitution. In this chapter I attempt to unravel some of the reasoning behind these divergent positions. I distinguish first between different kinds of constitutions and argue that the existing constitutional basis of the EU is minimalist at best, inadequate to deal with the tensions generated by the perceived lack of legitimacy of moves towards further European integration. There is, however, a strong case to be made *against* giving the EU a 'proper' constitution, based among other things on the view that there is no European people to give itself such a constitution. But standing still implies that the existing situation is stable, continuing with the *status quo* a viable option. I argue that this is not possible. Movement in the direction of adopting a constitution is necessary but the issue of what kind of constitution remains. We are moving rapidly, at the European (and very often the national) level, towards a new kind of multi-level, non-homogeneous polity in which traditional notions of citizenship and democratic constituency must be supplemented by new ones, divorced from national and ethnic identities.

I conceptualize such a movement as an open-ended process in which the construction of a European constitution goes hand in hand with the construction of an *active* European citizenry.

Constitutionalizing the European Union is a political project to be worked for at many levels: conceptual, practical institution-building and pressuring the existing structures from outside and from below. The concluding sections of this chapter advance some ideas on these themes.

Two constitutional traditions

No single approach dominates the history of constitutional thinking. There is, rather, a dialogue between two broad traditions: liberal and republican (Bellamy and Castiglione 1996). In the liberal tradition, in line with the focus of the liberal project on protecting individual rights (in particular property rights), political power has generally been seen as necessary but danger-ous, something that therefore ought to be restricted as far as possible. The purpose of a constitution is to set a framework for these limitations, to act as a curb on government in order to protect the individual. This usually involves both a separation and a delimitation of powers *and* of rights which are placed beyond the remit of the government.

The essence of a constitution, in this tradition, is well captured by William G. Andrews (1968: 26): 'Constitutionalism, deriving its authority from the belief in transcendental principles of justice and rights, controls government by limiting its authority and establishing regular procedures for its operation.'

More recently Ronald Dworkin has expressed a similar notion, viewing constitutionalism as no more than 'a system that establishes legal rights that the dominant legislature does not have the power to override or compromise' and remarking that 'constitutionalism so understood is an increasingly popular political phenomenon' (cited in Bellamy and Castiglione 1996: 436). The 'tyranny of the majority', the fear of which so exercised John Stuart Mill, is dealt with in the liberal tradition by putting a range of legal rights beyond the remit of government and, hence, of the majority.

In contrast to this is a republican tradition. While not at all opposed to rights, due process and impartial procedures, it refuses to found the guarantees of freedom and political order upon them. Rather, they have to depend ultimately on the citizenry itself. 'Central to republican theory,' says Michael Sandel,

> is the idea that liberty depends on sharing in self-government. This idea is not by itself inconsistent with liberal freedom . . . According to republican political theory, however, sharing in self-rule involves something more. It means deliberating with fellow citizens about the common good and helping to shape the destiny of the political community . . . (1996: 5–6)

To put the contrast sharply, while liberal constitutionalism tries to protect rights and the political order *from* politics, the ultimate guarantor for republicanism *is* politics. Or, in Sandel's felicitous juxtaposition, for liberalism 'liberty is defined in opposition to democracy'; for republicanism it is a 'consequence of self-government' (1996: 25, 26).

Thus for Thomas Paine in *The Rights of Man*, the essence of a constitution is that it should be 'the act of a . . . people constituting a government'. 'It is,' says Dieter Grimm, 'inherent in a constitution in the full sense of the term that it goes back to an act taken by or at least attributed to the people, in which they attribute political capacity to themselves' (1997: 248). Oppression, as Richard Bellamy puts it succinctly in his analysis of the US constitutional debate in the eighteenth century, 'is guarded against not by virtue of abstract principles, such as rights, that might covertly embody the values and interests of the hegemonic groups administering them, but through a political process which allows the people to voice their concerns for themselves' (Bellamy and Castiglione 1996: 455). From a republican vantage point the central task of government is to protect freedom by promoting civic virtue among the citizens; government in turn has to be accountable to the people in order not to become coercive or abusive.

It is clear, from this perspective that, if the EU has a constitution, it is not of the republican kind.

> Primary Community law, [Grimm points out] goes back not to a European people but to the individual member states, and remains dependent on them even after its entry into force. While nations give themselves a constitution, the European Union is given a constitution by third parties. The 'masters of the treaties', as it is sometimes put, are still the member states, who have not been, as it were, absorbed into the Union. (1997: 248)

It is the republican tradition, I believe, which needs to be revitalized and built on at EU level. The forms of democracy in the EU do not evoke much public interest or support and the project as a whole is lacking in legitimacy (part of the so-called democratic deficit). Quite simply the citizens of the European Union have not in any real sense consented to the project. (I have deliberately used the word 'citizens' rather than 'people' or 'peoples' but will pick up that issue later.) And unless something qualitative is done to alter the present realities, these problems will be exacerbated substantially by the enlargements of the Community envisaged in the next decade or two.

A constitution, a formal setting out of the rules in accessible form after an extensive public discussion or rather series of discussions among the multiple publics that constitute the population of the EU, would, in my view, go far to reverse the cynicism and disillusionment which is so widespread in relation to the European Union. But before elaborating some suggestions about the pursuit of such a project it is important to look at some of the problems with it – and the light these problems shed on the forms of a possible constitution.

Is a constitution – of any kind – what the European Union needs?

There are many kinds of danger in trying to give the EU a constitution of a different kind from the treaty-based constitution which currently underpins it. First, drawing up a constitution has historically been a statist project *par excellence* – one, that is, in which citizens define their relation to their state (Preuss 1996). Indeed, the core of any definition of the modern state goes back to Max Weber's: a body that successfully monopolizes the means of legitimate force over a territorial area. The European Union is not a state – or super-state – in that sense. It does not monopolize – and does not envisage monopolizing – the means of force over its 'territory' but rather shares sovereignty with its member states, some among them the earliest nation state formations in the world. Nor are its boundaries fixed. Rather, the very project of European union is one that is in principle open, flexible, dynamic and expansive. A commitment to closer integration internally goes hand-in-hand with a commitment to ever closer union among all the peoples of Europe, who, even with the haziness of the border of Europe to the east, are congregated in more than forty states.

The danger of a constitution is that it can freeze – or attempt to freeze – a historically specific set of social relations into some political structure which then limits and curtails future choices.[1] The issue is not just the traditional political science question as to whether a flexible rather than a rigid constitution is preferable, but how to conceptualize a constitution for the EU in a world in which the traditional notion of a constitution in any of its forms may be losing its relevance. Certainly, it is hard to simply apply traditional notions to an expanding EU characterized at the same time by increasingly rapid social and technological change. The US experience of an expanding federal polity does not provide a helpful model, for expansion there was achieved at the expense of difference and diversity of political tradition and formation, by riding roughshod over the Indian and Spanish American peoples whose territories it was to expand into.

Second, there seems little doubt that, if 'giving Europe a constitution' means replicating the model of representative parliamentary democracy existing in the member states, the limitations of that form of democracy are likely to be greatly exacerbated at European Union level. Each member of the European Parliament may well come to 'represent' around 700,000 citizens. Without the reinvigoration of existing democratic mechanisms and the invention of new participatory forms, the gap between representative and represented, already yawning in many of the member states (Judge 1995), may become unbearably large.

If democracy depends on formal structures and basic rights it depends no less on the existence of a range of political parties, associations and citizens' movements with the capacity to organize and make their influence felt on the policy process. There is great variation among member states when viewed in this light; how much greater the weaknesses at EU level. Dieter Grimm in his argument *against* a move towards such a constitution has spelled out well these limitations:

> Mediatory structures have hardly even been formed here yet. There is no Europeanised party system, just European groups in the Strasbourg parliament, and, apart from that, loose cooperation among pragmatically related parties. This does not bring integration of the European population, even at the moment of European elections. Nor have European associations or citizens' movements arisen, even though cooperation among national associations is further advanced than with parties. A search for European media, whether in print or broadcast, would be completely fruitless. This

makes the European Union fall far short not just of ideal conceptions of a model democracy but even of the already deficient situation in member states. (1997: 251–2)

Third is the issue as to who the people are who would be giving themselves a constitution. 'Can there be a democratization at the European level,' ask Joseph Weiler *et al.*, 'without there being a transcendent notion of a European people?' (1995: 5). The Treaty of European Union after all, calls for an ever closer union among the *peoples* of Europe. On this point let me immediately concur: there is not a single European 'people'. There is, rather, a multiplicity of peoples with a multiplicity of histories, cultures, languages and customs within Europe. While many of them overlap and intersect, others do not. Any attempted homogenization in the interests of forging a single 'people', as well as being bound to fail, would be politically and socially coercive.

The impossibility of standing still

These objections are strong, yet seem to be predicated on a belief that the existing situation is both stable and 'good enough', despite the democratic deficit readily identified within it. I have argued elsewhere (Kuper 1998) that this concept needs substantial extension to cover a whole range of democratic *deficits* along a series of axes: civil, social and economic as well as more narrowly institutional. There is no reason to expect the democratic deficit, however conceived, as likely to do anything in the medium term except worsen. Quite simply, the nation state in Europe is decreasingly capable of delivering the social and economic benefits on which its legitimacy in the post-World War II period came to be founded. This is not to posit the withering away of the nation state in the face of globalization but to recognize a number of factors which together have transformed realities in Western Europe.

First, there is the tendency towards globalization and the triumphant extension of the free-trade provisions of the GATT agreement with the completion of the Uruguay Round and the foundation of the World Trade Organization. The proposed Multilateral Agreement on Investment may have been withdrawn but it is extremely likely that its replacement will be another nail in the coffin of state regulation of the economy.

Second, paradoxically, is the existence and development of the EU itself, an international organization quite unlike any other, as shown by the impossibility of reaching any consensus on a phrase to describe it: among the wide variety offered have been such concepts as 'pluralistic security community', 'regime', *Staatenverbund*, *civitas europea*, 'concordance system', 'federal union', 'quasi state', 'regulatory state', 'multi-level governance', *condominio* (Wessels 1997: 268). Limitations on the nation state were already underpinning some of the drive towards a European Economic Community in the 1950s and the limited pooling of sovereignty which it permitted. But while it is plausible to interpret this development, as Milward does, as one which permitted the strengthening of the nation state (Milward 1993; Milward *et al.* 1993), it becomes less and less plausible to maintain this in the face of subsequent developments, especially since the Single European Act and the introduction of qualified majority voting. Nation states remain the actors who come together at crucial moments to (re)define the terms of their co-operation – that is, indeed, the truth of the intergovernmentalist approach. But what these nation states have already agreed has taken on a life of its own in such a way that is extremely difficult to reverse, as Pierson (1996) argues convincingly in his historical-institutionalist analysis of the EU dynamic. In so far as control over macroeconomic life is any longer possible, it occurs, if at all, at EU rather than nation-state level.

Third, the collapse of the Soviet Union has destroyed the global environment to which European economic union was so clearly a 'free world' response. With it, the need for the heavily armed and readily-mobilizable-for-war nation state (already transformed by the development of the bloc system from the 1950s onwards, of modern weapon systems and of modern communication systems) has all but disappeared in Europe.[2] Instead the pressure for a Common Foreign and Security Policy involving some form of supranational integration continues to mount.

Fourth, connected with these developments and contributing to them has been a profound communications revolution. New information technology (coupled with more mundane but nonetheless highly significant changes in transport systems) has transformed modern banking, finance, management, production and distribution profoundly. Nor is the process over. The regulatory agencies responding to and shaping the direction of these changes – which affect directly every aspect of the Single Market – are inevitably supranational, focused on the Commission and not the individual member states.

Indeed, it is hard any longer to see what core functions historically performed by the state are any longer carried out, largely and unambiguously, by the member states of the EU. For example, Michael Mann (1993) identifies five functions of the nation state. On top of responsibility for making war, macroeconomic planning and the provision of a communications infrastructure alluded to above, he identifies two others: guaranteeing social citizenship rights over the private sphere; and functioning as the site of political democracy. And it is precisely failures at both these levels, associated with the developments at suprastate level discussed above, which become so crucial in discussions of the democratic deficit and of European citizenship.

Democracy and citizenship in Europe

The truth is that interdependences among communities have escalated to such an extent that democracy can no longer be simply conceived – as it traditionally has been – as something within a sovereign, self-governing community of political equals who constitute a more or less homogeneous society. What are we now to make of so many concepts of democratic theory – such as legitimacy, constituency, representation, participation – traditionally so intimately attached to and located within the boundaries of the nation state? These are all put in question as more and more decisions affect other people beyond the territorial boundaries of the decision-making state.

The issue is well expressed by David Held in his discussion of cosmopolitan democracy (by which he understands a model in which citizens, wherever located, as well as governments, have a voice and representation in international affairs):

> [T]he problem of democracy in our times is to specify how democracy can be secured in a series of *interconnected* power and authority centres. . . . [D]emocracy within a particular community and democratic relations among communities are interlocked, absolutely inseparable, and . . . new organizational and binding mechanisms must be created if democracy is to survive and develop in the decades ahead. (1995: 106, 112)

Central to any notion of democracy is consent. But what is the relevant constituency which should consent in the multi-level, non-homogeneous, interlocking communities which constitute the polity today? The answer, immediately, is that there is not – and can no longer be – a single constituency with an associated single, supreme sovereign body one can appeal to as the ultimate source of authority. A homogenizing democratic project – creating a single European people – would be a disaster (witness the experiments at homogenization in Croatia or Serbia, and the even more chilling attempts in Bosnia and Kosovo). The only way to envisage democracy in a multi-level, non-homogeneous community is by a double conceptual disengagement: of citizenship from nationality and ethnicity and of democratic constituency from territory defined nationally, and in some cases from being defined in territorial terms at all.

To elaborate: on the one hand, the rights and obligations of being a member of the larger entity must be separate from and not dependent on (prior) membership of some community where membership is defined in national or ethnic terms. One may – usually will – have these identities as well, but they could pertain in particular to nations other than those which happen historically to have predominated in the definition of the multi-level, non-homogeneous wider supranational communities now emerging, of which the European Union is the pre-eminent example (as, in analogous but rather different ways, are the rapidly transforming, heterogeneous communities of Canada and Australia of the last two decades – see Kymlicka 1995; Castles 1994). On the other hand, the simple identification of the democratic constituency with the territory of the nation state and sub-order democratic communities with regional and local territorial divisions of that state becomes increasingly unsatisfactory. If by relevant constituencies we mean those most affected by particular decisions and therefore with some rights of representation in any process in which these decisions are taken, such constituencies may well prove to be other than territorial. For instance, self-defining cultural or religious communities, scattered over disparate geographical regions and countries, may be the appropriate constituency for certain kinds of issues and certain social groups for others. This is suggested by Iris Marion Young in proposing veto rights over changes in reproductive rights for women or land use policy in reservations for Indians (1990: 184).[3]

Multi-level governance may have its weaknesses as an analytical category but it does capture something of the emerging reality of decision-making in modern interdependent polities. It alerts us to the need to disentangle these various levels and identify the relevant constituencies in order to find representative forms and processes of involvement appropriate at each and every level.

But how to square this ever shifting terrain of multi-level, non-homogeneous, interlocking communities with the idea of a constitution which traditionally has seemed to imply fixity, constancy?[4] Given these realities, it would be unwise to envisage a founding *moment* when a constitution emerges. Far more plausible – and less threatening – is a view of an on-going, shifting process, hopefully of constructive learning and experimentation. One needs to conceptualize it precisely as constitution *building*, as an *on-going constitutionalizing process*, in which, *as a goal*, the EU can come to be perceived as a community created by its citizens. Or, to put it another way, a constitution makes sense in the EU today only if seen as permanently provisional, constructed with the widest possible input from the democratically organized voluntary bodies among the citizenry (parties and parliaments, churches, trade unions, women's groups, etc.). Not only can the interests and preferences of the European *demos* not be taken as given, waiting to find expression in a constitution at the EU level, but the *demos* itself (as opposed to the variety of existing *demoi*) does not exist. Paine's 'act of a . . . people constituting a government' needs to be reconceptualized for new circumstances in which a European citizenry creates and defines itself – as a citizenry without being a people – in the process of forging a wider European unity.

There is, inevitably, a voluntaristic element inherent in such a perspective. Habermas expresses it well when he writes in response to Grimm (cited above) that:

> I see the nub of republicanism in the fact that the forms and procedures of the constitutional state together with the democratic mode of legitimation simultaneously forge a new level of social integration . . . What unites a nation of citizens as opposed to a *Volksnation* is not some primordial substrate but rather an intersubjectively shared context of possible understanding. (1997: 262)

A condition then, of a European federal structure emerging 'worthy of the name of a democratic Europe', continues

Habermas, is the development of 'a Europe-wide, integrated public sphere . . . in the ambit of a common political culture: a civil society with interest associations; non-governmental organisations; citizens' movements etc; and naturally a party system appropriate to a European arena' (1997: 263). It is, in reality, a matter of *political will*.

But is the public sphere envisaged here not too thin, without emotional or moral resonance for its citizens? Such is the critique which Michael Sandel has elaborated of 'the procedural republic'. This is the term he uses to characterize what the US has become in its 200 year odyssey from its republican foundations, a development which he sees as threatening the very basis of that society.

The critique is powerful in the US context but I do not think it applicable to the realities of the European Union or the argument here. The concept of citizenship on which Habermas's integrated public sphere is predicated is in reality quite substantive, without being exclusive (and Castoriadis 1997 provides a strong argument for believing that any procedural approach is inevitably substantive). It would have to provide real returns to its citizens in terms of both the physical and the material security it secured as well as real opportunities for deliberation and participation and a sense of belonging. But – and this point must be stressed – there is no reason for it to have to become an individual citizen's sole or 'true' identity which is *the same as* that of every other citizen, least of all a citizen's identity defined in national terms. While providing a floor of civil, political and social rights as suggested by Marshall such citizenship need not – and should not – be the sole source of these. At the same time, it would need to go beyond Marshall in elaborating a framework which guaranteed cultural rights (and the resources to pursue them), while leaving their content to elaboration elsewhere (subject to guarantees of human rights and certain democratic norms and values).

In other words, one would recognize with Sandel (and against Rousseau) that there is no single, unitary and uncontestable common good (Sandel 1996: 320). And while Sandel doubts that transnational forms of governance can inspire identification and allegiance, which even states find difficult today, it is increasingly only at the transnational level that the conditions which will allow identification and allegiance to thrive and prosper (at whatever levels) can be guaranteed.

What is to be done?

The argument here is not predicated on the success of the project it outlines, merely on the belief that if democracy is to be safeguarded and extended into the twenty-first century in Europe it will have to come to terms with the issues outlined above.

There are at least three levels at which it needs to be pursued, all of which I would see as integral to 'the making of a constitution for Europe'. First is a theoretical/conceptual enterprise, second a practical institution-proposing and institution-building exercise and last, but certainly not least, practical campaigning in defence of, and for the extension of, the rights and interests of those currently socially, economically or politically disadvantaged (old age pensioners, the unemployed and resident non-nationals, for example, as a taster of what turns out to be a rather extensive list).

Theoretical/conceptual questions to explore cover a number of interlocking subject areas, three of which I would single out here: the division of powers between different levels of governance, the nature of European citizenship, and the constituency base of units in the federal polity.

Central to the first is the development and fleshing out of principles for a division of powers with some real elaboration of what subsidiarity might mean. I find the formulations of David Held (1995: 119 n. 19) the most precise so far, with his tests of extensiveness ('the range of people within and across borders who are significantly affected by a collective problem and policy question'), intensity ('the degree to which the latter impinges on a group of people(s) and, therefore, the degree to which regional or global legislation or other types of intervention are justified') and comparative efficiency ('concerned to provide a means of examining whether any proposed regional or global initiative is necessary insofar as the objective it seeks to meet cannot be realised in an adequate way by those operating at "lower" levels of national or local decision-making').

At the same time, one must query a view of subsidiarity which implies that there are sole and exclusive rights for the different levels; this all too easily insulates (and is probably intended to insulate) the upper levels against input from below. Rather, the model must be for constituencies from below to be represented on upper-level bodies as directly as feasible (always bearing in mind certain efficiency problems, exemplified in Scharpf's (1988) analysis of the 'joint-decision trap').

With regard to European citizenship, the attributes laid out in Article 8 of the Treaty of European Union are so thin that an interpreter as wise as Joseph Weiler (1997a) has been inclined to view them as a cynical exercise in public relations by the high contracting parties. Nonetheless, he and others have recognized 'the radical potential of Union citizenship . . . [in the way in which it provides] opportunities for redefining community, rethinking membership, rearticulating citizenship, and enhancing democratic decision-making that have sprung from the process of European political integration' (Kostakopoulou 1998).

Yasemin Soysal's analysis (1994) of citizenship in the European context is also highly pertinent here. She identifies a transformation in the conception of citizenship, already quite advanced, with the emergence of a new postnational model of citizenship predicated upon universal personhood rather than national belonging. Human rights principles have, in the postwar period, come to constitute a binding discourse that structures the limits of what is politically conceivable in national states. Soysal argues that once these principles have been codified in international agreements and conventions they also provide a focus for migrant and other interest groups to organize around.

Her study of six European countries (five EU member states and Switzerland) shows how social and civil citizenship rights in particular have been extended to non-citizen groups over time and how relatively unimportant national citizenship has been in this process:

> Contrary to what the national model of citizenship projects, it is no longer a simple task to differentiate noncitizen residents of Western nation-states in terms of the rights and privileges they hold. This is more and more the case even for temporary residents, particularly with regard to civil and social rights. (Soysal 1994: 130)

One can see the effects of this new discourse at work in the French Constitutional Council's annulling proposed legislation affecting family unification, reasoning that 'foreigners are not French, but they are human beings' (cited in Soysal 1994: 152).

Soysal recognizes that the process is not simple and unambiguous, that the same global-level processes and institutional frameworks that foster postnational membership also, ironically, reinforce certain aspects of the nation state. For postnational citizenship rights remain organized at the national level, where the nation state remains the regulator of social distribution. Yet this is the level at which notions of sovereignty still hold emotional sway, no matter to what extent they are in practice undermined. (It is also the level at which non-nationals experience insecurity, discrimination and harassment to a greater or lesser degree, a topic to which Soysal alludes (1994: 156–62) but might have paid a little more attention.) And it is to the extension of the political rights of citizenship, especially at national level, that hostility remains greatest. One can question how secure such transnational rights can ever be until such time as they have been recognized and embodied in new political structures in which the citizenry – all the citizenry – has its place.

This leads directly to the final theme to be explored under this theoretical/conceptual head: the problem of integrating the various constituencies and identities of the citizenry into the political structures of an evolving, living constitution of the European Union. By definition, many important identities do not find territorial expression; and many states have historically been destabilized, if not destroyed, by the clash of identities (particularly religious and ethnic/cultural) not adequately recognized or safeguarded. A reworked federalism does, however, provide the opportunity for meaningful innovation in this area by developing ideas of cultural or 'personal' federalism by the division of the community into non-territorial associations, membership of which is voluntary, to which the administration of cultural and educational affairs might be entrusted. There is both historical and contemporary experience to draw on, from the Austrian Social Democrats' pre-World War I approach, which proposed cultural associations (to be called 'national universities') which citizens would have the right to join regardless of where they lived, to elements of Belgium's constitution today, in which there is a Flemish-speaking community coinciding with a Flemish region, a French-speaking community (including francophones in Brussels) and a separate French region, and a German-speaking community but no German region (Bottomore and Goode 1978; Schwarzmantel 1991; Bogdanor 1995).

This last point leads straight into the more practical innovative and institutional side which I identified as the second string to the bow of constitution-building. The results of the massive pan-EU voter study co-ordinated by Cees van der Eijk and Mark Franklin focusing on the 1989 and 1994 European elections is helpful in providing evidence of the feasibility of reform, at least in terms of the attitudes and orientation of the electors. Their evidence points conclusively to the existence of a mature single European electorate as opposed to a series of national electorates, characterized by similar reasons across member-state boundaries both for participating (or not participating) and in the logic of their party choice, which, the evidence shows, is 'overwhelmingly instrumental' (Eijk *et al.* 1996: 365). But the significance of participation is stunted by the fact that established parties treat such elections as 'second-order national elections' rather than genuinely European elections. Their evidence suggests that there is every reason to believe that European voters would respond to the opportunity of being able to make real choices about alternatives at the European level. The solution to the democratic deficit, they argue, is not an increase in European Parliament power, because the core of the problem lies elsewhere. For them, what the European Parliament 'lacks most is not power but a mandate to use that power in any particular way' (Eijk *et al.* 1996: 7). So they advocate institutional changes to encourage the formation of trans-European political parties, the foundations of which already exist.

It is national politicians who have been reluctant to take the necessary steps because of a (well founded) fear that Europe-level issues cut across traditional party cleavages at the national level. Their refusal to allow European issues to be politicized has, ironically, contributed to the democratic deficit. The key reform for Eijk and Franklin would be 'the opening of the Council of Ministers to public scrutiny', seen by them as 'not only imperative from a normative democratic perspective but also a necessary prerequisite for any reforms whatsoever' (Eijk *et al.* 1996: 387).

That may well be the case, but the institutional reforms need to go *much* further, from encouraging transnational parties to encompassing a greatly enhanced role for European citizens at all political levels. Here I would highlight two important contributions to the debate. First that of Joseph Weiler and colleagues, commissioned by the European Parliament, to study certain problems of European integration (Weiler *et al.* n.d.).

Their proposals included the Lexcalibur proposal, a project to create a European public sphere by mirroring every *stage* of *each* Community decision-making project on the Internet with access for all legitimate lobbyists. It is, appropriately enough, illustrated on the net (for the address see Weiler *et al.* n.d.). Also, taking the view that the problem with human rights at EU level is not their existence but their effective vindication, they proposed adding to the treaty objectives the effective vindication of fundamental human rights in the sphere of application of Community law and the setting up of a Directorate General of Human Rights as part of 'a vigorous policy of Access-to-Justice'.

Second, Michael Nentwich has provided a comprehensive analysis of the opportunity structure for citizens' participation in the EU out of which he draws a dozen proposals 'to counterbalance the loss of participatory opportunities for the citizens of several EU member states due to the shift of many competencies to the supranational level' (1998). They include proposals for European deliberative polls, individual membership of trans-European parties, various forms of petitioning and of referendum, etc. Weiler *et al.* (n.d.), too, propose a European legislative ballot if enough signatories in say more than five member states request it. Their aim here is partly to provide a symbolic enhancement of the voice of citizens, partly to encourage the formation of trans-European pressure groups by really giving them a handle on the legislative process (even if they end up largely lobbying the Parliament).

Third, by way of bold assertion, is my belief that none of this will bear fruit without pressure on the current decision-makers, whether at European, national or regional level, by the practical campaigning activities of those in socially and politically progressive interest groups and social movements. The conditions for success are not easy to specify but the 'highly idiosyncratic opportunity structures defined by that unique combination of governmental bodies (at all levels) which share decision-making authority' in the European political space means 'we are apt to see the development and proliferation of multiple movement forms' (Marks and McAdam 1996: 275). And these activities, in any event, run back into those in the previous point whereby social movements are pursuing not just their particular goals but also their right to contribute to the relevant policy-making processes, i.e. to transform the political opportunity structures of the current set-up.

Conclusion

By way of conclusion it seems clear that principles for a division of powers, proposals for new forms of access to the existing institutions and even new forms of politics altogether cannot be divorced from more general considerations of the *purposes* of the Union – which in turn relate directly to the content of European citizenship. Just as it was the emergence and growth of social citizenship in post-war Europe which finally integrated the mass of the population positively rather than negatively into the emerging Christian and social democracies (neatly captured by T. H. Marshall's classic 1950 analysis) so a positive identification between various European publics and the EU is crucial to the healthy development of the Union. There is currently little perceived connection between the grand aims of Article 2 of the treaty and people's day-to-day experiences of the EU, and what there is is often negative.

Article 2 envisages 'a harmonious and balanced development of economic activities, sustainable and non-inflationary growth respecting the environment, a high degree of convergence of economic performance, a high level of employment and of social protection, the raising of the standard of living and quality of life, and economic and social cohesion and solidarity among Member States'. But until the subordination of social well-being to economic indicators is reversed and Article 2 becomes a reality, the ordinary citizen is bound to remain sceptical.

The core not just of the previous section on 'what is to be done?' but really of the approach in this chapter as a whole is to support a process of constitutionalization but to see it as possible only if it goes hand-in-hand with a process of constructing an active European citizenry. That empowering involves not simply an extension of effective political rights but some social underpinning to make the political rights a reality. Without it, the project of European union will take place increasingly behind the backs of and beyond the control of the peoples whose 'ever closer union' supposedly provides its principal form of legitimation.

Notes

1 As indeed can treaties – witness the Treaty on European Union's attempt to freeze a high point of neo-liberal monetarism into the very constitution of the single currency with its treaty commitment to the maintenance of price stability as 'the primary objective' of the proposed European System of Central Banks (Article 105).

2 For a full discussion of these themes see Kaldor (1995), whose arguments I find compelling.

3 Young explores well the tension between the universality of citizenship in democratic theory on the one hand and the actual richness of difference which exists in modern-day societies, from which people should not be forced to dissociate themselves when they act as citizens. She makes a strong case for the recognition of group representation of the oppressed or disadvantaged, a recognition which should include self-organization, the right to express group views on issues of concern to them and, in extreme cases, veto powers over especially sensitive policy proposals. The kinds of groups she has in mind include women, blacks and Native Americans but also gay men, lesbians and poor people, old people and disabled people, very disparate kinds of groups whose members may be but often are not geographically concentrated.

4 Although neither is concerned with the issue of a constitution at all, I was particularly struck by parallels between my work and attempts by two participants at the 1997 UACES research conference at which these ideas were first presented, Thomas Diez and Mishka Foster, to conceptualize the (increasingly) shifting sands on which the EU rests. From completely different theoretical perspectives (from mine and from each other's), they stress the open-textured nature of politics in the emerging EU. Diez (1997a) adopts a discourse approach, using it to explore nuances in the British debate(s) about European integration which are often lost in the prevalent and simplistic pro- and anti-EC characterizations; and (1997b) to construct two models of integration: the well known federal model and what he calls a Network Europe 'horizon' which, among other things 'does not provide a clear institutional blueprint . . . [and] blurs the boundaries between different territories, between the social and the political, between inside and outside . . . with its multiple and overlapping identities . . .'. Foster (1997), in turn, extends the insights of self-organization theory, which attempts to describe the spontaneous emergence of order in both living and non-living systems. She characterizes the EU as 'a self-organising system' evolving endogenously within a set of constraints, explained best by historical institutionalism, which limits the range of possible outcomes. In both Diez and Foster static models are eschewed.

References

Andrews, William G. (1968), *Constitutions and Constitutionalism*, Princeton NJ, Van Nostrand.

Bellamy, Richard, and Dario Castiglione, eds (1996), *Constitutionalism in Transformation. European and Theoretical Perspectives*, special issue of *Political Studies* 44 (3).

Bogdanor, Vernon (1995), 'Overcoming the twentieth century. Democracy and nationalism in Central and Eastern Europe', *Political Quarterly* 66 (1), 84–97.

Bottomore, Tom, and Patrick Goode, eds (1978), *Austro-Marxism*, Oxford: Clarendon Press.

Castles, Stephen (1994), 'Democracy and multicultural citizenship. Australian debates and their relevance to Western Europe', in Rainer Bauböck (ed.), *From Aliens to Citizens. Redefining the Status of Immigrants in Europe*, Aldershot, Avebury, pp. 3–27.

Castoriadis, Cornelius (1997), 'Democracy as procedure and democracy as regime', *Constellations* 4 (1), 1–18.

Diez, Thomas (1997a), 'Reading the EU. Discursive nodal points in the British debate(s) about European integration', UACES research conference, Loughborough, September.

Diez, Thomas (1997b), 'Visions of European order. Federal state, network horizon and international ethics', *Alternatives* 22 (3),

Eijk, Cees van der, Mark Franklin *et al.* (1996), *Choosing Europe? The European Electorate and National Politics in the Face of Union*, Ann Arbor MI, University of Michigan Press.

Foster, Mishka (1997), 'Institutional self-organization and the EU', UACES research conference, Loughborough, September.

Grimm, Dieter (1997), 'Does Europe need a constitution?' in Peter Gowan and Perry Anderson (eds), *The Question of Europe*, London, Verso, pp. 239–58.

Gustavsson, Sverker (1996), 'Preserve or abolish the democratic deficit?' in Eivind Smith (ed.), *National Parliaments as Cornerstones of European Integration*, London, Kluwer, pp. 100–23.

Habermas, Jürgen (1997), 'Reply to Grimm' in Peter Gowan and Perry Anderson (eds), *The Question of Europe*, London, Verso, pp. 259–64.

Held, David (1995), 'Democracy and the new international order' in Daniele Archibugi and David Held (eds), *Cosmopolitan Democracy*, Cambridge, Polity Press, pp. 96–120.

Judge, David (1995), 'The failure of national parliaments', *West European Politics* 18 (3), 79–100.

Kaldor, Mary (1995), 'European institutions, nation states and nationalism' in Daniele Archibugi and David Held (eds), *Cosmopolitan Democracy*, Cambridge, Polity Press, pp. 68–95.

Kostakopoulou, Dora (1998), 'EU citizenship as a model for citizenship beyond the nation state' in Michael Nentwich and Albert Weale (eds), *Political Theory and the European Union*, London, Routledge.

Kuper, Richard (1998a), 'The making of a constitution for Europe', *Contemporary Politics* 4 (3), 285–97.

Kuper, Richard (1998b), 'The many democratic deficits of the EU' in Michael Nentwich and Albert Weale (eds), *Political Theory and the European Union*, London, Routledge.

Kymlicka, Will (1995), *Multicultural Citizenship*, Oxford, Oxford University Press.

Mann, Michael (1993), 'Nation states in Europe and other continents. Diversifying, developing, not dying', *Daedalus* 122 (3), 1–23.

Marks, Gary, and Doug McAdam (1996), 'Social movements and the changing structure of political opportunity in the EU', *West European Politics* 19 (2), 249–78.

Marshall, T. H. (1950), *Citizenship and Social Class*, Cambridge, Cambridge University Press.

Milward, Alan S. (1993), *The European Rescue of the Nation State*, London, Routledge.

Milward, Alan S., Frances M. B. Lynch, Federico Romero *et al.* (1993), *The Frontier of National Sovereignty. History and Theory, 1945–92*, London, Routledge.

Nentwich, Michael (1998), 'Opportunity structures for citizens' participation. The case of the EU' in Michael Nentwich and Albert Weale (eds), *Political Theory and the European Union*, London, Routledge.

Nentwich, Michael, and Albert Weale, eds (1998), *Political Theory and the European Union. Legitimacy, Constitutional Choice and Citizenship*, London, Routledge.

Pierson, Paul (1996), 'The path to European integration. A historical institutionalist analysis', *Comparative Political Studies* 29 (2), 123–63.

Preuss, Ulrich K. (1996), 'Prospects of a constitution for Europe', *Constellations* 3 (2), 209–24.

Sandel, Michael (1996), *Democracy's Discontents. America in Search of a Public Philosophy*, Cambridge MA, Belknap Press of Harvard University Press.

Scharpf, Fritz W. (1988), 'The joint-decision trap. Lessons from German federalism and European integration', *Public Administration* 66 (3), 239–78.

Schwarzmantel, John (1991), *Socialism and the Idea of the Nation*, Hemel Hempstead, Harvester Wheatsheaf.

Soysal, Yasemin Nuhoglu (1994), *Limits of Citizenship. Migrants and Postnational Membership in Europe*, Chicago, University of Chicago Press.

Weiler, J. H. H. (1997a), Jean Monnet lecture, London School of Economics, March, unpublished.

Weiler, J. H. H. (1997b), 'The reform of European constitutionalism', *Journal of Common Market Studies* 35 (1), 97–131.

Weiler, J. H. H., Alexander Ballman, Ulrich Haltern et al. (n.d.), 'Certain Rectangular Problems of European Integration. Empowering the Individual. The Four Principal Proposals', Directorate General of Research, European Parliament, http://www.iue.it/AEL/EP. See also the simulation 'Lexcalibur. The European Public Square. The Decision-making Process of the European Community', http://www.iue.it/AEL/EP/Lex/.

Weiler, J. H. H., Ulrich R. Haltern and Franz C. Mayer (1995), 'European democracy and its critique', *West European Politics* 18 (3), 4–39.

Wessels, Wolfgang (1997), 'An ever closer fusion? A dynamic macropolitical view of integration processes', *Journal of Common Market Studies* 35 (2), 267–99.

Young, Iris Marion (1990), *Justice and the Politics of Difference*, Princeton NJ, Princeton University Press.

Acknowledgement

An earlier version of this chapter appeared in *Contemporary Politics* (Kuper 1998a).

9

Democratizing the EU: evidence and argument

CATHERINE HOSKYNS

The chapters of this book indicate how many different perspectives on and approaches to the issue of democratizing the EU there can be, even among those who have revealed at least a measure of agreement on objectives and values. The variation comes from standpoint, the mix of theoretical and empirical material used, and the weight given to the different interests in play. Thus, the feminized critiques of Sue Cohen in Chapter 2, which are based on direct and personal experience of EU processes, contrast sharply with the more formal theorizing of Sverker Gustavsson in Chapter 3. No one contributor is more 'right' than any other, and all these views, analyses and experiences (and many others) are needed if we are to be able to get a grip on the substantive issues and the context in which they are being considered.

Out of this varied material four issues stand out. First, what was called in Chapter 1 (after Altiero Spinelli) 'the substance of politics': that is, the extent to which political understandings and practices are developing across the EU which coexist with, and begin to challenge, the already well established elite exchange and socialization; second, the combined issues of transparency and accountability; third, the way in which 'constitutive' or 'agenda-setting' decisions are taken at EU level; and finally, the issue of values and how the EU asserts authority.

This chapter will examine these four issues in more detail, drawing on and expanding the material in the book. It will then go on in the light of these accounts to consider current trends at the level both of theoretical understandings and of practical politics. In so doing, I want to go beyond the usual mantras of saying, 'Nothing should change because the current situation is the least worst which can be envisaged' and 'The EU is a new political animal and therefore new forms of democracy are needed – but we cannot for the life of us think what they might be!' On the contrary, what becomes evident from the analysis is that there are a number of ways in which democracy could be strengthened at the EU level which would not require profound structural change. Far from transnational and national forms of democracy being in competition with each other, the introduction of the former may well be what is now needed to revitalize the latter.

The substance of politics

As Mary Kaldor points out in Chapter 7, viewed from Eastern Europe, what is surprising about the EU is not so much the democratic deficit in formal or institutional terms as the absence of a 'European domestic politics', a sense of civic belonging and access for the critical individual to channels of influence. This kind of politics began to develop in Poland and Hungary in the period before 1989, when 'change from below' was the only possibility. Now 'democracy' is being imposed from above on each state in Eastern Europe, leaving little space for transnational debate or citizens' action.

Sue Cohen suggests that considerable potential for such European domestic politics does now exist, and that many people and organizations are affected by and seek to influence EU policies. In the process, transnational links are made. Although the European Commission to some extent encourages such developments, the usual result is frustration rather than achievement. She describes in forceful terms the 'fudging' and disingenuousness which very often characterize Commission activities and discourse in this respect, and sees it as deriving from the conflict between the Commission's need to relate to a wider constituency and its inability to deliver when demands are made.

The European Parliament is the place where one might expect the substance of politics to be emerging. In Chapter 5 we suggest, however, that the tying of the Parliament to the Council of Ministers through the co-decision procedure, while in some respects an advance, hinders certain aspects of the Parliament's political role and keeps it from establishing an alternative legitimacy. The Parliament is arguably more effective when it sets out to challenge the EU bureaucracy than when it seeks to become a part of it. Recent developments which begin to present such a challenge include: raising issues of accountability, taking power over appointments, organizing inquiries and hearings, and creating committees which go beyond the scrutiny function to provide forums for transnational debate.

In justifying the absence of a democratic politics within the EU frame, practitioners and academics have argued that democracy depends upon there being a self-aware *demos*, or people, to make use of representative structures, and that in Europe this exists only at the level of the nation or the state. Richard Kuper argues in Chapter 8, however, that the very multiplicity of peoples in Europe, the diversity of cultures and traditions, and the fact that many identities are not territorially based, makes it all the more important to increase representation and 'voice' at the European level. Mark Leonard's study of popular attitudes to Europe supports this, suggesting that in many respects a European consciousness does exist across different groupings, but that the structures and values imposed on it by the prevailing EU system repress rather than encourage popular involvement (Leonard 1998).

It is unlikely that this situation will remain at stalemate or advance along predictable lines. The effects of the Single Market, and even more of the single currency, have yet to be felt throughout the system. However, the changes in material reality which these developments embody are already altering the status and power of certain social groups, for example those like lorry drivers and air traffic controllers upon whom key communications networks depend. Although demands resulting from these changes are at the moment mediated through national channels (as demonstrated by the French lorry drivers' blockade in the autumn of 1996) the effects are transnational.

The Danish vote against the Treaty on European Union (the Maastricht Treaty) in June 1992 took place in the course of a national referendum, but it has had a profound effect on attitudes at EU level, and can be seen as the trigger for most of the 'pro-democracy' moves which have been made since then. If national political procedures are all that are available, then these are what people will use. Increasingly, however, the effects are diffused throughout Europe. In this sense Spinelli's 'substance of politics' is beginning to emerge – but not in the forms he expected.

Transparency and accountability

Transparency

The issue of transparency – that is, the extent of public knowledge about and access to EU procedures and processes – comes up in a number of chapters and in different ways. It is after all one of the most fundamental of democratic rights. Stefano Fella in Chapter 4 shows that transparency and openness in the EU was an issue the British Labour Party focused on in its preparations for power, anticipating that it might at very short notice have to participate in debates on the subject in the final stages of negotiations over the Amsterdam Treaty. The schizophrenia of the European Parliament, we suggest in Chapter 5, is well demonstrated by its positions on the transparency issue. On the one hand, some of its actions and attitudes contribute to the culture of secrecy; on the other, a number of officials and MEPs have been at the forefront of campaigns on issues such as public access to documents. Valerio Lintner shows in Chapter 6 what a crucial issue transparency is both as regards the negotiations for Economic and Monetary Union (EMU) and the subsequent operations of the European Central Bank (ECB).

The issue of transparency has a number of aspects. It involves public knowledge about procedures and how and why decisions are taken, access to proceedings and documents and (possibly) greater public participation in decision-making. Controversies abound, particularly over the stage at which transparency should be required, and within which bodies. It can be seen both as a way of empowering the citizen and as a powerful inhibitor of corruption. As far as the EU is concerned, the key to transparency lies in the Council of Ministers.

The old 'Community method' as far as openness went (particularly as practised by the Commission) was to issue bland information summaries and public relations material and then leak 'real' documents where necessary to interested parties, and to journalists and academics who were felt to be sympathetic. It worked well until the 1980s and helped to create a protective and relatively benign smokescreen around Community activities. It also fitted in well with the more 'diplomatic' style of the Council proceedings and the assumption that they were still in essence international negotiations which did not require public scrutiny. Inevitably, however, it reinforced the elitism of the policy-making process and helped to create a system of differential access which favoured the well organized and well resourced.

Post-Maastricht this cosy situation began to change, triggered in part by the Danish referendum. However, it meant that, initially at least, the main concern was to make the EU more popular, not more democratic. Nevertheless, a raft of measures was adopted, including more information about the Council work programme and meetings, some open sessions and – most important – in December 1993 a Council decision on public access to documents (Bunyan 1999). The imminent entry to the EU of Sweden and Finland, where such access is regarded as a citizen's right, undoubtedly hastened the process. Even so there continued to be much debate as to whether openness required more summaries and 'after the event' accounts or access to 'real' documents in time for them to affect the policy process (Grønbech-Jensen 1998).

Accountability

Transparency leads directly on to the issue of accountability. Transparency and openness lay the basis of accountability but there still need to be visible and verifiable procedures for scrutiny and control, even more so in areas where public access is not considered appropriate. EU practices present particular problems in this respect because they fall uneasily between national and international patterns of regulation and control. Often what the release of documents reveals is that accountability mechanisms do not exist. Traditionally both the European Court of Justice (ECJ) and the Court of Auditors have provided important checks at European level, but more political and public mechanisms have been lacking.

The heart of the accountability issue as far as the EU is concerned (and the major demonstration of its absence) lies with the mass of administrative and management committees set up between the Commission and the Council, particularly since the adoption of the Single Market programme. This is the so-called 'comitology' phenomenon (Dogan 1997; Dehousse 1998). The committees ensure and supervise the implementation of Community policy over a wide range of policy areas. They have the power to 'fill in' and amend decisions and to adopt second-level administrative regulations. They are policy-specific and generally include Commission and national officials and experts, and sometimes industry representatives (Demmke

1998). In general, they can be said to be furthering the 'fusion' of a European bureaucracy – but outside either public scrutiny or involvement (Wessels 1998).

Much of this activity contributes to the dead wall which social movement activists come up against when dealing with European institutions (Chapters 2, 5 and 7). It also leads on to the problems of accountability which surface in respect of the more public activities of the EU, for example the operations of the ECB. As Lintner shows, making the ECB accountable to the European Parliament is inadequate, since neither practice nor procedures exist. In fact the ECB will have far more political and economic independence than national central banks, first because the Parliament (to which it is formally accountable) itself lacks legitimacy and second because there is no integrated political process at European level for it to engage with or fit into (Elgie 1998; Buiter 1999).

The absence of open and integrated politics in the EU allows decisions to be taken in a distorted way and removes some areas from public debate. For example, there is no discussion of the possibility of assisting the budget problems of the EU by levying a European business tax on the consolidated accounts of companies with interests in more than one state. Since large companies have hugely benefited from the creation of the Single Market, the suggestion that they should contribute directly to its maintenance has a certain logic. The single tax would make the operations of such companies more transparent and reduce their capacity for tax avoidance. However, at present such a proposal would have little chance of success, given the disproportionate influence which business exerts at European level and the reluctance of governments to cede revenue-raising powers. Much more minor proposals aimed at reducing unfair tax competition between states have come up against strong opposition. These may or may not be rational decisions in the circumstances. What is striking is the lack of any open forum where such issues can be debated and decisions evaluated – from a European rather than a 'national sovereignty' point of view (Picciotto 1992: 76).

Transparency and accountability are key issues in the democratic debate, and as the above examples suggest they play a role in shifting the balance from those who have power and influence to those who have not. To the extent that they open up the underside of elite politics and permit more popular understanding and participation, they are likely in the long run to increase the legitimacy of EU procedures. However, they also threaten established interests and disturb practices which have developed pragmatically to deal with at least one level of transnational decision-making. Since Maastricht new emphasis has been given to these questions but the move remains fragile. It can, however, be seen as part of a swing back from too much emphasis on liberty towards a greater concern with equality. That, as was said in Chapter 1, may be a necessary development for the twenty-first century.

Constitutive decisions and legitimacy

The term 'constitutive decisions' is used here in the context of the EU to refer to those decisions which determine the allocation of powers and the shape of the institutions, mark the basic compromises, and/or set the project off in a new direction. What is unique about the EU is the extent to which these involve the transfer of competences from the individual state to shared institutions and merged decision-making. Usually, though not exclusively, such decisions end up as part of the EU treaties and are approved as international legal obligations by each state according to its own procedures. Secondary legislation adopted under these treaties, however, becomes part of the EU's supranational legal order, and as such is directly binding in the member states. Examples would be the constitutive decisions made to establish the Single Market and EMU and the mass of secondary legislation needed to implement them.

Here one can see the EU free-floating between two paradigms. International treaties normally result from negotiations and bargaining between states in relatively closed procedures. Traditionally they mainly create external obligations for states, with little effect on the core concerns of the citizen. Treaties are regarded as 'legitimate' if the political systems of the states producing them are viewed as legitimate by their own citizens.

However, the transfer of competences, together with the strong enforcement of EU treaties and secondary legislation, moves into a new paradigm, much nearer to that of a unified polity. Furthermore, the scope of these measures is such that they increasingly impinge very directly on the concerns of the citizen. It is this situation that has caused some analysts to see the treaties as becoming *de facto* the constitution of the EU (Moravcsik 1993: 513; Weiler 1997: 97–8).

Since the treaties do embody constitutive decisions, one would expect a rather different negotiating process to be emerging, involving consultation and debate and some form of ratification by all those affected. In a democratic political system it is the constitutive decisions that most require popular involvement and sanction. However, in the case of the EU the political system is 'upside down', with far more strength in the units (the member states) than in the collectivity. Thus the governments of the member states wish above all to keep control of these constitutive decisions, and to continue to decide them by the well understood procedures of EU intergovernmental bargaining (Hix 1998). The dilemma is that the effects of these decisions are now such that, to retain legitimacy and engender support, clearer rules and values need to be established and a broader range of interests built in (Beetham and Lord 1998).

In 1984, as is discussed in Chapter 5, the European Parliament in the run-up to the adoption of the Single European Act produced its own alternative treaty. This was its response to being excluded from the negotiating process. It thus challenged the member state governments to adopt more open procedures. Since then, and particularly after the problems with ratifying the Maastricht Treaty, the governments acting through the Council of Ministers have arguably been engaged in damage limitation: trying to keep hold of the negotiating process for constitutive decisions while making some concessions to public opinion and to the Parliament.

The concessions follow two lines. The first involves some slight increase in consultation during the pre-negotiation process, for example, the more open procedures of the Reflection Group before the adoption of the Amsterdam Treaty. A gesture in this direction was also made by the British government in June 1998 when it sponsored the People's Europe conference in London two weeks before the Cardiff summit of the Council. The aim, in theory at least, was to provide a more 'informal' input into the proceedings. The second involves making changes in the substance of what is being agreed – for example, granting greater powers to the Parliament in the new co-decision procedure and enabling the adoption of provisions on European citizenship. Interestingly, both these routes are regarded as preferable to allowing any opening-up of the negotiating process

itself. The reason would seem to be the perception of EU governments that it is only behind closed doors and with a limited
number of actors with defined interests that the kind of package
deals which characterize these constitutive decisions can con-
ceivably be reached.

The example of EMU is relevant here. Accounts of the negotiation process strongly suggest that agreement was possible
only because the participants understood one another, had a
certain level of trust and common interest, and were able to use
log-rolling and 'side payments' to clinch the deal.[1] However,
that is not the full story. As Lintner argues in Chapter 6,
although agreement was reached, it may not have been in the
most appropriate form. The failure to consult a wider range of
interests in establishing the criteria for the convergence of
member-state economies and the terms of reference of the ECB
itself have landed the new social democratic governments of the
EU with a set of rules which are not entirely to their liking. To
change these criteria now would require a treaty amendment
and risk destabilizing the euro. Consulting a narrow range of
interests is by no means always the most efficient procedure if
stable and lasting arrangements are required.

Richard Kuper (Chapter 8) makes clear the difference
between a liberal constitution, which basically ensures individual rights, and a republican one, which in addition creates a participatory politics for people. If the EU is engaged in a
constitutionalizing process, it is certainly more in the direction
of the former than the latter. Nevertheless, the dilemma is that
legitimacy requires some move in the republican direction also.
Gustavsson (reflecting on the views of Sweden) and Fella (com-
menting on New Labour in Britain) suggest that the reflex at
least of these two governments is still to seek such participation
through revitalizing and involving national democratic structures in the EU process, rather than encouraging more transnational forms of democracy.

Legitimation, although a process involving people, is normally initiated by elites who seek to legitimate the processes
they are involved in by generating appropriate symbols, rituals
and common experiences (Miliband 1973). To a limited extent
this has been attempted at EU level, but the symbols chosen are
curiously blank (gold stars, bridges and towers on the new euro
notes, for example). As far as one can tell these symbols
have had little effect, primarily because the real legitimation

has continued to take place at national level and around national processes.

The ruling of the German Constitutional Court on the compatibility of the Maastricht Treaty with the German constitution shows how deep the need is to retain such national legitimacy. The court was dealing with a complaint that the ceding of economic sovereignty in the treaty infringed the democratic rights of German citizens. In reply, the judges asserted that the EU remains an 'association of states', with the states as 'masters of the treaty'. Any ceding of sovereignty was provisional and could be restored. Thus the democratic procedures of the German state could still be regarded as providing adequate protection for its citizens (Herdegen 1994).

Values and leadership

One of the tests of the legitimacy of particular political systems is that decisions are taken by policy-makers according to values they share with the bulk of the population (Beetham and Lord 1998: 3). This is difficult to apply to the EU, since until very recently it was accorded no values of its own (beyond applying the rule of law) but was committed to incorporating those common to the member states. However, the values implicit in the early moves to European integration have been identified by Joseph Weiler (1994) as 'peace, prosperity and supranationalism'. If this is an accurate delineation, it is likely that these values were shared at the time by the bulk of the populations in the six original member states. In particular, among those who noticed it, a level of supranational control seems to have been accepted as a necessary price to pay to achieve the other two objectives. This helps to account for the generally benign view of European integration held by the public during this period, despite or perhaps because of a lack of direct involvement.[2]

It was this benign disregard which enabled the EC to develop relatively unnoticed a set of economic values which were again implicit rather than explicit. Within the market system, they helped to develop the idea of economic interdependence as a mainly elite activity and to demonstrate the advantages, in terms of the avoidance of political controversy, of separating out the economic from the social and political. Thus, once basic relations between states were settled and the security framework in Europe was guaranteed by the Cold War, the economic imperatives of integration were accorded priority. This was encouraged in the 1970s by the entry of states such as Britain and Denmark whose desire for admission was driven by economic necessity rather than political commitment.

As a result, closer and more intense forms of economic integration went ahead while the social and political measures which might have balanced them were put on the back burner. In these circumstances, it was seen as unnecessary to proclaim values for the EC – and the formula of endorsing member state values was continued. The by then well established separation of the economic from the political and social matched and facilitated both the market liberalism of the 1980s and the increasing globalization of economic activity. In this the EC was the world writ small.

There were some exceptions to this marginalization of social issues, and the outcomes in those cases are revealing. The EU's policy on equal treatment for women, for example, developed strongly from the 1970s onwards mainly because of the demand for women in the labour market and the strength of second-wave feminism across Europe (Pillinger 1992; Hoskyns 1996). Nevertheless, women have remained generally wary of European integration. This is evident both in Eurobarometer surveys and in research done after the Danish and the French Maastricht referendums which showed that a substantially higher proportion of women than men voted 'no' across all social classes. In Denmark, many women saw Brussels as a male-dominated economic zone which they had little chance to influence (Bertone 1998: 18). Similarly, arguments that the EU policy on women's rights was more advanced than that of France carried little weight against the broader fears of a monetarist Europe (Mossus-Lavau and Sineau 1992). This gendered scepticism seems to be based on the perception that the EU is elitist and obscure and stands for no overarching or inclusive values – 'club class Europe' as Leonard terms it (1998). Similar reactions within the European Anti Poverty Network are examined by Cohen in Chapter 2. Limited and circumscribed policy advantages are therefore no answer to the absence of shared values and broader involvements.

These examples suggest that neither 'peace, prosperity and supranationalism' nor market-making on its own are now enough to create either benign disregard or a more positive popular acceptance of EU activity. Mary Kaldor suggests in Chapter 7 that what is needed is on the one hand respect for national cultures and institutions and on the other some grand collective projects which people can call their own, and which focus on the future of Europe rather than its past. The Amsterdam Treaty takes a tiny step forward in stating principles for the EU itself rather than deriving them from the practice of the member states, and the category of European citizen does now exist. There is, however, as yet no arena, no public space where these and other ideas can be put forward and their content debated.

The institutions of the EU, whether supranational or intergovernmental, are in no condition to provide leadership of that kind, since over the years they have developed along lines which suit either the international or the market-making models discussed above. EU politicians are first and foremost national leaders and ill equipped to speak for Europe as a whole. Studies of the European Commission show that popular leadership is not really its role (despite the rhetoric) and that a 'detached' attitude to particular principles or values is part of its strategy for success (Cram 1997). Page characterizes the EU system as 'leaderless pluralism' and demonstrates the way in which the institutions interact to undermine any emerging sites of influence (Page 1992). The problems which arose in 1998–99 over the choice of a governor for the ECB and of someone to speak for the EU in foreign policy matters make it clear what a difficult issue this is.

The emerging picture

These then are some of the main themes of the book. They present a picture of elite fusion at EU level managed by governments still essentially interacting according to the practices and norms of inter-state relations. At the same time, populations are becoming concerned and wary, while having slightly more information about and points of engagement with EU institutions and policy processes. It is this situation which is beginning to bring more vigour to set-piece confrontations, between the Parliament and the Commission on fraud, for example, or around the role of the ECB. The low turn-out in the 1999

European elections, however, demonstrates how little the wider public is really engaged and suggests continuing scepticism about the role and importance of the Parliament.

The issue of democracy is central in this situation. According to the mainly inter-state model, democracy in the EU is primarily ensured by the assumed legitimacy of the interacting member state governments, by the emphasis on the rule of law, and by some carefully controlled experiments involving the Commission and more recently the Parliament. Public involvement and/or dissent and indifference suggest that further reassurance is required. Such reassurance might be achieved on the one hand by reasserting national control in more visible ways and on the other by introducing appropriate forms of democratic accountability at the European level. As Gustavsson points out in Chapter 3, all such strategies, including attempting to preserve the *status quo*, involve risks.

Although this situation has been in the making for years, its consequences are now more felt and visible, and the resulting dilemmas have become a central concern for both theorists and analysts of European integration and for those involved in practical politics at the EU level. There have been important developments in both these areas in recent years.

The contribution of theory

One feature of the 1990s is that there has been increasing interest in the future of democracy, not only within nation states but also between them. The shaky reintegration of the former Eastern bloc into the international system, the pervasive imagery of globalization, the expanding scope of international regulation mean that this level of activity can hardly be ignored. Theorists have responded in a number of ways. On the one hand, those whose ideas of democracy are rooted in the history and experience of the nation state are pessimistic that these practices can ever be extended to the international level (Dahl 1998: 114–17). On the other hand, those who believe in the possibility of 'cosmopolitan democracy', based on the creation of transnational communities and forms of democratic participation beyond the nation state, appear to have little concrete upon which to build (Archibugi and Held 1995). Regulation at the global level is constantly expanding while the institutional and societal bases of its democratic underpinning are stretched to breaking.

The theories which come nearest to addressing these dilemmas – rejecting pessimism while keeping within the bounds of possibility – are those of deliberative or, as it is sometimes called, discursive democracy (Dryzek 1990; Benhabib 1996; Bohman and Rehg 1997). Deliberative democracy is concerned with negotiation and policy-making and is based on the principle that those who are affected by decisions should have some say in them. The debate centres on how to encourage participation, how difference can be accommodated rather than repressed, and what kinds of values are appropriate in a public space of this kind. The relevance to the international level is that such ideas go beyond democracy as representation and are concerned with exactly the kinds of procedures and structures upon which international bargaining is at present based.

The EU provides a test bed for such ideas, having both strong institutions and an urgent need of legitimation. As the early part of this chapter suggests, the various aspects of the democracy/legitimacy debate as they apply to the EU have become the subject of increasingly sophisticated, and detailed, analyses. A number of books in the 1990s demonstrate this general trend (Newman 1996; Andersen and Eliassen 1996; Lehning and Weale 1997; Chryssochoou 1998). Some initial attempts have also been made to relate the ideas of deliberative democracy to the situation of the EU (Cohen and Sabel 1997; Gerstenberg 1997). The debate gains in importance because it relates to concern about the international system as a whole.

The many issues intertwined in the concept of democracy are also beginning to affect the trajectory and emphasis of theories of European integration. Such theories are important because of the influence they have over the ways in which European integration is perceived and the questions posed. These new concerns help to transcend the false dichotomy between neo-functionalists and neo-realists which dominated debate on European integration up to the mid 1980s. Neither of these theories took seriously or sought to explain the absence of democratic principles and structures in the development of integration in Western Europe. Arguably, therefore, by focusing elsewhere they distracted attention from these characteristics and their possible implications (Featherstone 1994).

The situation is now very different, and a multiplicity of new analyses and pre-theories do more justice to the complexity of EU politics. The fact that they can fairly easily be subdivided into different groups according to how they conceptualize and deal with the issue of democracy demonstrates the extent of change.

Two-level games

The first of these groups is made up of analyses which directly or indirectly have the effect of justifying the separation of the international and the national and the different rules and norms which apply to each. One of the strongest proponents of this model for the EU, the 'two-level game' as he characterizes it, is Andrew Moravscik. He uses the term 'liberal intergovernmentalism' to describe a situation where national governments as the main players use the supranational level of the EU to achieve aims seen to be impossible by other means, and sometimes as a way of diverting political opposition (Moravcsik 1993). If a wider range of views need to be accommodated, it should be done at national level and taken account of in the 'preferences' which national governments assert in intergovernmental bargaining. Overall he sees the economic outcomes of European integration as justifying the means, and states that 'ironically, the EC's "democratic deficit" may be a fundamental source of its success' (1993: 518).

The work of Giandomenico Majone is analysed in depth in Chapter 3. Majone also in his way supports the 'two-level game', drawing a distinction between international (including European) policy-making, which is technocratic and largely about regulation, and policy-making at national level, which is in essence about redistribution. There can, he suggests, be different forms of accountability for the former (resting on a degree of openness and professional standards) without going down the route of parliamentary control (Majone 1996, 1998). This difference is necessary because 'economic integration without political integration is feasible only if economics and politics are kept as separate as possible' (1998: 7). Majone's work has been important in illustrating the way in which state functions are changing and in dissecting the characteristics of bureaucratic decision-making at the European level. However, his distinction between regulation and redistribution seems hard to justify. The evidence from within the EU is that regulation at European level is increasingly influencing and restricting the national capacity to intervene and redistribute (Everson 1995).

What is characteristic of both the above analyses is that they presume and/or seek to reinforce the entity of the nation state, at least in political terms, and deny the possibility of transnational politics at any but an elite level. This is also true of the attempts to apply the theories of consociation to the EU (Taylor 1996; Chryssochoou 1998). Consociation has been developed to explain political systems in countries which have sought to accommodate separate cultural groups or 'segments' within one state. It is being used to describe the 1997 peace agreements in Northern Ireland (O'Leary 1999).

Consociational arrangements are intended to preserve the cultural and political autonomy of the segments while protracted elite bargaining at the centre produces apparently efficient solutions without any need for inter-cultural mingling. Although such arrangements may be the only route forward in the short run (as in Northern Ireland), they may well over a longer period perpetuate and consolidate the differences they reflect. As applied to the EU, these ideas have considerable explanatory power. However, when viewed as a programme for the future they again preclude the recognition or encouragement of more cross-national processes.

Gustavsson in Chapter 3 also argues in favour of the separation of the international and the national, but he does so in a manner which takes democracy as the primary goal. Starting from the assumption that any proposals must be justified in terms of promoting results which are likely to be 'better' than the available alternatives, he suggests that the maintenance of the existing democratic deficit is to be preferred to attempts to overcome it. For its abolition might well jeopardize democracy within the member states without bringing about the conditions for its re-establishment at EU level. His preference is for a revitalization of democracy within the individual states. Paradoxically, he hopes that EMU will bring this about, because otherwise it could have highly damaging social and political effects.

All these accounts are engaging with real problems and issues and help to identify and explain important processes within the EU system. Gustavsson's argument is particularly challenging for its insistence on the social democratic approach of 'piecemeal social engineering' and as a salutary warning against judgements in terms of overall teleological purposes embedded in a 'European project'.

An integrated system?

The above analyses on the whole, though for different reasons, come back to supporting the *status quo* or proposing minor adjustments that do not upset the trajectory of what is basically inter-state bargaining and administration in a complex setting. However, alongside these accounts others are developing which identify and give priority to different aspects of the EU's complexity. Such interpretations twist the lens a bit and present the EU as a more integrated system and as having the potential and some basis for more open politics and different forms of accountability.

One of these new approaches is summed up in the term 'multi-level governance'. This maintains (in contrast to the Moravscik view) that the power of national governments is becoming diffused both by the need to bargain and compromise at the EU level and by the fact that governments are losing their right to mediate all domestic interests in the international arena. In the European context, these ideas have mainly come from those whose starting point has been the analysis of regional politics in the EU, and the policy processes surrounding the funding programmes (Marks *et al.* 1996; Jeffery 1997). Sub-regional mobilization is seen as increasingly important, though its effects are by no means clear and are often 'disorderly and subversive'. These analyses take account of the vast number of networks, programmes and projects which now exist in Europe, and see them as stretching beyond business and political elites and bringing new layers into the political process.

On this reading, the implementation of policy in the EU is itself beginning to create some of the prerequisites of wider participation. This emphasis is one which opens the way to more political and democratic interpretations of the EU's situation. Some would go further and argue that the real impetus to democracy in the EU is now coming from the fragmentation of the nation state and from new regional confidence within the EU frame.

A similar emphasis is evident in new trends in legal theory which extrapolate from the way the legal order has developed in the EU. In the decoupling of law from the state, and in the development of ways to deal with legal pluralism, it is argued that the

European legal order has outstripped its polity. This line of argument springs initially from the work of Joseph Weiler but has now taken on new forms and new dimensions (Joerges 1996). Legal analysts of this persuasion are likely to experience the EU system as an organic whole and feel at the same time that too much is being expected of the legal process. They thus make the transition to considering the political requirements of the system rather more easily than do those coming from other disciplines. This in turn can produce more acute perceptions of where the fault lines lie.[3]

One example of analysis from this perspective is Michelle Everson's dissection (1995) of economic rights within the EU. She shows that while individuals have gained rights to participate in the Single Market these economic rights are increasingly becoming dissociated from social and political rights. This is not primarily because such rights are absent from the treaties but because national governments which do guarantee them are losing control in the Single Market. Thus citizens may participate in the market but not share in its creation. Joerges supports this, arguing that Europe 'cannot, and should not, be based upon a dichotomous structure of (national) political rights and (European) economic liberties (1996: 105). This more organic view of the EU system provides a marked contrast to the analyses of Moravscik and Majone.

Two comments can be made about the above (necessarily brief) survey of some developments in European integration theory. The first is that the issue of democracy, and the need to counter or forward arguments for it, has moved to a much more central position in the debates about European integration. The second is that theoretical accounts of this kind go beyond description or explanation, and play an important role in closing off or opening up political possibilities. It is thus of considerable significance that the debate has shifted in the directions described. The final section will examine to what extent the politics of governments is moving in similar directions.

Treaty revision

The clearest indication of the collective priorities of governments towards the EU is given in the constitutive decisions they take, usually in the context of treaty revision. As discussed earlier in this chapter, these are still the purest form of inter-governmental decision-making in the EU system. During the 1990s treaty-revising bargains were struck in Maastricht in 1991 and in Amsterdam in 1997.[4] In order to estimate whether government attitudes are changing, these decisions will be ana-lysed in terms of the extent to which they increase formal democracy (measured by changes in the institutional structure and towards the codification of rights and values) and informal democracy (measured by changes which have the effect of encouraging debate, participation and collective awareness). The extent to which these developments support the 'two-level game' or 'integrated system' models will also be considered.

The pressure for some form of democratization was present at the time of the Maastricht negotiations. It was relatively 'silent' and came from the institutions, particularly the Parliament, some governments and as backwash from the EMU decisions. With such a huge transfer of economic sovereignty on the table the need for some 'balancing' mechanisms was hard to deny (Duff et al. 1994). By the time of Amsterdam the public had made themselves heard. The concern after that was for govern-ments to appear to be listening, to adopt an agenda which had relevance to what the public were perceived to want, and above all to make sure that there would be no further problems with ratification. At Amsterdam there were also three new states to accommodate – Austria, Finland and Sweden.

In terms of formal democracy the major development was the introduction of co-decision for the Parliament – initiated at Maastricht and refined at Amsterdam. It was not as big a leap as may appear at first sight, owing to the particular policy areas covered and the restrictions placed on future legislation. However, it represents a substantial disturbance of established procedures and its effects are unpredictable. Maastricht and Amsterdam also gave the Parliament more say in the appoint-ment of a new Commission. The terms of the two institutions have been linked together, and Parliament now has to approve both the member governments' nomination for president and the full Commission team before they can take office.

In addition to the measures directly relating to the Parliament, both Maastricht and Amsterdam introduced other aspects of formal democracy. The most important was the rec-ognition of European citizenship.[5] However weak the content, this has finally and irrevocably moved the EU on from its early concern with people only in their capacity as economic actors towards a broader view of its constituency. The right of citizens to vote in local and European elections anywhere in the Union begins in a small way to establish the idea of a common political space and caused the majority of member states to amend their constitutions to give recognition to other EU nationals. However, the fact that European citizenship is at present conferred only on those with nationality in a member state (and therefore excludes third-country residents) means that what establishes democracy at one level creates exclusions at another. This illustrates very clearly the contradictions inherent both in European integration and in democracy itself.

Maastricht also introduced the concept of 'subsidiarity', which, while often unclear in effect and purpose, has the potential to justify a more layered approach to governance. This was given a further nudge by the decision to set up the Committee of the Regions, giving advisory powers and some presence at EU level to sub-national units. Amsterdam supplemented these moves by defining subsidiarity more carefully in a lengthy protocol and by identifying the Union as marking a new stage 'in which decisions are taken as openly as possible and as closely as possible to the citizen'. These are developments which when taken together can be seen as shifting the EU very gradually towards a more structured division of powers (Duff 1997).

At Maastricht the category of citizen was not associated with any fundamental rights, except that of free movement. At Amsterdam, though the actual citizenship provisions were left virtually unchanged, it was stated in an amendment, now included in the preamble to the treaty, that the Union itself was founded 'on the principles of liberty, democracy, respect for human rights and fundamental freedoms'. Gender equality has also been included among the aims of the Union and the way opened for further anti-discrimination measures. Thus some move was being made in the direction of stating values for the Union itself while ensuring that they were rooted in what was already common to the member states.

Informal democracy

Can any of the measures adopted at Maastricht and Amsterdam be seen as going beyond the formal attributes of democracy to encourage more debate and greater participation – to move, as it were, from liberal to republican constitutionalism? Here we need to look for aspects of the treaties which empower people and encourage engagement, and which have the effect of opening up the interstices of elite politics. As one might expect, there is less here than in the formal category – but still something.

In the first place, some of the developments discussed above have or could have an effect on public involvement. This is particularly true of the notion of European citizenship, which, despite its limitations and the lack of debate (or even publicity) surrounding its adoption, for the first time concretizes the link between people and the European system and puts in place one of the building blocks for the construction of a European public space. Beyond that there are a few hints which begin to suggest how that space might be filled in, and which use a new language. Political parties at the European level, for example, are to be encouraged as a way of forming 'a European awareness' and 'expressing the political will of citizens'. Although such parties have been slow to develop, there were signs in the run-up to the 1999 European elections of more serious attempts to hammer out common manifestoes. As discussed in Chapter 5, the commitment at Maastricht and Amsterdam to 'a uniform procedure' for European elections, or one based on common principles, has prompted some imaginative proposals, and here again a new language.

Probably the most significant contribution to informal democracy is the new emphasis on transparency and accountability. This was hinted at in Maastricht and developed more fully at Amsterdam, after the secrecy of EU policy-making was revealed as one of the main causes of Danish dissent. As a result, and under certain conditions, access to documents of Community institutions (including the Council) has been made a right of all EU citizens.[6] Tony Bunyan of Statewatch illustrates cogently how these provisions, by tipping the balance slightly, are beginning to give the public some purchase on EU officialdom (Bunyan 1999). The provisions run in parallel with the work of the Ombudsman, set up under Maastricht and empowered to investigate complaints about maladminstration by Community bodies, and with the Parliament's own new power to establish temporary committees of inquiry into fraud in the application of Community law.

Finally, at Amsterdam the agreement on social policy went into the treaty, the environment policy was strengthened and a chapter added on employment. Although the commitments on employment are weak and the provisions on the environment and social policy open to extensive prevarication and dilution, the additions did (and were intended to) suggest greater concern with policies which addressed public needs and interests. Some new points of access have thus been created.

The balance sheet

Putting all these commitments together is in a sense misleading, since it ignores the strength of the intergovernmental and 'state protecting' measures which were adopted alongside them, and the system in which they are embedded. 'State protecting' measures are not necessarily anti-democratic, but they rest on and reinforce the view that it is only the national state which can embody democracy. The emphasis on pillars, opt-outs and flexibility at Maastricht, together with the check on new legislation and the retention of the veto in key areas, were characteristic of this view. At Amsterdam the smaller countries fought to retain their privileges as states, and saw it as the best way of protecting democracy.

These commitments need also to be examined against the strength of the system being challenged. The market-making and international paradigms are deeply rooted in the EU, and even when important changes are made implementation can easily limit their effect. Significantly, no move was made at Maastricht to control or regulate comitology despite the fact that in its submissions Parliament had made this a key area of concern. At Amsterdam a declaration was attached asking the Commission to propose amendments to its 1987 decision which established the comitology procedures. As discussed in Chapter 5, at the time of writing this was producing a power struggle between institutions rather than a debate about democracy.

The two-level game is still the dominant paradigm. However, it retains within it some basic contradictions, the most important of which is the need for legitimation if economic objectives are to be pursued effectively. Making necessary concessions to the Parliament and projecting other concepts (for example, accountability) to the European level trigger new forms of interaction which can begin to suggest a different politics. The outcomes remain entirely unpredictable.

Evidence and argument

Arguments about democratizing the EU remain hard to evaluate. However, it is significant that debate is now more open and that unpredictable events like the March 1999 confrontation between Parliament and Commission are for the first time bringing genuinely European political issues to public attention. However, in the absence of any real structures for participation and debate, such developments are as likely to result in cynicism and apathy as they are to create pressure for further involvement. The results of the elections to the European Parliament in June 1999 (discussed in more detail in Chapter 5) make this very clear.

Despite this, arguments that maintain either directly or by implication that the nation state is still the only feasible guarantor of democracy are appearing increasingly unsatisfactory. Such views are often self-serving, and they deny the implications and realities of the transfer of power and fail to recognize the political changes taking place. Principles and procedures need to be devised which, while not replacing the state as a focus of democracy, supplement its safeguards and supportive structures in ways appropriate to international and transnational policy-making. Slow organic change still appears to be the only feasible route for democratization in the EU, but there is beginning to be a more solid pressure behind the process.

In this last section I want to return to the three approaches to democratization discussed by Michael Newman in Chapter 1. By examining them in the context of the above arguments, I hope to identify more precisely in what directions the EU democratization process is going, where and why particular gaps exist, and suggest some new ways forward.

Approach 1 focused on the activism of social and political movements and saw the gradual democratization of institutions and political systems at the European level springing out of that activity and the demands it poses. This focus is important, especially as it has received little academic or scholarly attention until recently. However, the evidence suggests that while on the surface this activity is given some encouragement by EU institutions and processes, there is in reality a brick wall as far as real influence is concerned. Furthermore, the recent treaty revisions are almost entirely silent on this crucial area.

What is needed to encourage this kind of involvement is the

establishment of a 'third channel' of influence running along-side those already available via state mechanisms and the European Parliament. A third channel would aim to achieve a level playing field as far as influence and involvement in the policy-making of the EU is concerned between experts, bureau-crats and social actors. The ideas of deliberative democracy dis-cussed earlier provide some guidance here about the principles and practices to be employed. Essentials in the process would be openness, the encouragement of debate, the application of pro-fessional standards and the requirement to provide reasons for decisions taken.

While this may seem hard to achieve, given the present balance of forces in the EU, it provides at least a gaol to be aimed for. The revision of the comitology decision, and the greater involvement of the European Parliament which it seems likely to produce, may provide some openings. Such developments would have the great advantage of relieving the frustrations of activists (amply demonstrated in this volume) without having radically to alter institutions and structures. It could also provide space for establishing in a real sense the 'substance of politics'.

Approach 2 concerns fundamental rights and the level at which they are effectively guaranteed. The ECJ has for a long time been the main enforcer of economic rights, particularly in the sense of fair competition, free movement and access to ser-vices. Member states have also accepted equal treatment between men and women at work as a principle of European law. At the same time, a broader range of rights is guaranteed through the European Convention on Human Rights (ECHR), although EU member states accede and make use of it in differ-ent ways. It has frequently been proposed that the EU itself should accede to the ECHR, and the ECJ has for some time undertaken to apply its provisions.

There are some rights, however, which need to be guaranteed at EU level even if already covered by the ECHR because it would have symbolic value and place them in the same space and enforceable in the same way as economic rights. Nothing at present in the ECHR matches the consciousness-raising effect of the working out of detailed provisions and their implementa-tion in the EU context. Despite their limitations, the gender equality measures demonstrate this most clearly. One category of rights which require this treatment is those concerned with race and other forms of discrimination, as was partially recognized in the Amsterdam Treaty. Such moves have great significance and begin the process of creating and codifying a level of shared values which stretches beyond the economic.

Approach 3 concerns the development of a European collective consciousness which would support and lay the basis of a more transnational politics. As can be seen in this book, opinions vary over the extent to which European peoples remain wedded to the nation state and whether there is in fact a more collective *demos* waiting to be revealed. Surveys of public opinion suggest that people have very little affective attachment to the European system and rely for protection on the familiar structures of their own country. On the other hand, they have been given little occasion or encouragement to experience anything else in a self-aware way. The workings of the Common/Single Market have created exchanges and interactions at a popular as well as an elite level over a long period, but the results are hard to estimate. Consociation (the attempt to explain how different cultural groups can work together in the same polity) does not, however, seem the right model for the EU. Economic integration has gone too far and too much 'intermingling' is already taking place.

What has been conspicuously lacking so far is any lead from the top in Europe to encourage people to feel that they can have a collective political as well as economic identity, and that such an identity would support rather than threaten national solidarity and continuing diversity. An important move in this direction would be to take and ratify EU constitutive decisions in more collective and open ways, and for significant Europe-wide political occasions to be more strongly promoted. As we have seen, there is likely to be strong resistance from governments to such developments, although Amsterdam did take a small step in that direction.

'Europe' needs to be sold to the people by its governments as something positive which serves their interests. As Miliband argues, in the end legitimation has to come from the top. But for it to be convincing it has to be true. The intermingling of ideas from activists, practitioners and theorists presented in this book suggests some ways forward which could improve policy-making and legitimacy without requiring extensive structural change. The EU is a test bed for such developments. If international processes cannot be given democratic legitimacy in these favourable circumstances, there is little chance elsewhere.

Notes

1 'The Money Changers. The Struggle for the Euro' (BBC-2, April 1998, three programmes). These detailed programmes give a fascinating account of how since the 1960s the issue of EMU has gradually risen up the EC/EU agenda. The final programme shows that the series of negotiations which led to the decision to adopt a single currency involved a shrewd understanding by key participants of what interests had to be accommodated, what feathers smoothed, and who and what could be marginalized at any particular point in time.

2 During the 1950s and 1960s the populations of Europe were primarily concerned with the setting up of welfare systems on a national basis. These were their reward for the rigours of the war and a consequence of the political changes that followed it. During the same period the infrastructure of European integration was tiny in comparison with what exists today.

3 Debates along these lines, involving both lawyers and political scientists, have been conducted for some time now in the pages of the *European Law Journal*. See particularly the special issue on 'Legal Theory in the European Union', *European Law Journal*, 4 (4), December 1998.

4 Evaluating the measures in the two treaties is by no means easy. The Maastricht intergovernmental conference drafted the new Treaty on European Union (TEU) and also amended or added to the Treaty establishing the European Community (TEC), the former Treaty of Rome. The Amsterdam Treaty contains amendments to both the TEU and the TEC. Subsequently a consolidated version of the two foundation treaties has been produced, incorporating all the amendments and renumbering the articles. On the whole, additions and amendments to the Treaty of Rome carry more legal weight than those to the TEU.

5 The proposal on citizenship was apparently introduced by the Spanish government and at one time was thought might be a central theme of the treaty. The concept was progressively weakened during the negotiations and detached from any substantial link with fundamental rights. In the end, no one opposed its inclusion (Anderson *et al.* 1994).

6 Article 255, Treaty of Rome (consolidated version).

References

Andersen, S., and K. A. Eliassen (1996), *The European Union. How Democratic is it?* London, Sage.

Anderson, M., M. den Boer *et al.* (1994), 'European citizenship and co-operation in justice and home affairs' in A. Duff (ed.), *Maastricht and Beyond*, London, Routledge, pp. 104–22.

Archibugi, D., and D. Held (1995), *Cosmopolitan Democracy. An Agenda for a new World Order*, Oxford, Polity Press.

Beetham, D., and C. Lord (1998), *Legitimacy and the European Union*, London, Routledge.

Benhabib, S., ed. (1996), *Democracy and Difference. Contesting the Boundaries of the Political*, Princeton NJ, Princeton University Press.

Bertone, C. (1998), *Bringing Gender into the Debate on the EU/EC*, Aarhus, University of Aarhus.

Bohman, J., and W. Rehg, eds (1997), *Deliberative Democracy. Essays on Reason and Politics*, Cambridge MA, MIT Press.

202 DEMOCRATIZING THE EUROPEAN UNION

Buiter, W. H. (1999), 'Alice in Euroland', *Journal of Common Market Studies* 37 (2), 181–209.

Bunyan, T. (1999), *Secrecy, Democracy and the Third Pillar*, London, Kogan Page.

Chryssochoou, D. N. (1998), *Democracy in the European Union*, London, Tauris.

Cohen, J., and C. Sabel (1997), 'Directly deliberative polyarchy', *European Law Journal* 3 (4), 313–42.

Cram, L. (1997), *Policy-making in the European Union. Conceptual Lenses and the Integration Process*, London, Routledge.

Dahl, R. A. (1998), *On Democracy*, New Haven CT, Yale University Press.

Dehousse, R. (1998), *Citizens' Rights and the Reform of Comitology Procedures. The Case for a Pluralist Approach*, Florence, European University Institute.

Demmke, C. (1998), 'The secret life of comitology, or, The role of public officials in EC environmental policy', *Eipascope* 3, 14–23.

Dogan, R. (1997), 'Comitology. Little procedures with big implications', *West European Politics* 20, 31–60.

Dryzek, J. S. (1990), *Discursive Democracy. Politics, Policy and Political Science*, Cambridge, Cambridge University Press.

Duff, A., ed. (1997), *The Treaty of Amsterdam. Text and Commentary*, London, Sweet & Maxwell.

Duff, A., J. Pinder *et al.*, eds (1994), *Maastricht and Beyond. Building the European Union*, London, Routledge.

Elgie, R. (1998), 'Democratic accountability and central bank independence. Historical, contemporary, national and European perspectives', *West European Politics* 21 (3), 53–76.

Everson, M. (1995), 'Economic rights within the EU' in R. Bellamy, V. Bufacchi and D. Castiglione (eds), *Democracy and Constitutional Culture in the Union of Europe*, Lothian Foundation Press, pp. 137–52.

Featherstone, K. (1994), 'Jean Monnet and the "democratic deficit" in the EU', *Journal of Common Market Studies* 32 (2), 149–70.

Gerstenberg, O. (1997), 'Law's polyarchy. A comment on Cohen and Sabel?', *European Law Journal* 3 (4), 343–58.

Grønbech-Jensen, C. (1998), 'The Scandinavian tradition of open government and the EU. Problems of compatibility?', *Journal of European Public Policy* 5 (1), 185–99.

Herdegen, M. (1994), 'Maastricht and the German Constitutional Court. Constitutional restraints for an "ever closer union"', *Common Market Law Review* 31 (2), 235–62.

Hix, S. (1998), 'Elections, parties and institutional design. A comparative perspective on EU democracy', *West European Politics* 21 (3), 19–52.

Hoskyns, C. (1996), *Integrating Gender. Women, Law and Politics in the European Union*, London, Verso.

Jeffery, C., ed. (1997), *The Regional Dimension of the European Union. Towards a Third Level in Europe*, London, Frank Cass.

Joerges, C. (1996), 'Taking the law seriously. On political science and the role of law in the process of European integration', *European Law Journal* 2 (2), 105–36.

Lehning, P. B., and A. Weale, eds (1997), *Citizenship, Democracy and Justice in the new Europe*, London, Routledge.

Leonard, M. (1998), *Rediscovering Europe*, London, Demos.

Majone, G. (1996), *Regulating Europe*, London, Routledge.

Majone, G. (1998), 'Europe's "democracy deficit". The question of standards', *European Law Journal* 4 (1), 5–28.

Marks, G., L. Hooghe *et al.* (1996), 'European integration from the 1990s. State-centric *v.* multi-level governance', *Journal of Common Market Studies* 34 (3), 341–78.

Miliband, R. (1969), *The State in Capitalist Society*, London, Weidenfeld & Nicolson.

Moravcsik, A. (1993), 'Preferences and power in the EC. A liberal intergovernmentalist approach', *Journal of Common Market Studies* 31 (4), 473–524.

Mossus-Lavau, J., and M. Sineau (1992), 'Les femmes et Maastricht. Une vote critique', *Libération* (Paris), 10 November, p. 6.

Newman, M. (1996), *Democracy, Sovereignty and the European Union*, London, Hurst.

O'Leary, B. (1999), 'Assessing the British-Irish agreement', *New Left Review* 233, 66–96.

Page, E. C. (1992), *Political Authority and Bureaucratic Power. A Comparative Analysis*, London, Harvester Wheatsheaf.

Picciotto, S. (1992), *International Business Taxation*, London, Weidenfeld & Nicolson.

Pillinger, J. (1992), *Feminizing the Market. Women's Pay and Employment in the European Community*, London, Macmillan.

Taylor, P. (1996), *The European Union in the 1990s*, Oxford, Oxford University Press.

Weiler, J. H. H. (1994), '*Fin-de-siècle* Europe' in R. Dehousse (ed.), *Europe after Maastricht. An ever closer Union?*, Munich, Beck, pp. 203–16.

Weiler, J. H. H. (1997), 'The reform of European constitutionalism', *Journal of Common Market Studies* 35 (1), 97–131.

Wessels, W. (1998), 'Comitology: fusion in action. Politico-administrative trends in the EU system', *Journal of European Public Policy* 5 (3), 209–34.

Index